THE RATIONALITY OF INDUCTION

The Rationality of Induction

D. C. STOVE

CLARENDON PRESS · OXFORD
1986

Oxford University Press, Walton Street, Oxford OX2 6DP

Oxford New York Toronto
Delhi Bombay Calcutta Madras Karachi
Kuala Lumpur Singapore Hong Kong Tokyo
Nairobi Dar es Salaam Cape Town
Melbourne Auckland
and associated companies in
Beirut Berlin Ibadan Nicosia

Oxford is a trade mark of Oxford University Press

Published in the United States
by Oxford University Press, New York

British Library Cataloguing in Publication Data
Stove, D. C.
The rationality of induction.
1. Induction (Logic)
I. Title
161   BC91
ISBN 0-19-824789-3

Library of Congress Cataloging in Publication Data
Stove, D. C. (David Charles)
The rationality of induction.
Bibliography: p.
Includes index.
1. Induction (Logic). 2. Logic. 3. Probabilities.
I. Title.
BC91.S76 1986   161   85-21434
ISBN 0-19-824789-3

Set by Cotswold Typesetting Ltd, Cheltenham
Printed in Great Britain by
Billing & Son Ltd, Worcester

To the memory of

DONALD CARY WILLIAMS

1899–1983

Author of 'The Ground of Induction'

ACKNOWLEDGEMENTS

For some things which are not in this book, I am indebted to Dr Paul Hyland, Dr Peter Forrest, Professor David Armstrong, and Dr John Bacon, who pointed out to me errors in earlier drafts.

For things which are in the book, I am indebted to Dr Hyland and Dr Forrest again, to Mr Vic Dudman, to Dr Grahame Priest, to Dr Len O'Neill, to Dr Chris Mortensen, to Mr Michael Warby, to Mr Ken Gemes, to Mr Peter Kintominas, and especially to Mr Robert Kuhn. These debts are all mentioned at the appropriate place in the text, except one; so I should add here that Mr Kuhn gave me not only the organizing idea of Chapter VI, section (iii), but mathematical help without which I could not have completed the preceding section.

But easily the greatest intellectual debt which the book owes is to the late Professor D. C. Williams, author of *The Ground of Induction*, published by Harvard University Press in 1947. Accordingly I have dedicated the book to his memory.

I have also to thank the Senate of the University of Sydney for granting me leave for the second half of 1983: leave which gave me leisure to write Part Two of this book.

D. C. STOVE

CONTENTS

PART ONE

INDUCTION

I

INDUCTION PRESUPPOSES ANGELS

(i)

(1) That all the many observed ravens have been black is not a completely conclusive reason to believe that all ravens are black.

The truth of (1) is obvious to everyone, including those philosophers who say that all the many observed ravens having been black is not a reason at all to believe that all ravens are black.

Nor is the truth of (1) merely contingent. Of course (1) *mentions* two propositions which *are* contingent, namely

(2) All the many observed ravens have been black,

and

(3) All ravens are black.

But (1) itself is not contingent. For it is enough to entail the truth of (1) that it is logically possible that (2) be true and (3) false, whereas something's being logically possible is not enough to entail the truth of any contingent proposition.

Indeed, there are no contingent instances of the schema

(4) p is not a completely conclusive reason to believe q,

when p is a proposition about what has been or might have been observed, and q is a proposition about the unobserved. For with these values it will always be logically possible that p be true and q false, and this logical possibility is enough to entail the truth of the corresponding instance of (4); whereas something's being logically possible is not enough to entail the truth of any contingent proposition.

Proposition (1), then, being true and not contingent, is a necessary truth.

Here is another way of saying just what (1) says:

(5) The inference from (2) to (3) is fallible.

So, (5) is a necessary truth too.

(When I say that the inference from (2) to (3) is fallible, I mean what I say and no more. I do not mean, for example, that the inference from (2)-*and-r* to (3) is fallible, for any *r*: that would very obviously be false. And the same holds in general: when I say that the inference from *p* to *q* is fallible, I mean that the inference to *q from p* is fallible, and I mean no more.)

The inference from (2) to (3) is an inductive one: an inference from the observed to the unobserved. So there is at least one inductive inference of which it is necessarily true that it is fallible.

Since there are no contingent instances of (4) when *p* and *q* take values such as to make the inference from *p* to *q* inductive, what (5) truly says of one inductive inference is true in the same way, that is, necessarily, of any other inductive inference as well. So it is a necessary truth that any inductive inference is fallible.

'There can be no demonstrative arguments for a matter of fact and existence', as Hume was always saying: in other words, necessary truths have no contingent consequences. Hence the necessary truth that any inductive inference is fallible has no contingent consequences; or, as we may say, the fallibility of induction has no contingent consequences. And therefore, using the word 'presupposition', when a presupposition is ascribed to a proposition or a state of affairs, in the sense of 'consequence', we may say that the fallibility of induction has no contingent presuppositions.

The proposition,

(6) That all the many observed ravens have been black is a reason to believe that all ravens are black,

is like (1) in being obviously true. It is further like (1) in that it is not contingent.

Of course (6), like (1), mentions the contingent propositions (2) and (3). But, again like (1), it does not *assert* either of those propositions. Its truth, therefore, does not depend on what their truth-values happen to be. Suppose that those truth-values are the 'worst' possible: that is, suppose the conjunction of (2) with the negation of (3). Even this contingent proposition, it should be evident, is not inconsistent with (6). (In order for *p* to be a reason to believe *q*, it is not necessary that the inference from *p* to *q* be *infallible*.) Every other contingent proposition, *a fortiori*, is consistent with (6). A proposition is contingent, however, only if there is some contingent proposition which is inconsistent with it. So (6) is not contingent.

Since (6) is true and not contingent, it is a necessary truth. Here is another way of saying just what (6) says:

(7) The inference from (2) to (3) is rational.

So (7) is a necessary truth too.

(When I say that the inference from (2) to (3) is rational, I mean what I say and no more. I do not mean, for example, that the inference from (2)-*and-r* to (3) is rational, for any *r*; that would very obviously be false. And the same holds in general; when I say that the inference from *p* to *q* is rational, I mean that the inference to *q from p* is rational, and I mean no more.)

Since the inference from (2) to (3) is inductive, there is at least one inductive inference of which it is necessarily true that it is rational. Necessary truths have no contingent consequences. So the necessary truth (7) has no contingent consequences; or, we may say, the rationality of the inductive inference from (2) to (3) has no contingent consequences. We may therefore say, too, that the rationality of the inductive inference from (2) to (3) has no contingent presuppositions.

It is not possible, however, to generalize (7) universally, as it is possible to generalize (5). For while it is true that all inductive inferences are fallible, it is not true that all inductive inferences are rational. The inference, for example, from (2) to

(8) All ravens are observed,

is inductive but not rational.

Still, it is obvious that what (7) says truly of one inductive inference is true in the same way, that is, necessarily, of any other inductive inference which *is* rational. That is, if you take any inductive inference whatever, then to say of it that it is rational is to say of it what is necessarily true of it if true at all. Necessary truths have no contingent consquences. Hence to say truly, of an inductive inference, that it is rational, has no contingent consequences. Or we may say, the rationality of inductive inference has no contingent consequences. And so the rationality of induction, just like the fallibility of induction, has no contingent presuppositions.

We have seen that the schema

(9) *p* is a reason to believe *q*,

has no contingent instances, when *p* is a proposition about the observed and *q* is a proposition about the unobserved. I believe, indeed, though I will not assume in what follows, that (9) has *no* contingent instances, whatever *p* or *q* may be.

This may seem against common sense. Does it not sometimes depend on a contingent proposition *r*, whether or not *p* is a reason to believe *q*? Well, it is true that we often say, with the appearance of truth, things of the form '*p* is a reason to believe *q*, if and only if *r*', with *r* contingent. For example, even good philosophers sometimes say things like this, that 'Abe is a raven' is a reason to believe 'Abe is black' if and only if more than half of all ravens are black. Well, that is just false, because, let the majority of ravens be coloured as they may, 'Abe is a raven' is *not* a reason to believe that Abe is black, or that he is green, or that he is colourless. Still, what the person who says this means by it is almost certainly something else, and something which *is* true. He means that 'Abe is a raven and more than half of all ravens are black' *is* a reason to believe 'Abe is black', and that 'Abe is a raven' is *not* such a reason. And all of *this* is not only true but (I think) necessarily true, and *a fortiori* consistent with saying that (9) has no contingent instances.

Saying that *p* is a reason to believe *q* if and only if contingent *r*, instead of saying that *p* is not a reason to believe *q* and that *p*-and-*r* is, is one of the varieties of what I have elsewhere called 'misconditionalization'.[1] In many cases misconditionalization will not matter, since in order to avoid it one needs only to take care to say what one means, instead of something one does not mean. In other cases, though, misconditionalization really is a part of what people mean to say, and then it often will matter. For its usual (though not its invariable) effect is to imply that what the logical relation is between two contingent propositions depends upon some further contingent proposition; and that must always be false.

---

[1] Stove (1972).

Nor is misconditionalization the only thing which ever contributes to the mistaken belief that a proposition like (6) is contingent. Another process which sometimes does so is one that might be called 'value-conditionalization'. For example, because (6) is true, one might say, and say with the appearance of truth, that

(9a) *p* is a reason to believe that all ravens are black, if *p* is 'All the many observed ravens have been black'.

Whereas misconditionalization always results in a conditional proposition, and typically results in one which is necessarily false, value-conditionalization always results, as it does here, in a pseudo-conditional which is in fact not a proposition at all. Thus (9a) for example is not a conditional, and not even a proposition, because its 'consequent', '*p* is a reason to believe that all ravens are black', is neither true nor false. Still, we all sometimes do things like saying (9a) instead of (6). And when we do, the fact that *p* could take other values than the one mentioned here, and values which are *not* reasons to believe that all ravens are black, is bound to suggest to us that (9a) is contingent, and hence to suggest that (6) is contingent too.

(ii)

But now we seem to be, and indeed we are, headed for a collision with Hume, and what is more, with all philosophers since. For Hume said, of course, that inductive inference presupposes something contingent, namely, that nature is uniform, or that the unobserved resembles the observed, or that the future will be like the past. And how many philosophers are there who have disagreed with this dictum of Hume's? Not one that I know of. (Yet people say that philosophers never agree!)

It is true that there is no outright collision between us yet, at any rate in words. Hume's *subject* and mine are not quite the same. For he says that inductive *inference* has contingent presuppositions, whereas I said that *the rationality of* inductive inference has no contingent presuppositions. But no one will expect *this* difference to avert the impending collision between us, because no one will doubt that Hume would agree to say instead that the rationality of inductive inference has contingent presuppositions, if he could be persuaded to attend at all to a distinction so trifling.

Again, Hume's sense of 'presupposition' cannot be quite the same as mine. For I used 'presupposition', as I said, in the sense of 'consequence', and accordingly I use 'presuppose' in the sense of 'entails'. But it makes no sense, strictly speaking, to say of an *inference* that it entails a certain proposition or has it as a consequence. So when Hume said that inductive inference presupposes something contingent, he cannot have meant, by 'presupposes', 'entails'. But this difference is not going to prevent the threatened collision either. Because no one will doubt, again, that Hume would agree to say instead that the rationality of induction has contingent consequences or entailments; if only, again, you could overcome his aversion to microscopic quibbling.

We should know, though, what Hume *did* mean by 'presuppose', when he said that inductive inferences presuppose something contingent. So let us look at what he said. The following are all the relevant texts.

Hume says that 'all our experimental conclusions *proceed upon the supposition* that the future will be conformable to the past';[2] that 'all inferences from experience *suppose, as their foundation*, that the future will resemble the past';[3] that 'all reasonings from experience *are founded on the supposition*, that the course of nature will continue uniformly the same';[4] that 'all probable arguments *are built on the supposition* that there is this conformity betwixt the future and the past';[5] that 'probability is *founded on the presumption* of a resemblance, betwixt those objects, of which we have had experience, and those, of which we have had none.'[6]

In order to extract from these quotations the dictum which I and all others ascribe to Hume, that inductive inferences presuppose (etc.), only two things are needed. Substitute the word 'presuppose' for the variety of Hume's phrases which I have italicized above. I do not think there can possibly be any objection to this.

---

[2] Hume (1748), p. 35.
[3] Ibid., p. 37.
[4] Hume (1740), p. 651.
[5] Ibid., p. 651.
[6] Hume (1739), p. 90.

Then, substitute 'inductive inferences' for Hume's 'inferences from experience', 'reasonings from experience', 'experimental conclusions', 'probable arguments', and 'probability'. There cannot be any serious doubt about the propriety of this, either. A few people in the present century, it is true, have managed to misunderstand Hume's phrase 'probable arguments'.[7] But to the philosopher in the street it seems and always has seemed obvious that Hume's subject, in the passages quoted above, was simply inductive inferences; and the philosopher in the street is right.

Consider, then, some inference which Hume and we would agree is a paradigm of inductive inference: the inference from (2) to (3) will do. Hume says that this inference presupposes that unobserved ravens resemble the observed ones in colour, or presupposes that nature is uniform with respect to the colour of ravens, or presupposes that future ravens resemble past ones in colour.

It must have seemed to Hume that this dictum is obviously true. For it was a *premiss* of his argument, and one which (as we see) he often repeated, without ever a hint of an explanation as to what he meant by any of those phrases which I have translated as 'presuppose'. And as I have said, the dictum has seemed obviously true as well to nearly all philosophers since. To me, however, Hume's dictum seems obviously false, or else completely unclear; and it is the main object of the present section to bring other people to see it in that light.

When some one says that a certain proposition is presupposed by a certain inference, I understand him, to the extent that I understand him at all, to be referring to a proposition distinct from any that is *asserted* at any stage of the inference, whether as the conclusion of it or as a premiss. If the etymology of the word 'presupposition' counts for anything, and it can scarcely count for nothing, a presupposition of an inference is a proposition 'below' or 'before' that inference. It is hidden; or at least, by comparison with the conclusion or any premiss, it is hidden. This is fearfully vague, to be sure. But as far as it goes it is, surely, part at least of what philosophers generally understand when an inference is said to presuppose a certain proposition.

Accordingly, there would be no difficulty in agreeing with

[7] Cf. Stove (1965).

some one who said, for example, that the inference from 'All ravens are black' to 'Abe is black' presupposes that Abe is a raven. This saying would seem to me, and I think to everyone else, to be true; and *a fortiori* we would understand well enough what this person means by 'presupposes'. His sense of 'presupposes' would be this, or something very like it: an inference from *p* to *q* presupposes that *r*, if and only if no one could, on account of believing *p*, rationally believe *q*, unless he also believes *r*. Now it is true that no one could, on account of believing 'All ravens are black', rationally believe 'Abe is black', unless he also believes 'Abe is a raven'. So it is true that his inference presupposes, in the above sense of 'presupposes', that Abe is a raven.

Suppose, however, that some one were to say that that same inference—the one from 'All ravens are black' to 'Abe is black'—presupposes that Abe is black, or that Abe is coloured. In that case his saying would seem to me obviously false, or else what he means by 'presupposes' would be altogether unclear to me; and I would expect other people to be baffled in the same way by this saying. One should reply to such a person, obviously, in some such way as the following. 'Look, that inference does not presuppose that Abe is black. It *concludes* that Abe is black. It does not presuppose that Abe is coloured. Part of what the conclusion *asserts* is that Abe is coloured. You are calling the conclusion of the inference, or a consequence of the conclusion, a presupposition of the inference. Yet you can hardly *mean*, by "a proposition presupposed by an inference", "a proposition entailed by the conclusion of the inference". So what *do* you mean, when you say of a certain inference that it presupposes a certain proposition?'

This example, although imaginary, should remind us that in real life one often wants to say something like that to beginners in philosophy and to bad philosophers. These people are the world's greatest presupposition-detectors. Accusing inferences of presupposing something is the very breath of their nostrils, and it must be a rare inference indeed that can survive their scrutiny. If some one infers 'Abe is black' from 'Abe is a raven', they will say that the inference presupposes that all ravens are black. But let some one infer 'Abe is black' from 'Abe is a raven and all ravens are black': why, they will still say the same thing, that the inference presupposes that all ravens are black! That a premiss of a certain inference should be also a presupposition of it, is no trouble at all to them. Nothing else is either. Do you think to elude the vigilance of such critics, by making your inferences as explicit and as cautious as an inference can be? Your hopes are vain. If your inference is only from 'There is at least one raven, or none', to 'There is at least one raven, or none', still there is bound to be some philosophical ass who will tell you that your inference presupposes something or other; and you may consider yourself lucky if he does not discover that it presupposes something contingent.

But surely (it will be said) this reminder of the squalor of *ordinary* philosophical life cannot have any bearing on *Hume's* saying that inductive inferences presuppose something? Well, we shall see.

Hume says that the inductive inference from (2), 'All the many observed ravens have been black', to (3), 'All ravens are black', presupposes that unobserved ravens resemble observed ones in colour. Now, it simply cannot be denied that this saying is, at least on the face of it, exactly like the baffling saying referred to a moment ago: that the inference from 'All ravens are black' to 'Abe is black' presupposes that Abe is black. For the inference from (2) to (3) does not *presuppose* that unobserved ravens resemble observed ones in colour. It *concludes* that unobserved ravens resemble observed ones in colour. It does not *presuppose* that nature is uniform with respect to the colour of ravens: that nature is uniform in that respect, is part of what the conclusion *asserts*. It does not *presuppose* that future ravens are like past ones in colour: the conclusion of the inference *says that*, among other things. Hume seems to be calling the conclusion of the inference, or a consequence of the conclusion, a presupposition of the inference. Yet he can hardly *mean*, by 'a proposition presupposed by an inference', 'a proposition entailed by the conclusion of the inference'. What, then, *does* Hume mean, when he says that the inference from (2) to (3) presupposes that nature is uniform (etc.)?

Here is one possible answer: an answer which is natural in itself, and which worked well, as we saw, in another case in which a certain inference was said to presuppose a certain proposition. The suggestion is this. By saying that the inference from (2) to (3) presupposes that unobserved ravens resemble observed ones in colour, perhaps Hume meant that no one could, on account of believing (2), rationally believe (3), unless he *also* believes that unobserved ravens resemble observed ones in colour.

In this case, however, this suggestion is evidently hopeless, and the reason is essentially the same as the one I just gave for finding Hume's dictum baffling in the first place. It is merely ridiculous to imply that some one who believes (3), 'All ravens are black', might or might not also believe that unobserved ravens resemble observed ones in colour. Believing that all ravens are black just *is* believing, among other things, that unobserved ravens resemble observed ones in colour. And of course the same goes for the uniformity of nature. To believe (3) is to believe, among other things, that nature is uniform with respect to the colour of ravens.

Here is a second suggestion as to what Hume meant, when he said that the inference from (2) to (3) presupposes the proposition that unobserved ravens resemble observed ones in colour. Perhaps he meant that that proposition is the least that you would have to add to (2), in order to turn the inference to (3) into a valid one.

If you take any invalid inference from p to q, then there will be many propositions which, conjoined with p, suffice to turn the inference to q into a valid one. Let us call the weakest of these propositions, 'the validator' of the inference from p to q. Then the present suggestion is that Hume meant by his dictum that the validator of the inference from (2) to (3) is the proposition that unobserved ravens resemble observed ones in colour.

The suggestion has several merits, which I have pointed out elsewhere.[8] One of its merits is that (within the limits of accuracy to be expected in such exegeses) it makes Hume's dictum true. For the validator of any invalid inference from p to q is the material conditional $p \supset q$, so that the validator of the inference from (2) to (3) is the conditional $(2) \supset (3)$; and $(2) \supset (3)$, since it is false if and only if the observed ravens have all been black and some unobserved raven is not, may be said to be the proposition that the unobserved ravens do resemble the observed ones in colour.

But then, of course, the material conditional $p \supset q$ is simply

---

[8] See Stove (1973), pp. 43–4.

part of what q itself asserts. And $(2) \supset (3)$, in particular, is simply part of what the conclusion of the inference from (2) to (3) asserts.

So, even on this second suggestion as to what Hume means by 'presuppose', we are up against the same objection as was fatal to the first suggestion, and the same objection to his dictum as I made at first. In dealing with Hume we are dealing with some one who seems resolved to call a proposition, which is the conclusion or a consequence of the conclusion of the inference from (2) to (3), a *presupposition* of the inference from (2) to (3). This really is like dealing with those baffling people mentioned earlier, who are resolved to call one of the *premisses* of a syllogistic inference a presupposition of that inference. Our response, accordingly, should be essentially the same as it was at first. When Hume says, as on this present interpretation he does say, that the inference from (2) to (3) presupposes that $(2) \supset (3)$, we should simply say this. 'You either use the word "presupposes" in a way which is altogether unclear, or you are mistaken. The inference from (2) to (3) does not presuppose that $(2) \supset (3)$. It *concludes* that $(2) \supset (3)$, among other things.'

(iii)

The meaning of Hume's dictum, then, is not at all clear. It is clear though, from the texts, what he immediately went on to infer from it.

From

(10) Inductive inference presupposes that nature is uniform,

Hume inferred

(11) That nature is uniform cannot be rationally inferred by
      induction.

The idea is, of course, that since induction presupposes uniformity, induction *to* uniformity 'must evidently be going in a circle, and taking that for granted, which is the very point in question'.[9]

---

[9] Hume (1748), p. 36. The same thing is said again on the following page; in Hume (1739), p. 90; and in Hume (1740), p. 651.

I said before that I do not know one philosopher who has disagreed with Hume's dictum (10). Well, neither do I know one
who has objected to this reasoning of his from (10) to (11). Quite
the contrary, this piece of reasoning has passed current for a
master-stroke, as far as I know, for nearly 250 years.

This is something I cannot help marvelling at. This reasoning
should impress no one. The conclusion (11) is obviously false.
For it is obviously true, as was said in (i) above, that for example

(6) That all the many observed ravens have been black is a
reason to believe that all ravens are black;

while, as was said in (ii) above, a reason to believe that all ravens
are black is a reason to believe that nature is uniform with
respect to the colour of ravens. So (11) is false: it *can* be rationally inferred by induction that nature is uniform. Since (11) is
false, either it does not follow from (10), or Hume's dictum (10)
is false too, whatever it may mean.

Yet no one has ever said that, as far as I know, or said anything
like it. Quite the contrary: what Hume's dictum (10), and his
inference from it, have in historical fact inspired, has been not
criticism, but imitation. Philosophers beyond counting have been
moved by Hume's example to search for still other presuppositions of induction. Nor have they searched in vain. And when
they have discovered these additional presuppositions of induction, they have usually concluded, just as Hume did, that these
propositions presupposed by induction could not themselves be
rationally inferred by induction.

People often say that philosophy is fruitless, but this is merely
from ignorance. Those who say so can know little, for example,
of that part of philosophy which deals with the presuppositions
of induction; for that is an area where philosophical researches
have been fruitful to a degree little short of prodigious. Hume
discovered that induction presupposes that nature is uniform:
well enough, no doubt, for its day. But who, that is not blinded
by reverence for the achievements of antiquity, can compare it
with what has been done since then in the same way? Why, since
Hume, it has been discovered that induction presupposes the
Law of Universal Causation; presupposes that the apparent freedom of the will is an illusion; presupposes that the universe is,
precisely as the prescient genius of Newton anticipated, simple;

presupposes that the universe is, precisely as many geniuses even in our century foresaw, intelligible; presupposes that the future is fixed, and that the apparent flow of time is a delusion; presupposes that God's providence is steady; presupposes that God cannot suspend the laws it has pleased him to impose on his creation, and hence that reports of miracles are all false; presupposes that catastrophism in geology is false; presupposes that position in space or in time is causally inefficacious; presupposes that causation is more than constant conjunction; presupposes that properties are so distributed among individuals that individuals fall into 'natural kinds'; presupposes that the sources of qualitative variety in nature are not infinite in number; presupposes that the possible causes of any given event are humanly surveyable; presupposes that the human race is perfectible, cognitively at least, and anyway has an indefinitely long future before it. And this, I should emphasize, is but a handful drawn from among the presuppositions of induction which the march of mind has brought to light *already.* Induction itself bids us believe that we will have reason in the future to be still more grateful to the industry of philosophers for further and still more interesting discoveries of the same kind.

Many philosophers have followed Hume, then, in claiming to discover a presupposition, *p*, of induction; and most of them have followed him also, in concluding from this that the proposition *p* itself could not be rationally inferred by induction. But most of them have done so with an intention very different from Hume's, and even opposite to it. These philosophers have usually not been sceptics about induction, but quite the reverse. The only effect that they expected the discovery that *p* is a presupposition of induction to have, was the effect of putting the proposition *p* in a peculiarly invulnerable position. For what could be more firmly established than induction, whose authority, as Hume most truly said, 'none but a fool or madman will ever pretend to dispute'?[10] Why, nothing, except some proposition which induction itself presupposes, and which therefore cannot owe anything of *its* authority even to induction.

But this industry, of discovering presuppositions of induction, however conservatively it may have been intended, was bound to

---

[10] Hume (1748), p. 36.

have quite an opposite effect, once the weight of opinion shifted decisively to the sceptical side, as it has done in this century. The discovery that induction presupposes *p* may appear to make *p* safe, while confidence in the rationality of induction is strong. But once it is weak, every new discovery or allegation of a pre-supposition of induction has merely the effect of making *induction* seem *less* safe. Giving fugitives sanctuary in your house may make *them* safe, while the pursuing power is weak; but once it is strong, the only effect of the practice is to make your house unsafe.

Consider the list which I gave three paragraphs back, of pre-suppositions of induction which philosophers have claimed to discover. Of course I do not intend to suggest that all of these claims are false; or even that a single one of them is false. Far from it: it is almost out of the question that anyone should ever be in a position to say whether any of them is false or not, in view of the difficulty of discovering what it is that philosophers mean, when they say of an inference that it presupposes some proposition or other. But will any rational man, on reading through that list, lay his hand on his heart and say 'Goodness, what a lot of presuppositions induction has'? You would have to be an idiot to say so. No, the only moral that a rational man could draw from such a list is that the entire terminology of inferences-presupposing-that is a kind of intellectual poison gas, and that you should let it altogether alone.

This is a discouraging moral. In fact it may not be obvious at once just how discouraging it is. But the fact is, unfortunately, that the terminology of inferences-presupposing-that, with its ramified family of cognates, is so ubiquitous, not just in the philosophy of induction, but in philosophy generally, that our profession at large would be struck almost dumb if it had to give up saying of inferences that they presuppose, rest on, are based on, assume (etc.) some proposition or other. The terminology of inferences-presupposing-that, it would be no great exaggeration to say, is not so much a cancer of the language of philosophy, as the language of philosophy itself.

That induction is rational is, we saw in (i) above, a necessary truth. Hence it can have no presuppositions: at least, it can have no contingent presuppositions. How, then, can it have come about, that men of the most penetrating intelligence, beginning with Hume, should have persuaded themselves and others of the contrary: that the rationality of induction *does* have contingent presuppositions?

Easily. Indeed, as Hamlet says, "'tis as easy as lying', or rather, much easier: it is as easy as using language in the way that philosophers use it. The fact is, Hume and all his imitators, sceptical or conservative, have stopped quite unnecessarily short in this business. It is easy to discover a contingent presupposition of induction which has escaped the notice of all previous investigators. Indeed, you can virtually leave it to the language of philosophy to do the job for you. I hope now to convince you of this, by 'proving' that induction presupposes the existence of angels, or of something very like them. My premisses will be few and weak: only two in fact, one of them a necessary truth of the most impeccable triviality, and the other a proposition which most philosophers would regard as a necessary truth, and which perhaps really is so. And every step in my 'proof', I undertake, will be one which either is actually faultless, or the fault if any in it will not be of a sort, or of a size, which any of the detection-equipment currently in use among philosophers is capable of picking up.

(iv)

(A) The conclusion of the inference from (2) to (3) presupposes that all the unobserved ravens resemble the observed ones in colour.

∴ (B) The inference from (2), that (3), presupposes that nature is uniform with respect to the colour of ravens.

∴ (C) The inference from (2) to (3) presupposes that nature is uniform with respect to the colour of ravens.

∴ (D) The presupposition of the inference from (2) to (3) would fail, and the inference would have a false conclusion and true premiss, if unobserved ravens did not resemble the observed ones in colour.

∴ (E) The inference from (2) to (3) would be invalid if it were not the case that nature is uniform with respect to the colour of ravens.

∴ (F) The validity of the inference from (2) to (3) presupposes that nature is uniform with respect to the colour of ravens.

∴ (G) The inference from (2) to (3) would not be rationally conclusive if unobserved ravens were not like the observed ones in colour.

∴ (H) There would be no rational foundation for the inference from (2) to (3) unless the colour of ravens were uniform, not in our experience merely, but in nature.

∴ (I) It would be unreasonable to conclude (3) from (2) if it were merely an accident that all the observed ravens have been black, while other ravens might quite well not be black.

∴ (J) The inference from (2) to (3) would be irrational if the blackness of all the observed ravens were not owing to the operation of natural laws which in some way connect blackness with ravenhood.

∴ (K) The rationality of the induction from (2) to (3) presupposes the existence of natural laws of which the blackness of all the observed ravens is a manifestation.

(The next proposition is the second premiss of the 'proof'. All philosophers, I believe, regard part (a) of it as a necessary truth. Most philosophers, I think, regard part (b) of it as a necessary truth too; and they may well be right.)

(Z) A law of nature (a) is not a physical agent, and has no spatial parts; (b) is not merely a statement that the course of nature is universally such-and-such, but is something which in some sense constrains the course of nature to be what it is.

∴ (L) The existence of things which, though they have no spatial parts and are not physical agents themselves, are able to constrain the course of nature, and to manifest themselves in physical phenomena (such as the colour of the feathers of certain birds), is a presupposition of the rationality of the inference from (2) to (3).

∴ (M) Inductive inference from (2) to (3) presupposes the existence of angels or of something very like them.

(v)

Since there is nothing mysterious about how the second premiss (Z) contributes to this 'proof', and hence to this 'discovery' of a new presupposition of induction, we may set it aside. But as for the rest, the 'proof' is surely more than a little mysterious. Its only other premiss is (A), and (A) is very obviously true. *Of course* it is presupposed, by 'All ravens are black', that all the unobserved ravens resemble the observed ones in colour, or that nature is uniform with respect to the colour of ravens. In fact (A) is a necessary truth, and a trivial one at that. Yet all we did was to take this little dry stick of necessary truth, drop it into a strong solution of things that philosophers do with language, and slosh it around for five minutes. Then we pulled it out, and it had become (M), and the homely inductive inference about the ravens has become as thickly encrusted with metaphysical pre-suppositions as the deepest philosopher could wish. We have evidently stumbled upon the philosophers' stone, or rather the philosophers' solution. We will be rich, if only we can determine the chemical composition of this solution.

Whether my chemical analysis is complete, I do not know. But I can identify six ingredients of the solution, and I think that these together do most of the work.

First, there is a certain way of talking about laws of nature: a way which was the usual one in the nineteenth century, and which has lately come into favour again among philosophers, but which I have never been able to understand. I mean, talking about laws of nature as though they were *causal* agents of some kind. Laws, according to this way of talking, can 'manifest' them-selves, though they need not; also, they 'operate'; their 'opera-tions', moreover, can be 'interfered with', for example by the 'operation' of other laws; their 'operations' may even be able to be 'suspended' by the operations of another causal agent more 'powerful' than laws; and so on. I have nothing to say about this ingredient, except that since I cannot understand the suggestion that laws of nature are causal agents, I think we ought not to talk about laws as though they are causal agents.

This is the least important of the six ingredients of my 'proof' that I can identify, because it is the most specific. Besides, it comes into my 'proof' only at a point when most of the damage has already been done.

Second, there is an ingredient which I will call 'severity-shift'. You will notice that the words or phrases which are employed in my 'proof' to express an unfavourable evaluation of the inference from (2) to (3) (or, rather, of that inference *unaided* by the pre-supposition which is going to rescue it), steadily but insensibly increase in severity as the 'proof' goes along. At least, I intended all these increases to be insensible. If I have not succeeded, and you in fact felt some little bumps in this respect, that will not matter much. Because I could certainly smooth those bumps out just by dragging out the 'proof' to greater length. In addition to the unfavourably evaluative expressions which I have made use of, I still have in reserve 'fallible', 'incorrect', 'unreliable', 'falla-cious', 'precarious', 'groundless', 'unreasonable', not to mention twenty others that I could as easily have employed.

This ingredient of severity-shift is an indispensable one. A philosopher who claims to have discovered a presupposition of the rationality of induction has to convince us that induction unaided by the presupposition he sponsors would be irrational. Yet the worst that he can *begin* by assuming, by way of an evaluation of inductive inference, is that it is fallible; and that is not yet a severe enough verdict on it. After all, the inference from '99 per cent of ravens are black and Abe is a raven', to 'Abe is black', is *fallible*; but hardly anyone would consent to have it concluded from that, that it is irrational. So the best thing for our philosopher to do is to construct a severity-continuum which will link fallibility with irrationality, as I have done. The only alternative would be to introduce some sort of deductivist thesis as an express premiss; and no philosopher is ever silly enough to do that. The beauty of a thing like (G), for example, is that it is perfectly Janus-faced, looking both forward and back. It can be read, with equal ease, either as the mildest of reproofs to unaided induction, on account of its fallibility, or as damning it as irra-tional.

The third ingredient of my 'proof' is misconditionalization. This begins at the step from (D) to (E), and is never absent after that. This ingredient is quite as essential as that of severity-shift. No 'discovery' of a contingent presupposition of induction can ever take place without at least some assistance from this great engine for turning truths into falsities; and the reason is evident. To allege that induction has a contingent presupposition is to put forward a conditional scheme for the *redemption* of inductive inferences. An inference such as that from (2) to (3), although intrinsically devoid of all merit, is to have merit miraculously *bestowed on it*, or *imputed to it* (as theologians say), by grace: by the grace of some contingent fact about the universe. (Some one like Hume differs from the optimistic 'discoverers' of presuppositions of induction, only in thinking that we have no reason to believe in the existence of this saving grace.) Misconditionalization, then, not to mention a trifle like theological incomprehensibility, is inseparable from any would-be discovery of a contingent presupposition of induction. But this fact is obvious enough not to need dwelling upon.

The fourth ingredient of my 'proof' is the strong preference which it exhibits for the subjunctive mood over the indicative. This ingredient is not an absolutely indispensable one, as severity-shift and misconditionalization are. But it is much more nearly indispensable, and also much more helpful to the plausibility of the 'proof', than it may at first sight appear.

It is nearly indispensable, because as I indicated a moment ago, to allege that induction has a certain contingent presupposition *p*, is to utter a conditional threat: 'If *p* were to fail, the heavens would fall on induction'. And to utter a conditional threat is to speak subjunctively.

The value of the subjunctive mood, for the plausibility of a 'proof' like mine, lies in this: that it *softens the harsh effects of misconditionalization* by (as it were) setting them some distance off. Compare, for example, (G) above with the following, which differs from it only by being entirely in the indicative mood:

(G′) The inference from (2) to (3) *is not* rationally conclusive, if unobserved ravens *do not* resemble observed ones in colour.

You do not need to be as sensitive as some people are to misconditionalization in any of its forms, to think that (G′) gives out a decidedly tinny sound by comparison with (G). In fact, (G′) might awaken the indignation of even the most insensitive philosopher. For it says, altogether too brutally, that the question whether a certain inference is rationally conclusive—a question

which is, after all, in the jurisdiction of philosophers and logicians, and is an *a priori* matter—is decided elsewhere, decided by
a contingency, and even decided by, of all things, the colour of
the feathers on some lousy birds! Of course (G) really says the
same thing; but, thanks to the subjunctive, it says it much more
politely.

The fifth ingredient is what I will call 'subject-drift'. I mean
that, in my 'proof', and whenever a philosopher claims to discover a presupposition of induction, the subject, in the sense of
that to which the presupposition is ascribed, drifts about. It drifts
about, more specifically, among the following four points of the
compass: induction or inductive inference itself; the *truth of the
conclusions of* inductive inference, or in other words the success
of induction; the *validity* of induction; and the *rationality*
of induction. In the above 'proof', for example, a presupposition
is ascribed at least once to each of these four very different
things.

Of these four subjects, it is only the rationality of induction
which should ever engage the attention of philosophers for long.
Since induction is necessarily, as we saw in (i) above, fallible or
invalid, the validity of induction is a subject easily exhausted.
And as to the *truth of the conclusion of* an induction, or whether
the conclusion of an induction with true premises is true, or
whether more of such conclusions are true than are false: well,
these of course are all contingent matters, with which philosophers have nothing to do. The success rate among inductions is
as little the concern of philosophers as the blackness rate among
ravens. Hume, in particular, was as little concerned as the next
philosopher with what the long-run success rate of induction
might be, and of course he *said* nothing about this subject; and *a
fortiori*, he said nothing discouraging about it. Yet there are
philosophers who do not shrink from the absurdity of implying
that, in order to 'answer' what Hume said about induction, we
would need to establish something *encouraging* about the long-
run success rate of induction. Some people just like to make rope
neckties for themselves. But, in general, it is scarcely possible to
exaggerate the harm that has been done to the philosophy of
induction by philosophers who drift from the success of induction to the rationality of induction, and back again, and all over
the place. Squalor rules, OK?

The first three propositions in my 'proof' are entirely free from all of the devices illustrated so far. In (A), (B), and (C), there is no causal talk about laws, no severity-shift, no misconditionaliza-tion, and no subjunctive mood. In fact (A), (B), and (C) seem entirely free from any fault of importance, whatever may happen later in the 'proof'. (A) is obviously true. And in the transition from (A) to (B) there is nothing to set off any alarm signals in the philosophical control tower. Nor is there, in the transition from (B) to (C). If there is any one fault in my 'proof' which is critically responsible for the absurdity of the end-result, it can scarcely be in (A)–(C).

The truth is exactly the reverse. They say that after a man is beheaded, it is his *first* step that matters, and it is certainly like that here. The single most critical contribution towards proving that induction presupposes angels has already been made once we have reached (C). That contribution is the subject-drift by which the presupposition of uniformity, which in (A) was ascribed to *the conclusion* of an inductive inference, becomes ascribed in (C) to *the inference* itself. This first battle of the war was the decisive one, and we lost; or, rather, we surrendered without a fight.

This battle is known, or should be, as 'Hume's drift'. For why does Hume, and why do most philosophers, think that (C) is obviously true? Because (A) *is* obviously true, and because subject-drift, between the truth of the conclusion of an inference, and the inference itself, is no trouble at all to them. That is why the transition from (A) to (C) does not alert the monitoring system of philosophers, or even show up on it. And this is also, once (C) is generalized, the reason why Hume's general dictum,

(10) Inductive inference presupposes that nature is uniform,

seems obviously true. The uniformity of nature *is* a presupposi-tion, that is, a consequence, of the *conclusions* of induction; and subject-drift does the rest.

The historical assertion which I have just made will be accepted, if it is accepted, less because the details of Hume's text bear it out, than because philosophers find, by introspection, that this is indeed the way in which Hume's dictum (10), or any other allegation of a contingent presupposition of induction, came to seem to them obviously true. If, for example, it seems to you obviously true that induction presupposes the existence of natural laws, it may not be beyond the power of introspection to disclose that this owes all its apparent obviousness to something else, which really is obviously true: that the existence of natural laws is a presupposition, that is, a consequence, of some of the *conclusions* of induction.

But as it happens there is striking confirmation of what I say in the very quotations given above, from which arose the entire industry of discovering presuppositions of induction. For there you may see that it was no trouble at all to Hume to change the subject, to which the presupposition of uniformity is ascribed, from 'experimental *conclusions*', to '*inferences* from experience', inside two pages of the *Enquiry*. And of course no one notices. (How could they possibly notice? Philosophers are interested only in the big questions.) More generally, Hume often—and not only when he is writing about induction—uses 'inference' and 'conclusion' interchangeably.[11] How many philosophers do not? Subject-drift in philosophy, like commerce between the states of our commonwealth, shall be absolutely free and unrestricted.

Of course, there is a price to be paid. It is in the nature of liberty that great gains in one area will result in some losses in others. One of the penalties attached to subject-drift in a 'proof' like mine, or in Hume, is that the word 'presupposes' cannot retain in (C) the sense that it had in (A), of 'entails'. For as was said in (ii) above, it makes no sense to say that an *inference* entails some proposition. What the word 'presupposes' *does* mean in (C) or in (10) becomes, therefore, as we saw in (ii) above, a matter of some difficulty. But surely that is a very small price to pay for a major philosophical discovery, such as Hume's (10), that induction presupposes the uniformity of nature?

And then, think of the benefits. Once you have got to (C), it is perfectly plain sailing thereafter. What is there that any philosopher can possibly object to, in the transition from (C) to (D)? Or in that from (D) to (E)? Or in that from (E) to (F)? There is nothing in any of this to disturb what Hume called 'the calm, though obscure, regions of philosophy'.[12] And with (F) we have

---

[11] See for example Hume (1739), pp. 88 and 139; Hume (1748), p. 37; Hume (1882), vol. 2, p. 391.
[12] Hume (1882), vol. 4, p. 363.

the presupposition of uniformity ascribed to the *validity* of the inductive inference in question: the *third* subject to which we have so far drifted.

It is even easier after that. For now you can leave everything to another ingredient of the 'proof', severity-shift. All you have to do is to slide down the smooth incline from 'invalid' to 'fallacious', to 'unjustified', to 'unreasonable', to 'irrational', and the job is done. And now you can ascribe the presupposition of uniformity to a fourth and final subject, as in (K): *the rationality of* the inductive inference in question. Home at last!

Once a presupposition *p* of the rationality of induction has been thus 'discovered', Hume or his imitators are sure to ask, 'What reason have you to believe *p*?' To ask, for example, as Hume of course does ask, 'What reason have you to believe that nature is uniform?' This question passes, in our profession, for a hard though sensible one. But it is not.

The question means, at least on the face of it, 'What reason have you to believe that nature is uniform with respect to the colour of ravens, for example?' That is, it means 'What reason have you to believe the *truth of the conclusions of* induction?' This is a very easy question. We have countless such reasons. For example, that all the many observed ravens have been black. That is a reason to believe that all ravens are black, and hence a reason to believe that nature is uniform with respect to the colour of ravens.

If the question does not mean 'What reason have you to believe the truth of the conclusions of induction?', what does it mean? Well, remembering how easy subject-drift is in this part of philosophy, it might well mean: 'What reason have you to believe that *induction is rational*?' But this too is an excessively easy question to answer. It is a necessary truth that induction is rational, as we saw in (i) above, and a necessary truth very easily recognized to be such. And that it is a necessary truth that induction is rational, and easily seen to be so, is a very sufficient reason to believe that induction is rational.

In reality, however, when a philosopher asks, 'What reason have you to believe that nature is uniform?', the likeliest thing is, that he does not mean the first of the two questions just mentioned, nor yet the second, but neither, and both: in short, that he is simply adrift, in the usual way, among the truth of the conclusions of induction, the rationality of induction, and various other points of the compass.

If some one were to ask, '*Why* is it a necessary truth that induction is rational?', his question would no longer be an easy one, but it would not be a sensible one either. There can be no explaining why that is not otherwise, which could not *be* otherwise.

Of course, one can in some cases *prove* a certain necessary truth. But, even then, the proposition proved does not owe its necessary truth to the proof. And a necessary truth is not the less a necessary truth if there happens to be no proof of it.

The sixth and last ingredient that I can detect in my 'proof', and in all other cases that I know of in which some one has 'discovered' a contingent presupposition of induction, is this: a marked preference for using substantive nouns when something evaluative is to be said about an inductive inference.

When you want to express a qualitative evaluation, favourable or unfavourable, of an inference, you can always do so, if you want to, just by using adjectives. You can say that the inference is valid or invalid, rational or irrational, justified or unjustified, and so on. But you can always express your evaluation, if you prefer to, by means of a substantive noun. Thus you might say that the inference has a, or has no, rational *foundation*, or that there is, or that there is not, *justification* for it, or that it has, or that it lacks, a *basis* in logic, and so on.

Now you might say that whatever else might matter in philosophy, a difference so slight and so superficial as this one could not possibly matter. Well, against that, I say it *must* matter. I say so, because it is a fact of intellectual history that a philosopher, if he is engaged in making out a claim that induction has a certain presupposition *p*, is far more likely to say, for example, that the inference from (2) to (3) would *have no rational foundation* but for *p*, than to say that it would be *irrational* but for *p*. For the purposes of evaluating inductive inferences, he reckons ten adjectives not worth one substantive noun. Now there must be reasons for this. And I think I can, to some extent, point out what they are.

First, anyone who alleges that an inference from *p* to *q* has a certain presupposition, is intending, as I said in (ii) above, to direct your attention to some proposition below or before the manifest inference from p to q. And if that is his intention, then adjectival evaluations will not suit him, because they do not point beyond the manifest inference. Substantival evaluations, on the other hand, are just the thing, because they do point to some proposition beyond the manifest inference.

Second, anyone who wants to make out that induction has a certain presupposition p has an evident interest in evaluating as unfavourably as he can inductive inferences which are unaided by the presupposition p of which he is the sponsor: the sicker the patient, the more necessary the doctor's ministrations. And an unfavourable substantival evaluation *is* more unfavourable than the nearest adjectival one. Nor is the reason far to seek. Compare, for example, 'has no rational foundation', with 'is irrational'. The former is more unfavourable than the latter, because, while it directs attention beyond the manifest inference being evaluated, it also reports back that, even out there, there is no help for this unfortunate inference. The two evaluations differ, therefore, much as a *cancelled reprieve* from being hanged differs from an order for your hanging. And that is a real enough difference.

Third, substantival evaluations are more rotund expressions than adjectival ones. Here I must expect to forfeit any last vestige that may remain of my readers' patience. Will I say that mere rotundity of expression plays a part of any importance in philosophy?

Yes. In fact I know it does, and anyone else can satisfy himself of the fact by trying the same experiment as I have. Tell a philosopher—yourself will do as well as another—that induction presupposes nothing, and see whether the incredulity with which this meets does not find expression in certain characteristic words.

The response will be something like this. 'Impossible: there must be *some* foundation, some ground, some basis of induction. How could one rationally infer the colour of future ravens from the colour of past ones, if there were not some connection between birds so "loose and separate", or if there were not some universal cement connecting blackness with ravenhood, or *something*, anyway, about the universe, which is that-which-makes-inductive-inference-rational?'

Of course I am not now suggesting that there is any merit in this kind of response. For all it is, of course, is the beginnings of

a 'proof' like the one in (iv) above. But what is worth attention is
this: that if some one says, what is true, that induction presupposes nothing, then what comes bubbling up in protest are none
of your thin adjectives, which are fit only for defending inductive
inferences in all their nakedness, or not at all. No, it is the round
old substantive nouns, the ones that fill the mouth if not the
mind, and which point to a beyond: 'foundation', 'ground', 'justification', 'connection', and the like. It is only these veterans that
rise to the occasion, battered yet irrepressibly buoyant, like
balloons made of some indestructible stuff and filled with
helium. Hume's favourite is 'foundation'[13]; but if one took the
writers in this vein, Hume plus all his imitators together, the
single most important word would probably be 'connection'.

I made the 'proof' in (iv) above as long as it is, for the same
reason as a pathologist puts a specimen under the microscope: in
order to be able to identify its small-scale components. For the
same reason, the six components which have now been identified
were introduced into that 'proof' one at a time. These are
obvious measures to take, where one's object is to expose the
fraudulence of the 'proof'. For such a 'proof' to be at its most
persuasive, contrariwise, and therefore for a really plausible 'discovery' of a presupposition of induction, the opposite measures
are indicated. That is, the thing should be as short as possible,
and the various ingredients should be introduced, as far as
possible, all at once.

The following quotation will go some way to illustrate how
much can be, and has been, achieved in this respect. Hume writes
that when we infer an unobserved effect from an observed cause,
or an unobserved cause from an observed effect, 'it is constantly
supposed that there is a connection between the present fact and
that which is inferred from it. Were there nothing to bind them
together, the inference would be entirely precarious.'[14]

It is all over in a second, and yet surprisingly many of the
ingredients I have distinguished in such 'proofs' are present here,
or represented by an obvious surrogate. The second sentence,
for example, exhibits misconditionalization, cushioned, as is

---

[13] See Hume (1748), pp. 32 (twice), pp. 33 and 37.
[14] Ibid., p. 27.

usual, by the subjunctive mood. There was no room, of course, in such a microscopic version, for evaluative expressions to undergo severity-shift. But the obvious surrogate for that is the quite masterly ambiguity of 'entirely precarious'. When a writer calls a certain inference 'precarious', the only thing we can be certain he means is, that it is fallible; and he might mean no more than that. If he calls it 'entirely precarious', it is still impossible to say with any confidence how much, if anything, more than that he means. Yet at the same time, the adverb sets up a suggestion, powerful though indefinite, that it is really some far more severe verdict than that of mere fallibility which is being passed on the inference in question.

The last two paragraphs will serve to remind the reader of what the real-life originals of the parody in (iv) above are like; and in particular, of how slight and innocent-seeming they can be. They also serve to illustrate a general truth, of a depressing kind: that two lines of print may suffice to generate a philosophical 'problem', which twenty pages of print scarcely suffice to show has nothing in it.

II

'THE PROBLEM OF JUSTIFYING INDUCTION'

HUME thought that inductive inference is unreasonable or un-justified. But he also thought that this proposition, although true, is unbelievable. Now there certainly can be true propositions which are unbelievable, but surely in this instance Hume simply underestimated his own powers of persuasion, or else the ease with which some people can be persuaded. It is true that in the eighteenth and nineteenth centuries there was not a single con-vert to his sceptical estimate of inductive inference. But our own century can boast of many. Sir Karl Popper has been an avowed Humean sceptic about induction all through his career,[1] and he has been one of the most influential philosophers of the last fifty years. His many followers, accordingly, not only believe that inductive inference is irrational, but treat this proposition as a settled thing and a mere starting-point.[2] So wide of the mark has Hume's reassuring thesis of the unbelievability of inductive scepticism proved to be.

Most philosophers, however, are not sceptics about induction even now, and they therefore enjoy, to this extent, the advantage of not outraging common sense. The disadvantage of their posi-tion is, of course, that they then face the problem of justifying induction. And this problem has proved so utterly intractable that it has diffused over the philosophical profession a general sense of helplessness and a half-assent to the sceptical position, or at the least a deep respect for it.

The upshot is that nowadays the philosopher in the street will admit, or rather he will hasten to affirm, that there is indeed a problem, and a peculiarly difficult problem, of justifying induc-tive inference. Philosophers, he will say, are in Hume's debt for bringing this problem before their minds, and in debt to Hume's followers (such as Popper) for keeping it there. To say so much is

---

[1] See for example Popper (1974), pp. 1015 and 1018–9.
[2] Cf. Stove (1982), ch. III.

thought to be no more than a proper respect for Hume requires. In any case, it is thought to be true.

It is not true, though. There is no such thing as the problem of justifying induction.

Of course it can properly be asked whether there is any instance of inductive inference which is reasonable or justified inference. But equally of course, the same question can properly be asked concerning any kind of inference whatever, (syllogistic inference for example). And whether it is asked about inductive inference or about some other kind, the answer to this question is either that there are instances of that kind of inference which are justified or reasonable inferences, in which case there is no 'problem of *justifying*' those instances; or the answer is that there are no instances of that kind of inference which are justified or reasonable, in which case again there is no 'problem of justifying' any inference of that kind.

It is nonsense to speak of justifying inductive inference, because it makes no sense to speak as though it might be possible for some one to *do* something which has the *effect* that inductive inferences become justified or reasonable ones. It may perhaps be true that the justification of *men* is by works (though even there all the better authorities are on the opposite side of the question). But the justification of inductive inference is certainly not by works. It is never a contingent matter (as we saw in Chapter I(i) above) whether

(9) *p* is a reason to believe *q*,

where *p* is a proposition about the observed and *q* is a proposition about the unobserved; whether, that is, an inductive inference is or is not a rational one. A necessary truth results, or else a necessary falsity, the moment that concrete values of the above kinds are substituted in (9) for *p* and for *q*. In other words, an inductive inference is a rational one, and is justified, or else it is unjustified and irrational, just by its premiss and its conclusion being the ones that they are. Nothing else comes into it; and least of all, what anyone *does*, or might do. (All of this is equally true, evidently enough, of any inference at all, inductive or other.)

Contrary, then, to what is nowadays constantly implied by philosophers who are not inductive sceptics, there is no problem of justifying induction. Cheerful acceptance of onerous but imaginary obligations is more typical of the history of religion than of the history of philosophy, but the widespread acceptance by non-sceptics in this century of a supposed obligation to justify induction shows that even in philosophy the phenomenon is not unknown. How were non-sceptics persuaded to take upon themselves this imaginary, or rather incomprehensible, obligation? The answer is, in essentially the same way as that in which philosophers, beginning with Hume, were enabled to 'discover' contingent presuppositions of induction: that is, by falling prey to tricks of language apparently so trifling that it is difficult even to concentrate attention on them. The crucial thing here is in fact a certain instance of the last matter discussed in Chapter I.

The question over which the inductive sceptic and the non-sceptic disagree is this: whether inductive inference is justified or not. Now it seems utterly harmless if the question over which they disagree is said instead to be that of whether there is or is not any justification of induction. But this re-description, apparently so trivial, in fact gives an entirely different orientation to the disagreement, and one which is fatal to the non-sceptic's side of it. The first question was, and the question really is, whether inductive inference has or lacks a certain property, the property of being justified or rational inference. The non-sceptic, if he allows himself to speak at all of the justification of induction, can only mean by that to affirm, what he believes and the sceptic denies, that induction does indeed have that property. But of course the natural meaning of the phrase 'the justification of induction' is, the *justifying* of induction: the *doing* of something which is necessary and sufficient for the effect that induction becomes justified. Once this phrase is admitted at all, the non-sceptic's fate is sealed. For he is vividly aware, of course, that nothing which has that amazing effect on induction has been done by himself or anyone else up till *now.* (As he well might be, since no one could do any such nonsensical thing.) Therefore the justification of induction inevitably comes to appear to the non-sceptic, not as what it is, a property or *proprium* of induction, but as an *agendum*; not as what it is, a timeless logical fact, but as a future duty hanging over him; not as what it is, a truth, but as a task.

In this way, and no other, the non-sceptic's 'problem of justifying induction' is conjured into existence.

Although no one could possibly 'justify induction', there is something which some one might do, and which does have some connection with the fact that induction is justified. Namely, some one might *prove* that induction is justified. That it *is* justified, is a truth (as was implied in Chapter I(i)) known to everyone. But it might be possible to prove this truth.

It would, of course, be utterly absurd to say that there is a '*problem* of proving that induction is justified', at least if this were understood as entailing that some one has some obligation to prove that proposition. Even the non-sceptics who are most respectful towards inductive scepticism would draw the line at saying that. For it is evident that no one has any obligation to prove that induction is justified, or even to try to do so. Besides, no one is in any position to say that this proposition, true though it obviously is, is one which can be proved at all. But then again, perhaps it can be. Certainly some one might try to prove that induction is justified, and no one is in any position to say that such an attempt could not succeed.

If there were a successful attempt of this kind, say in 1714 or 1947 or 2000 first of all, what one must *not* say is that induction was then justified for the first time, since that would have the idiotic implication that before that date induction was unjustified. But whether or not any such attempt ever does succeed, the idea of proving that induction is justified at least makes perfect sense; and it is the nearest thing, that does make sense, to the idea of 'justifying induction'.

Moreover, certain arguments which were thought of, either by those who advanced them or by others, as attempts to justify induction, actually were, or are best regarded as having been, something very different, namely, attempts to prove that induction is justified. This is the case, for example, with the old argument which is revived in Chapter VI, and with the arguments advanced in Chapter V.

What sort of thing would a proof that induction is justified be?

The same sort of thing, evidently, since it would be *the same* thing, as a disproof of the contradictory proposition: as a disproof, that is, of the sceptical thesis that induction is *not* justified or rational inference.

And what sort of thing would a disproof of the sceptical thesis be? Well, that depends, of course, on what kind of proposition the sceptical thesis is, and on what it says.

III

THE SCEPTICAL THESIS ABOUT
INDUCTION

HUME says that 'even after the observation of the frequent or
constant conjunction of objects, we have no reason to draw any
inference concerning any object beyond those of which we have
had experience . . .'.[1] Popper says that 'induction . . . is in no
sense justified'.[2] These are representative passages, and we are
therefore on safe ground in attributing to both these authors the
thesis that induction is unreasonable or unjustified. Our object in
this chapter is to find out exactly what these authors meant by
passages such as those just quoted, and what kind of proposition
it is that they are there asserting. It is Hume's text, of course,
which is basic here; for Popper, *qua* sceptic about induction, is
avowedly a mere follower of Hume.

At least in the *Treatise*, Hume showed some sympathy with
what he there called 'scepticism with regard to the senses'.[3] Since
the premisses of induction inference are propositions about what
has been or might have been observed, Hume therefore inclined,
at least at one time, to a certain scepticism about the *premisses* of
induction. But this is obviously something quite independent of
his scepticism about the kind of *inference from* propositions
about the observed, to propositions about the unobserved, that
humans and animals make. And it is only the latter kind of
scepticism with which we are concerned here.

A person is sceptical about a certain kind of *inference*, only if
he thinks that inferences of that kind are less conclusive, that is,
that their conclusions are more uncertain, or less probable, in
relation to their premisses, than they are thought to be by people
who are not sceptical on that subject. So a sceptic about inductive inference is one who thinks that inductive inferences are less
conclusive, that is, that their conclusions are more uncertain, or

---

[1] Hume (1739), p. 139.
[2] Popper (1974), p. 1015.
[3] Hume (1739), bk. I, pt. IV, sect. II.

less probable, in relation to their premisses, than they are thought to be by people who are not sceptics about induction.

When the sceptic says that inductive inference is unjustified, he means, of course, that *no* inductive inference is justified. He does not mean that some particular inductive inferences, or some particular kinds of inductive inference, are unjustified, though others are justified. The sceptical thesis, in other words, is a universal one.

This is obvious enough from the texts. The last thing that Hume or Popper intends to do is to *pick and choose* among inductive inferences. Their scepticism concerns inductive inference as such.

But the point does not depend on textual details. The sceptical thesis about induction not only has been a universal proposition, as a matter of historical fact, but must be so. The reason is that, while everyone knows that many inductive inferences are justified or rational ones, everyone also knows that others are not. Thus everyone knows (to use again an example given in Chapter I above) that the inference from

(2) All the many observed ravens have been black

to

(8) All ravens are observed

is not justified. Hence if the sceptic, when he says that inductive inference is unjustified, meant only that *some* inductive inferences are unjustified, then he would not be saying anything with which non-sceptics disagree; whereas, of course, he is.

Concerning any inductive inference which non-sceptics think *is* a justified one, the sceptical thesis says, then, at least that its conclusion is less probable in relation to its premisses than non-sceptics suppose. (Hence it says, among other things, that contrary to what non-sceptics suppose, no inductive inference is such that its conclusion has *high* probability in relation to its premisses.) But of course the sceptical thesis says more than this. Hume did not maintain only that the premiss of an inductive inference is *less* reason to believe the conclusion than it is usually thought to be. He maintained, as we have seen, that it is *no* reason. Now, what did he mean? What is his scepticism, over and above the minimum just mentioned?

There are many different things it might have been, because there are many different assessments of how probable the conclusions of induction are in relation to their premisses, all of which have the consequence that the premiss is no reason to believe the conclusion. For example, Hume's scepticism about induction might have been, or entailed, the thesis that the probability of the conclusion of an induction, in relation to the premiss, never exceeds 0·01. That is (employing standard abbreviations) it might have been the thesis

(12) For all e and all h such that the inference from e to h is inductive, $P(h/e) \leqq 0·01$.

But this suggestion is not worth pausing over. For there is, of course, nothing in Hume's text that would support the attribution of (12) to him.

Here is another possibility. Perhaps when Hume said that the premiss of an induction is no reason to believe the conclusion, part at least of what he meant was that it is no more reason to believe the conclusion than to believe the negation of the conclusion. We can safely neglect the (merely logical) possibility that Hume thought that the premiss of an inductive inference *is* a reason to believe the *negation* of the conclusion. But perhaps his inductive scepticism was or entailed the thesis that the conclusion of an induction, in relation to the premiss, is never more or less probable than its negation is. In other words,

(13) For all e and all h such that the inference from e to h is inductive, $P(h/e) = P(\sim h/e)$.

This is a much more promising suggestion than (12). The thesis (13) belongs to a class of propositions which J. M. Keynes named, with obvious aptness, 'judgments of indifference',[4] and it is true that in some parts of Hume's philosophy, his sceptical assessments of the conclusiveness of certain inferences do take the general form of judgements of indifference.[5] Then there is the fact (which I know from experience), that students of Hume will often say, once (13) is suggested to them, 'That's it! That is exactly what Hume does think about inductive inferences.' What is more, a recent writer has lent his authority to the suggestion

---

[4] Keynes (1921), p. 54.
[5] Cf. Stove (1979).

that Hume's scepticism about induction is (13), or something very like it. For Professor Stroud (1977) explicitly attributes to Hume the thesis that a proposition about the observed is no more reason to believe a proposition about the unobserved than it is to believe its negation. Indeed, Stroud must have regarded this as a very easy piece of exegesis, because although he attributes this thesis to Hume three times,[6] he does not once refer to Hume's text in support of the attribution.

But are there not passages to which he could have referred? Well, there are certainly passages in which Hume says that, both *a priori* and in the light of experience, inconsistent hypotheses about the future, or about the unobserved generally, are equally likely. For example, prior to experience, he says, motion in a billiard ball about to be hit by another is only one of

a hundred different effects [which] might as well follow from that cause. May not both those balls remain at absolute rest? May not the first ball return in a straight line, or leap off from the second in any line or direction? All these suppositions are consistent and conceivable. Why then should we give the preference to one which is no more consistent or conceivable than the rest?[7]

And Hume is going to say, of course, a little later on, that even after 'a long course of uniform experiments',[8] we are still not really any the wiser about the future than we were prior to experience: that all these contrary possibilities are still open, and equally likely (though not equally believable) even after we have witnessed a thousand billiard-ball collisions.[9]

Such passages, with that sort of continuation, are the nearest thing that I know of to textual grounds for attributing (13) to Hume. But they are so far from supporting that attribution, that they are actually inconsistent with it. Hume holds indeed, we see, that in relation to any observational evidence *e*, there are various hypotheses h, h^1, h^2, etc., about the unobserved, each of which is equally probable and each of which is a contrary of every other. But anyone's common sense, or the principles of probability, should tell him that, if h, h^1, h^2, are contraries of one

[6] Stroud (1977), pp. 14, 54, and 162.
[7] Hume (1748), pp. 29–30.
[8] Ibid., p. 36.
[9] Ibid., pp. 43 and 75.

another and $P(h/e)=P(h^1/e)=P(h^2/e)>0$, then h and its *contra-dictory*, not-h, are *not* equally probable in relation to e.

There is in fact not a single passage of Hume's text, as far as I know, which supports the suggestion that his sceptical thesis about induction is or entails (13).

Hume's sceptical thesis about induction was in fact a certain member of a class of propositions which Keynes called, again with obvious aptness, 'judgments of irrelevance'.[10] Schematically speaking, a judgement of irrelevance is the assertion that q is neither more nor less probable, in relation to r-and-p, that it is in relation to r alone. In short, p is irrelevant to q in relation to r, if and only if $P(q/r.p)=P(q/r)$. And Hume's sceptical thesis about induction was at least the thesis that, in relation to propositions knowable *a priori*, propositions about the observed are in this sense irrelevant to propositions about the unobserved. In other words, it was that the conclusion h of an inductive inference is neither more nor less probable, in relation to e-and-r, where e is the premiss and r is any proposition knowable *a priori*, than it is in relation to r alone.

Some of the decisive evidence in favour of this suggestion is the following.

Each time that Hume, in his very repetitive writings, comes to the sceptical conclusion that propositions about the observed are no reason to believe any proposition about the unobserved, this thesis is a deliberate 'echo' of another thesis which he had asserted at the outset of his argument for scepticism. This was the thesis that we have no reason to believe any proposition about the unobserved, *prior to* experience, or 'unassisted by experience',[11] or '*a priori*',[12] or (as he likes to say) in the situation of Adam when he had just been created:[13] in other words, in rela-tion to propositions knowable *a priori*. Of course there is nothing sceptical about *this* thesis. On the contrary, it is a thesis with which every empiricist will agree, and in fact Hume uses it pre-cisely to secure a broad (not to say commonplace) basis of agree-ment with which to begin his argument. But the argument *ends* with Hume saying *the very same thing* about propositions about

[10] Keynes (1921), p. 54.
[11] Hume (1748), p. 27.
[12] Ibid., p. 27.
[13] Hume (1740), pp. 650–1; Hume (1748), p. 27.

the unobserved, namely, that we have no reason to believe them—*even after* experience.

'We have no reason to believe any proposition about the unobserved, prior to experience': that is the preliminary empiricist commonplace ('Bacon's bell', as I have elsewhere called it[14]). But the ultimate sceptical conclusion ('Hume's bell'), says, in a shocking parody of that, 'We have no reason to believe any proposition about the unobserved *even after* experience!' This is, evidently, to say at least that experience does nothing to make conclusions about the unobserved more probable than they were *a priori*. And, neglecting again the merely logical possibility that Hume considered the conclusions of induction *less* probable in relation to their premisses than they are *a priori*, we have precisely the judgement of irrelevance which I have above attributed to him.

Here are five places at which Hume, actually using the phrase 'even after', and evidently thereby echoing his earlier empiricist thesis that we have no reason to believe anything about the unobserved prior to experience, says that we are no better off after experience than we were before: *Treatise*, pp. 91 and 139; *Abstract*, pp. 652 and 655; *Enquiry*, p. 32.

These passages leave us no option but to suppose that Hume, when he said that the premiss of an inductive inference is *no reason* to believe the conclusion, meant at least that it is no *more* reason than a proposition knowable *a priori* is; or in other words that in relation to propositions which are knowable *a priori*, a proposition about the observed is irrelevant (in Keynes's sense) to any proposition about the unobserved.

But there would be sufficient textual grounds for attributing this thesis to Hume, even if the 'even after' passages did not exist.

As every reader of Hume knows, he says that *one instance is no better than none*, as a reason for belief in a proposition about the unobserved.[15] Indeed, Hume says, one instance is no better than none even as a *cause* of such belief. ('It is only after a long course of uniform experiments in any kind, that we attain a firm reliance and security with regard to a particular event.'[16] 'It would have been necessary . . . for Adam (if he was not inspired)

---

[14] Stove (1975), p. 17.
[15] See, e.g. Hume (1748), p. 74.
[16] Ibid., p. 36.

to have had *experience* of the effect, which followed upon the impulse of [billiard] balls.'[17] Etc.)

He also says, as every reader knows, that a hundred or a thousand instances, though very different from one instance as a cause of belief about the unobserved, are no better than one as a reason for such belief.[18]

But now we need only put together these two undoubtedly Humean theses to arrive at the same conclusion as we reached before. If 'All ravens are black' is not more (or less) probable in relation to 'All of the 1000 observed ravens have been black' than it is in relation to 'The one observed raven was black'; and if it is not more (or less) probable in relation to the latter than it is in the absence of all experience; why, then, experience of ravens, many or few, as being black, is simply irrelevant to the proposition that all ravens are black.

Whether every proposition knowable *a priori* is a tautology, is a question to be asked; though not one to be answered here. But it hardly admits of dispute that every tautology is a proposition knowable *a priori*. Part at least, then, of the content of Hume's sceptical thesis about induction is this:

(14) For all *e* and all *h* such that the inference from *e* to *h* is inductive, and for all tautological *t*, $P(h/t.e) = P(h/t)$.

That Hume's scepticism about induction is or entails (14), first dawned on me in 1968, though it first appeared in print in 1973.[19] I should have realized the fact before then. For I knew before then that Popper, an avowed follower of Hume concerning induction, had maintained, on grounds of his own, two theses which are in fact special cases of (14).

Popper maintained that the initial probability, that is, the probability in relation to a tautology, of any unrestrictedly universal contingent proposition, is zero;[20] that is,

(15) For any *h* which is contingent and unrestrictedly universal, and for all tautological *t*, $P(h/t) = 0$.

[17] Hume (1740), p. 651. Italics in text.
[18] See Hume (1739), p. 88; Hume (1748), pp. 36, 43, and 75.
[19] Stove (1973), p. 61.
[20] Cf. Popper (1959), Appendix *vii.

It is a principle of probability, and an obvious one, that

(16) If $P(q/p)=0$ then, for all r, $P(q/p.r)=0$.

From (16) and (15) it follows that

(17) For all e and all h such that h is contingent and unrestrictedly universal, and the inference from e to h is inductive, and for all tautological t, $P(h/t.e)=P(h/t)$.

And (17) is, of course, a special case of (14).

Popper also maintained a thesis which is sometimes called that of 'instantial irrelevance'.[21] That is,

(18) For any two distinct non-overlapping individuals x and y, and for any predicate F such that the inference from Fx to Fy is inductive, $P(Fy/t.Fx)=P(Fy/t)$.

And (18), too, is a special case of (14).

Somehow or other, though, these facts failed to suggest to me what they should have, namely, that the sceptical thesis about induction is the thesis (14) of which both (17) and (18) are special cases. But once the suggestion is made, on the basis of Hume's texts, that the sceptical thesis is in fact (14), it is some independent confirmation of this suggestion that Hume's most explicitly sceptical follower should have been led to embrace (on whatever grounds) two special cases of (14).

We saw in Chapter I(i) above that there are no contingent instances of

(9) p is a reason to believe q,

when p is a proposition about the observed and q is a proposition about the unobserved. A proposition is non-contingent if and only if its negation is non-contingent. So there are no contingent instances, either, of

(19) p is not a reason to believe q,

when the values of p and of q are restricted in the same way. Now, with the values of p and q so restricted, (19), or in other words

---

[21] Cf. ibid., Appendix *vii.

(20) The premiss of an inductive inference is no reason to believe the conclusion,

is precisely the sceptical thesis which Hume maintained about induction. So the sceptical thesis about induction is not a contingent proposition.

I have argued above that when Hume said that the premiss of an inductive inference is no reason to believe the conclusion, he meant at least that the premiss of an induction is initially irrelevant to the conclusion. Supposing that I was right in this, then (14) is part at least of the content of (20), and (14) too, therefore, is not a contingent proposition.

But (14) is non-contingent on any supposition. It is a certain assessment of logical probability, that is, of the probability of propositions in relation to propositions, and no assessment of logical probability is contingent. Of course assessments of another kind of probability can easily be contingent: for example assessments of what is often called (following Carnap) 'factual probability' or 'probability$_2$'.[22] But it is not so with assessments of the probability of a proposition in relation to another. If we take, for example, any judgement of irrelevance, then it is obvious that the truth-value of such a proposition is fixed the moment that concrete values are submitted for p, q, and r in $P(q/r.p) = P(q/r)$. Whether these particular values are contingently *true* or not, and in general, how the universe *actually* is, does not come into it.[23]

Of course people will often misconditionalize. If we let T be some tautology, E be 'Abe is a raven', H be 'Abe is black', and E' be 'More than half of all ravens are black', people will say things like

(21) $P(H/T.E) > P(H/T)$ if and only if E'.

That is necessarily false, but then, almost certainly, it was not what the speaker really meant. He meant, rather, to say that

(22) $P(H/T.E.E') > P(H/T.E)$

and that

(23) $P(H/T.E) = P(H/T)$.

---

[22] Cf. Carnap (1962), ch. II.
[23] Cf. ibid., ch. II.

And both of *these* are not only true but necessarily true.

The idea of initial logical probability (probability of a proposition in relation to a tautology) makes some philosophers uneasy. It should not. There are countless assessments of initial logical probability, the truth of which is obvious to everyone. This is so even where the probability in question is that of a contingent proposition. Thus everyone knows, for example, that

(24) $P(\text{Abe is black}/T) < 1$;

that

(25) $P(\text{Abe is black}/T) > P(\text{Abe is black. Abe is a raven}/T)$;

that

(26) $P(\text{Abe is black}/T) < P(\text{Abe is black}/T.$ Abe is a raven. Most ravens are black);

and so on. There cannot be any question, then, of the legitimacy of the idea of the initial probability of a proposition.

In any case, the inductive sceptic himself needs that very idea, or a generalized version of it, even to state his thesis. For as we have seen, it is precisely in a certain comparison, of the probability of propositions about the unobserved after *and before* experience, that his sceptical thesis consists.

IV

WHAT SORT OF THING A PROOF THAT INDUCTION IS JUSTIFIED WOULD BE

THE sceptical thesis about induction is, then, a certain non-contingent universal proposition about how probable the conclusions of induction are in relation to their premisses. In its minimal form, the thesis is that such conclusions never have, in relation to their premisses, as high probability as non-sceptics suppose. In its non-minimal form the thesis is that the premiss of any inductive inference is initially irrelevant to the conclusion.

Hence to disprove the sceptical thesis in its non-minimal form it would be necessary and sufficient to prove, of some inductive inference, that its premiss is not initially irrelevant to its conclusion. I try to do this in Chapter V. To disprove the sceptical thesis in its minimal form it would be sufficient (though not necessary) to prove, of some inductive inference which non-sceptics think has high probability, that it does have high probability. I try to do this in Chapter VI.

To disprove the sceptical thesis, that induction is unjustified, is the same thing as to prove that induction is justified. Hence if the argument of Chapter V is a disproof of the non-minimal sceptical thesis, or the argument of Chapter VI is a disproof of the minimal sceptical thesis, then it will have been proved that induction is justified.

It deserves to be emphasized that, since the sceptical thesis is a universal proposition, one counter-example would suffice to disprove it. In other words, to prove that induction is justified, it would be sufficient to prove that the premiss of some *particular* inductive inference is not initially irrelevant to its conclusion, or that some *particular* inductive conclusion, which non-sceptics think is highly probable in relation to its premiss, really is so. It is not necessary, therefore, in order to prove that induction is justified, to prove that every inductive inference of a certain kind, or that every inductive inference of a certain logical form, is justified. It is not necessary to prove *any* universal proposition. (Still less, of course, is it necessary to 'prove' that *every* inductive inference is justified: a proposition which, as has been pointed out twice already, is false.)

It deserves even more emphasis that a proof that induction is justified would not be a proof of a contingent proposition. It would be a proof that the probability of the conclusion of a certain inductive inference in relation to the premisses is different from what that probability would be if the sceptical thesis were true. Hence it would be a proof of a certain assessment of the probability of one proposition in relation to another. And assessments of the probability of a proposition in relation to another are never contingent.

When philosophers have tried to 'justify induction', or to defend induction against sceptical attack, or to prove that induction is justified, the single greatest impediment to their efforts has usually been a certain failure of their own: failure to see that they were not required to prove something contingent. Mill, for example, imagined that in order to prove that induction is justified, he was required to prove nothing less than 'the Law of Universal Causation'.[1] More recently, many philosophers have implied that, in order to prove that induction is justified, it would be necessary to prove some contingent proposition, of an encouraging kind, about the long-run *success* of induction.[2] And there are—as was implied in Chapter I(iii)—many other forms of the same mistake.

The source of this mistake is the failure of these philosophers to realize that the thesis *against* which they are contending, the sceptical thesis about induction, is a *non-contingent* proposition *itself*. For no one would mistake a proposition *p*, which he wishes to prove, for a contingent one, if he had fully realized that not-*p* is non-contingent.

The source of *this* failure, in turn, is a certain kind of misuse of language in which inductive sceptics all engage, and which has been current among most philosophers writing about induction ever since Hume. Hume writes as though his scepticism about induction were the consequence of a recognition on his part of a

[1] Cf. Mill (1843), bk. III, chs. III and XXI.
[2] e.g. Salmon (1965), p. 277.

contingent fact about the cosmos, a fact which had escaped the notice of non-sceptics: the fact that future ravens and past ones are 'entirely loose and separate'[3] from one another, or that there is no 'necessary connection'[4] between them, or that 'cement of the universe'[5] is entirely lacking between ravenhood and blackness, and indeed everywhere else as well. And this kind of *suggestio falsi* is not at all accidental, but on the contrary is absolutely indispensable for generating 'the problem of justifying induction'. To this day it is true that a philosopher's interest in induction, however severely intellectual it may finally become, *begins* in feelings of insecurity: feelings which are generated by the illusion that the sceptic has shrewdly detected the absence of something making for security which might have been present in nature. And no beginner in philosophy ever 'sees the problem' about induction, until he has been brought to *feel* the fact, that unobserved ravens are 'loose and separate' from observed ones, as a part of some alarming cosmic deficiency.

Yet it should always have been obvious that this way of using language is misleading, and metaphorical at best. The suggestion that Hume had discovered that tomorrow's ravens and yesterday's are *literally* more separate from one another than other people think, or that he had discovered that blackness is *literally* more loosely attached to ravens than non-sceptics suppose: these are suggestions too evidently nonsensical to be taken seriously by anyone. (The 'curiosity'[6] and 'inquisitive disposition'[7] on which Hume congratulates himself, and in which the non-sceptic is presumed deficient, are precisely as real as the 'discoveries' to which they led him; though they constitute, no doubt, a typical enough specimen of that 'wonder' in which philosophy begins.)

There is another reason why it should have been obvious all along that the sceptical thesis about induction is not contingent. This is the fact that that thesis is obviously *universal*. Whence, if it were also contingent, then the sceptical thesis about induction would be just another contingent universal proposition like (3) 'All ravens are black', and in the same epistemic boat as that one.

---

[3] Hume (1748), p. 74.
[4] Ibid., sect. VII, *passim.*
[5] Hume (1740), p. 662.
[6] Hume (1748), p. 38.
[7] Ibid., p. 32.

Any *empiricist* philosopher, such as Hume, would therefore have had to conclude, from the sceptical thesis about induction, that there is no reason to believe the sceptical thesis about induction. And since it is obvious that inductive scepticism, when combined with empiricism, does not commit suicide in this obliging manner, it should have been obvious that the sceptical thesis about induction is not a contingent proposition.[8]

A proof, whatever else it is, is a valid inference of which all the premises are true. That induction is justified, is a certain assessment of logical probability. So a proof that induction is justified would be, whatever else it is, a valid inference, of which the conclusion is an assessment of logical probability, and of which all the premises are true.

Now, with only trivial exceptions, an assessment of logical probability cannot be validly inferred except from premises which include other assessments of logical probability. There is nothing suspicious about this, and nothing even peculiar to logical probability. The same thing holds for assessments of any kind of probability. With only trivial exceptions, an assessment of factual probability, say 'The probability of a human birth being male is 0·51', cannot be validly inferred except from premises which include other assessments of factual probability. A proof that induction is justified, therefore, will have other assessments of logical probability among its premises.

With only trivial exceptions, one assessment of probability can be validly inferred from others only *via* principles of probability. This too holds whatever the kind of probability may be that is being assessed. Principles of probability are propositions which stand to assessments of probability in essentially the same relation as that in which, in a geometry, general principles of length stand to assessments of particular lengths. Thus Pythagoras' theorem, for example, does not assess, either truly or falsely, the length of any side of any particular right-angled triangle. But, given assessments of the length of two sides of such a triangle, one can validly infer, *via* Pythagoras' theorem, an assessment of the length of the remaining side.

Here our concern is only with logical probability, and the

---

[8] Cf. Stove (1982), pp. 74–6.

principles which will be made use of below are few and obvious. The principal ones are the negation principle,

(27) $P(q/p) + P(\sim q/p) = 1$;

the conjunction principle,

(28) $P(p.q/r) = P(p/r) \times P(q/r.p) = P(q/r) \times P(p/r.q)$;

and the principle (16) mentioned near the end of Chapter III.

So far, then, a proof that induction is justified would be a valid inference, the premisses of which are all true and include both assessments and principles of logical probability.

It is obvious that these conditions are not sufficient. Otherwise, derivation *via* the negation principle (27), from some true assessment of logical probability 'P(H/E)=0·7', of 'P($\sim H/E$)= 0·3', would have to be a proof of the latter assessment. But it is obvious that it need not be any such thing. What, then, *does* a proof that induction is justified require, beyond the conditions stated a moment ago?

I cannot answer this question. But this has nothing at all to do with the special case with which we are concerned, where the conclusion is the proposition that induction is justified. It is simply because I cannot answer the much more general question, 'What is proof?', beyond mentioning validity, truth of premisses, and a few other obviously insufficient conditions like those.

But even in the absence of a satisfactory answer to the general question 'What is an *F*?', one can often rationally decide whether *x* is an *F*. For there may be paradigm-cases of *F*, that is, other instances *y*, *z*, etc., which are *F*'s beyond dispute, and such that the resemblance, however unanalysed, between *x* and these other cases, is so close as to compel rational assent to the proposition that *x* too is an *F*.

This is the case here. There are many valid inferences with true premisses which are, beyond dispute, proofs of the assessments of logical probability which are their conclusions.

I will give here only one such paradigm case, though it will be obvious, from this case, that many other such cases could easily be supplied. But to make up for this small number of cases, I will choose one which is especially 'close' to the case in which we are here interested. That is, my example of a proof of a certain assessment of logical probability will be one in which what is proved is the falsity of a thesis *like* (14), the sceptical thesis about induction.

The thesis disproved will be this:

(29) For all *e*, all *e'*, all *h*, all *h'*, such that the inferences from *e* to *h* and from *e'* to *h'* are both inductive, $P(h/e) = P(h'/e')$.

This is, of course, *not* a consequence of the sceptical thesis (14) about induction. But I hope no one will think that (29) is not even *like* (14) on the ground that (29) is silly. Of course it is silly, but that counts for nothing. All sceptical theses, actual or possible, about induction, are silly; that is, their falsity is so extremely obvious as to be known to everyone, including, of course, those philosophers who believe them. In fact, however, some one who is a sceptic about induction might very easily embrace (29). One who thinks that all inductive inferences are irrational, might well maintain, as a way of saying that there is nothing to choose between one inductive inference and another, precisely (29). In any case, there is this decisive consideration: (29) actually *is* a consequence of (13), a proposition which, as we have seen, has in historical fact been taken, and by no means without excuse, to be the sceptical thesis about induction.

The most natural way to prove (29) false is by *reductio ad absurdum*. So suppose (29) true.

Let '*a*', '*b*', '*c*', be short for the names 'Abe', 'Bob', 'Charles', of distinct non-overlapping individuals; let 'Abe is black' be abbreviated as '*Ba*', and so on.

Then the inference from '*Ba*' to '*Bb*' is inductive, and so is the inference from '*Ba*' to '*Bb.Bc*'.

Whence by (29),

(30) $P(Bb.Bc/Ba) = P(Bb/Ba)$.

By the conjunction principle of logical probability (28),

(31) $P(Bb.Bc/Ba) = P(Bb/Ba) \times P(Bc/Ba.Bb)$.

It follows from (30) and (31) that

(32) $P(Bc/Ba.Bb) = 1$.

But

(33) $P(Bc/Ba.Bb) < 1$.

Whence the supposition (29) is false. That is,

> (34) There are e, e', h, h' such that the inferences from e to h and from e' to h' are both inductive, and $P(h/e) \neq P(h'/e')$.

This argument is very short and childishly simple. But for all that it is evidently a proof of its conclusion (34). For a proposition so obviously false as (32) is sufficient to prove the falsity of any other assessment of logical probability which has it as a consequence.

(The falsity of (32), for all of its obviousness, is of course not contingent. Some one who believed that the inference to 'Bc' from '$Ba.Bb$' has the highest degree of conclusiveness that an inference can have, would be making a mistake of a logical, not a contingent kind.)

Every inductive inference, we saw in Chapter I(i), is fallible. Proposition (32) implies the opposite, and therefore can be accurately described as a thesis of inductive *infallibilism*. There is, of course, a certain element of piquancy in being able to show, as here, that a thesis about inductive inference which is of a *sceptical* flavour, such as (29), entails that certain inductive inferences are actually infallible.

In answer to the question, what a proof that induction is justified would be like, we can now do more than say that its premisses would be all true, would include both assessments and principles of logical probability, etc. We can point to the argument just given against (29), and say: it would be *like that*.

Of course I am not proposing to *analyse* this 'likeness', or to say what degree of it must be preserved by another argument which is to be a proof of the falsity of the sceptical thesis (14) about induction. But the above proof of the falsity of (29) is in fact, as I have already implied, also a proof of the falsity of (13). And the arguments now to be advanced against (14) will be, by any standards, sufficiently like the one just given against (29) and (13).

V

AN ATTEMPT TO PROVE THAT INDUCTION IS JUSTIFIED: THE RELEVANCE OF EXPERIENCE

Here is a proof of the falsity of the sceptical thesis about induction

(14) For all e and all h such that the inference from e to h is inductive, and for all tautological t, $P(h/t.e) = P(h/t)$.

From the conjunction principle of probability (28), it follows that

(35) $P(p/r) \times P(q/r.p) = P(q/r) \times P(p/r.q)$.

Whence, substituting for r some tautology T,

(36) $P(p/T) \times P(q/T.p) = P(q/T) \times P(p/T.q)$.

It follows from (36) that

(37) If $P(p/T)$ and $P(q/T)$ are each > 0, then $P(q/T.p) = P(q/T)$ if and only if $P(p/T.q) = P(q/T)$.

We may call (37) the principle of the symmetry of initial irrelevance. For it says that (as long as p and q are each initially possible) p is initially irrelevant to q if and only if q is initially irrelevant to p.

From the negation principle (27) it follows that

(38) $P(p/T.q) = P(p/T)$ if and only if $1 - P(\sim p/ T.q)$
    $= 1 - P(\sim p/T)$.

Whence

(39) $P(p/T.q) = P(p/T)$ if and only if $P(\sim p/T.q) = P(\sim p/T)$.

That is, q is initially irrelevant to p if and only if q is initially irrelevant to the negation of p.

From (37) and (39) it follows that

(40) If $P(p/T)$ and $P(q/T)$ are each > 0, then $P(q/T.p) = P(q/T)$ if and only if $P(\sim p/T.q) = P(\sim p/T)$.

From (37) it follows that

(41) If $P(\sim p/T)$ and $P(q/T)$ are each > 0, then $P(q/t.\sim p) = P(q/T)$ if and only if $P(\sim p/T.q) = P(\sim p/T)$.

From (40) and (41) it follows that

(42) If $P(p/T)$, $P(\sim p/T)$, and $P(q/T)$ are each > 0, then $P(q/T.p) = P(q/T)$ if and only if $P(q/T.\sim p) = P(q/T)$.

That is, if p, $\sim p$, and q are each initially possible, then p is initially irrelevant to q if and only if the negation of p is initially irrelevant to q.

For q substitute H, which is short for 'There are Australian ravens and all of them are black'; and for p substitute E, which is short for 'All the observed Australian ravens have been black'.

Then it follows from (42) that

(43) If $P(E/T)$, $P(\sim E/T)$, $P(H/T)$ are each > 0, then $P(H/T.E) = P(H/T)$ if and only if $P(H/T.\sim E) = P(H/T)$.

(44) $P(E/T) > 0$.

(45) $P(\sim E/T) > 0$.

(46) $P(H/T) > 0$.

Whence

(47) $P(H/T.E) = P(H/T)$ if and only if $P(H/T.\sim E) = P(H/T)$.

(48) The inference from E to H is inductive.

Whence from the supposition (14) it follows that

(49) $P(H/T.E) = P(H/T)$.

Whence, with (47),

(50) $P(H/T.\sim E) = P(H/T)$.

But, while (46) is true,

(51) $P(H/T.\sim E) = 0$.

Whence

(52) $P(H/T.\sim E) \neq P(H/T)$.

Whence the supposition (14) is false.

In short, if the observation-statement, 'All the observed Australian ravens have been black', were initially irrelevant to the hypothesis that all Australian ravens are black, as the sceptical thesis (14) about induction says it is, then 'Not all the observed Australian ravens have been black' would also be initially irrelevant to that hypothesis. But it is evidently not so.

Here is another proof of the falsity of (14).

Let H and T be as before, but let E now be 'All the Australian ravens observed between 1900 and 1980 were black'; and let E' be 'All the Australian ravens observed before 1900 were black'.

By the conjunction principle (28),

(53) $P(H/T) \times P(E/T.H) = P(E/T) \times P(H/T.E)$.

Whence by the symmetry of initial irrelevance (37),

(54) If $P(H/T)$ and $P(E/T)$ are each > 0, then $P(H/T.E) = P(H/T)$ if and only if $P(E/T.H) = P(E/T)$.

Again,

(46) $P(H/T) > 0$.

(55) $P(E/T) > 0$.

(56) The inference from E to H is inductive.

Suppose (14).

Then

(57) $P(H/T.E) = P(H/T)$.

Whence, with (54), (46), (55),

(58) $P(E/T.H) = P(E/T)$.

Obviously

(59) $P(E/T.H) = 1$.

Whence

(60) $P(E/T) = 1$.

From the negation principle (27) and the principle

(16) If $P(q/p) = 0$ then, for any r, $P(q/p.r) = 0$,

it follows that

(61) If $P(q/p) = 1$ then, for any r, $P(q/p.r) = 1$.

Whence, with (60),

(62) $P(E/T.E') = 1$.

But

(63) $P(E/T.E') < 1$.

Whence the supposition (14) is false.

In short, the sceptical thesis (14) about induction has the consequence, as we see from (62) and (60), that a thousand, or any number of instances, *are* as good as none—but in a sense rather different from that which Hume intended! The sceptical thesis (14), in fact, has the same fatal consequence as the thesis (13) disproved in Chapter IV: that some inductive inferences are actually infallible.

The two arguments just given are improved variants of the argument which I gave against (14) in Stove (1973)[1]. I learnt that argument from Dr Manfred von Thun when he was a graduate student. I likewise owe these two variations on it to two of my fourth-year students of recent years: the first to Mr Michael Warby, the second to Mr Ken Gemes.

---

[1] Stove (1973), pp. 68–9.

VI

ANOTHER ATTEMPT TO PROVE THAT INDUCTION IS JUSTIFIED: THE LAW OF LARGE NUMBERS

THE argument to be advanced here, unlike those advanced in Chapter V, is an attempt to prove the falsity of the *minimal* sceptical thesis about induction. In particular it is an attempt to prove that there is at least one inductive inference, thought by non-sceptics to have *high* probability, which really does so.

The basic idea of this attempted proof is an old one, going back at least to Laplace. In order for the version of it which I give in (iii) below to be properly understood, some account of the history of the argument, and especially of its more recent history, is an essential preliminary.

(i)

Suppose I learn that a certain coin is a fair one: that is, that any time it is tossed the probability of its coming up heads is $\frac{1}{2}$. Then I confidently infer that if it is tossed a large number of times, say 3000 times, it will come up heads about half of those times. I do not infer, with anything like the same degree of confidence, that it will come up heads about half the time if it is tossed a small number of times, say four times.

Everyone else, obviously, makes that same inference, and the same non-inference, as I do. Equally obviously, there is nothing special about the value $\frac{1}{2}$. If we learn that a coin is biased in such a way that at each toss with it the probability of heads is $\frac{1}{3}$, we confidently infer that in a large number of tosses the relative frequency of heads will be about $\frac{1}{3}$, and we do not infer with anything like the same confidence anything about the relative frequency of heads in a small number of tosses. Equally obviously, the kind of inference of which I am speaking is not confined to cases of coins, but is made whenever we learn something of the form 'The probability of the event E at each trial is x'.

In other words we all believe, or at least we all reason in countless cases as though we believe, 'the law of large numbers': that if the probability of the event E at each trial is x, then the probability is extremely high that in a large number of trials E will occur with a relative frequency which is close to x. Nor is this a belief which has become universal only recently, or only as a result of scientific discoveries: the opposite is obviously the case.

Here, then, is a kind of inference—'direct inference', to give it its old name—concerning which everyone believes that the difference between a large and a small number of cases or 'trials' makes all the difference to how conclusive the inference is. Everyone believes, for example, that

> (64) This coin will come up heads about half the time in 3000 tosses,

is highly probable in relation to

> (65) The probability of heads at each toss with this coin is $\frac{1}{2}$;

and everyone believes, on the other hand, that, in relation to (65) it is *not* highly probable that

> (66) This coin will come up heads about half the time in four tosses.

It is obvious, moreover, that these beliefs are true.

((65) is, of course, a contingent proposition, and in particular, an assessment of factual probability. But in speaking of the probability of (64) or (66) in relation to (65), we were of course speaking of *logical* probability: the probability of a proposition in relation to another. To make it less likely that the two concepts of probability should be confused with each other in what follows, I will sometimes signal the occurrence of the factual concept of probability in the way that Carnap did, thus: 'probability$_2$'. But it may be worth while to point out in addition that, although various assessments of factual probability are *mentioned* in this book, none is *asserted*; whereas, of course, many assessments of logical probability are asserted here.)

Human nature is so firmly wedded to belief in the law of large numbers, in fact, that we all have an inveterate tendency to go beyond the law, and to believe that a fair coin, if it is tossed a large number of times, is *certain* to come up heads about half the time. This belief has been reproved as a vulgar error by most of the better sort of writers on probability; and so it is. But the error is by no means confined to the vulgar. It was one of the greatest philosophers of the modern period who wrote that 'if you suppose a dye to have any biass, however small, to a particular side, this biass, though, perhaps, it may not appear in a few throws, will certainly prevail in a great number . . .'.[1] Again, what is the frequency interpretation of probability$_2$, but this error, proclaimed as a conceptual truth?

Still, even if this exaggeration of it is false, the law of large numbers itself is true. It is also believed, as I have said, *semper et ubique*. Proof of it, however, had to wait until the publication in 1714 of Jacques Bernoulli's *Ars Conjectandi*. That this book does contain such a proof is one of the principal things which entitle the theory of probability, in the period from about 1650 to 1850, to the glorious name of the *classical* theory.

It may well be asked, though, where is the glory? Everyone believes the law of large numbers, everyone always has believed it, and the belief is true. What, then, does a proof of it matter? There is merit in this question, because it is only too easy to misunderstand the nature of Bernoulli's achievement.

What Bernoulli proved for the first time was that direct inference has high probability when the number of trials is large; or, we may say, *a fortiori*, what he did was to prove that, where the number of trials is large, direct inference is justified. Now it is easy to let oneself say, instead of that, that in *Ars Conjectandi* direct inference to large numbers was justified for the first time. To say this makes Bernoulli's achievement much more momentous, of course, but it does so at the price of absurdity, since it implies that before 1714 direct inference to large number was not justified! No, what Bernoulli did was to prove for the first time the proposition—the *truth* of which everyone knew before—*that direct inference to large numbers is justified.*

Now it is true that a proof of a proposition which everyone knew before cannot matter *very* much. It can have a certain importance, however, and Bernoulli's proof does, if only for a reason I will now explain.

Direct inference is not the only kind of inference concerning

[1] Hume (1882), vol. 3, p. 175.

which everyone thinks that the difference between a small and a larger number of cases makes all the difference to the conclusiveness of the inference. Another kind is what I will call 'gamblers' inference'.

Every one of us, if he learns that

(67) At all of the 20 tosses with this fair coin it has come up heads,

is disposed to have an increased degree of belief in the proposition

(68) It will not come up heads next time;

whereas we are not so disposed by learning that

(69) At the two tosses with this fair coin it has come up heads.

Yet of course (68) is *not* more probable in relation to (67) than it is in relation to (69). Here, then, is a case of a universal belief, or at least a universal tendency to belief, that the difference between a larger and a small number of trials makes an inference more conclusive, but a case in which we are all *mistaken* in so believing or tending to believe.

Now suppose that some influential philosopher had taken it into his head to maintain that we are all mistaken, in the same way, about *direct* inference too: that the difference which large numbers seem to make to the probability of direct inferences is hallucinatory (as it certainly is in the case of gamblers' inference). This philosopher would have been wrong, of course, and everyone would have known he was wrong. But it could not have been proved, before 1714, that he was wrong, whereas after that date, it could be. Here, then, is a reason why a proof of the law of large numbers has at least a certain conditional importance: it is a disproof of silly philosophical scepticism, should that ever arise, about direct inference.

(Has it ever arisen in fact? In particular, was Hume a sceptic about direct inference, as he was about inductive? He certainly should have been, because of his extreme deductivist bias; but there is more direct evidence as well that he was. Section XI of Book I, Part III of the *Treatise* appears to be a discussion of direct inference, or of something very like it, and a sceptical evaluation of the kind of inference there discussed is certainly implied by the first two sentences of section XIII. It is impossible, however, to be sure of this matter. The main reason is that Hume shows scarcely any interest in the *evaluation* of the inferences he is discussing in XI: his interest is absorbed in their psychodynamics. Anyway, if he was a sceptic about direct inference, no one noticed; whereas everyone, of course, noticed his scepticism about inductive inference.)

As well as direct inference and gamblers' inference, there is a third kind of inference concerning which we all think that the difference between large number of trials or cases and a small number makes all the difference to the probability of the inference. This is what used to be called 'inverse inference', that is, direct inference turned round, or what we call inductive inference. Thus everyone believes that the inference to

(70) The probability$_2$ of heads with this coin is about $\frac{1}{2}$ at each toss

from

(71) This coin came up heads in half of 3000 tosses

is justified, and that the inference to (70) from

(72) This coin came up heads in half of two tosses,

is not. That is, just as everyone thinks and always has thought that direct inference to large numbers is justified, and to small numbers not, so everyone thinks and always has thought that induction *from* large numbers is justified, and from small numbers not. These universal beliefs further resemble the corresponding beliefs about direct inference in being obviously true. And to complete the parallel, there is even an inveterate tendency in the inductive case, as there is in the direct, to go beyond the truth: to believe that, for example, if a coin has come up heads half the time in a large number of tosses, then it is *certain* that the coin is an approximately fair one.

Because of these parallels, and because the theory of probability is, as Laplace said, only 'bon sens reduit au calcul', it was natural to expect, after Bernoulli, that what the theory of probability had done for direct inference to large numbers, it could do for inductive inference from large numbers. There were some people indeed, both before and after Laplace, who thought that the law of large numbers itself proved that induction from large numbers is justified, at the same time as it proved that direct inference to large numbers is justified. That is a natural enough belief, especially if the law of large numbers is formulated as saying, for example, that between the relative frequency of an event in a large number of trials, and the probability of the event at each trial, there is most unlikely to be any wide divergence. Others however, of whom Laplace was one, thought that, as inductive inference is the 'inverse' of direct inference, what was required to prove it justified was a proof of an 'inverse', as distinct from the 'direct', law of large numbers: the proposition that if the relative frequency of an event E in a large number of trials is x, then the probability is extremely high that the probability of E at each trial is close to x. And Laplace in fact advanced what he claimed was a proof of this proposition.[2]

But whereas Bernoulli's argument for the 'direct' law has never been seriously challenged, Laplace's argument for an 'inverse' law of large numbers met with a very different reception. At first, indeed, it seemed to carry conviction with most readers, and with some it continued to do so for a long time. (You can find strong traces of it as late as 1892, for example in Karl Pearson's *The Grammar of Science*.) But there was always a critical reaction to it as well, and in the longer run it was this reaction which seemed to prevail entirely. By about the middle of the twentieth century Keynes,[3] Kneale,[4] and other weighty authorities, had pronounced Laplace's argument a tissue of absurdity and confusion.

No one ever doubted the existence of God, it has been said, until the Boyle lecturers tried to prove it; and there is deep truth in this old joke. For it is a fact, although the process is evidently not an entirely rational one, that the failure, or what is believed to be the failure, of an attempt to prove a certain proposition, prompts people to wonder whether the proposition is true at all. Accordingly, Laplace being judged to have failed in his attempt to prove that induction from large numbers is justified, some people began to wonder whether induction, even from large numbers, *is* justified. That large numbers make all the difference

---

[2] Cf. Todhunter (1865), pp. 554 ff.
[3] Cf. Keynes (1921), ch. xxx.
[4] Cf. Kneale (1949), pp. 201 ff.

to the conclusiveness of *direct* inferences, no one, as I have said, (with the possible exception of Hume), has ever doubted. But now the thought was bound to arise, that perhaps *induction* is different. Perhaps the difference that large numbers seem to make to the conclusiveness of inductive inference is simply a universal hallucination, as it is in the case of gamblers' inference.

The Boyle-lecturers' effect (as we might call it) was assisted in this case by another and much more important historical circum-stance: the fact that, between the death of Bernoulli and the birth of Laplace, an influential philosopher *had* taken it into his head to maintain, and with all possible emphasis, what I have just mentioned as a dawning suspicion. To maintain, that is, that in inductive inference the superiority which we all ascribe to a large over a small number of cases is entirely imaginary. This was Hume, of course. 'Reason is incapable of any such variation', he wrote, as that by which 'we draw, from a thousand instances, an inference which we are not able to draw from one instance . . .'[5]

This cloud, the cloud of scepticism about induction, was scarcely bigger than a man's hand in Laplace's time; and in any case Laplace claimed and was at first widely believed (as I have said) to have dispersed it. But it was not dispersed. On the contrary, by the mid-twentieth century the cloud covered the sky. An influential minority of philosophers (Popper and his fol-lowers) actually embraced Hume's inductive scepticism;[6] and even the majority who did not were (as I indicated in Chapter II) 'half in love with easeful death' in its sceptical form. The suspi-cion that the value ascribed to large numbers is illusory in the case of induction, just as it is in the case of gamblers' inference, had penetrated almost every mind. And whether or not anything else could 'justify induction', one thing which by 1950 every competent philosopher was supposed to know was that at any rate the theory of probability could not.[7] The Laplacean argu-ment, consequently, seemed to be as dead as a doornail.

It was therefore entirely against the run of play when D. C. Williams published *The Ground of Induction* in 1947, a book which in essence resurrected the Laplacean idea, and purported to justify induction by means of a certain version of the law of

[5] Hume (1748), p. 43.
[6] Cf. Stove (1982), ch. III.
[7] Cf. von Wright (1957), pp. 153 and 176.

large numbers. (In fact, since Williams denies the need for any 'inversion' of the law of large numbers, his position is even closer to certain *pre*-Laplacean ideas than it is to Laplace himself.) Williams gives two versions of his central argument. The following is a summary of the second and better version.

Consider a certain class of inferences which are not inductive, but are in fact closely related to direct inferences: a class which Williams calls 'proportional syllogisms'. These are the instances of the schema

(73) $\frac{m}{n}$ ths of the *F*'s are *G*
      x is an *F*
      _____
      x is *G*.

Williams thinks that, while many philosophers are sceptical or uncertain about the probability of inductive inferences, no one is sceptical or uncertain about the probability of proportional syllogisms. If you take any instance of (73), everyone knows that the probability of the conclusion in relation to the premises is $\frac{m}{n}$: for example, that the probability of the inference

(74) 95% of ravens are black
      Abe is a raven
      _____
      Abe is black

is 0·95. The same holds for inferences which are proportional syllogisms in a slightly widened sense, where the major premiss has an *indefinite* quantifier, such as 'The great majority . . .' or 'At least $\frac{2}{3}$ . . .'. Thus everyone knows, for example, that the inference

(75) At least $\frac{2}{3}$ of ravens are black
      Abe is a raven
      _____
      Abe is black

has high, though indefinite, probability (viz., at least $\frac{2}{3}$).

Now, in view of the existence of this fund of common knowledge, it will be sufficient to justify *inductive* inference, Williams thinks, if it can be shown that there exist inductive inferences which have the same high (even if indefinite) degree of probability as for example (75) has.

This can be proved, Williams thinks, with respect to instances of the schema

(76) $\frac{m}{n}$ths of a large sample S of the F's are G
     About $\frac{m}{n}$ths of the population of F's are G.

For there is a purely arithmetical law of large numbers, he says, which states that for any finite population F, any attribute G, and any proportion $\frac{m}{n}$ in which G occurs in F, the vast majority of large samples—samples, say, of 3000 or more—must have approximately the same proportion of G's in them as the population F itself does. (Williams sketches the proof of a micro-instance or two of this law. Perhaps the best way to approach it first is to try the experiment of imagining the opposite: a population of F's in which most of the large samples are very *unlike* the population in the proportion of G's that they contain.)

Suppose, then, that our experience has been such as to furnish us with a large sample S of ravens, of which just 95 per cent are black. By the arithmetical law of large numbers, the vast majority of large samples of ravens must nearly match the raven population with respect to the proportion of black ravens that they contain. Hence any large sample of ravens is almost certain to be one of these near-population-matching, or in other words representative, samples. Hence, by the principle of the proportional syllogism, our large sample S is almost certainly a representative sample. Hence the population of ravens very probably contains about 95 per cent of black ones. 'This is the logical justification of induction.'[8]

The reception of Williams's book was such as could have been predicted from the state of opinion that I have sketched. It was thought to be an ignorant or a perverse attempt to revive an argument justly discredited long before. After attracting considerable attention, all unfavourable, at the time of its publication, the book was virtually forgotten soon afterwards.

I first read *The Ground of Induction* about 1955, and no other philosophical book has ever influenced me so much. It seemed to me the complete answer, not only to the inductive sceptics, but to the majority of philosophers who nowadays, without being sceptics about induction, are afflicted with 'modern nervousness' on that subject. Such people, echoing Hume, ask 'Why should I believe that the unobserved resembles the observed? True, I have seen many ravens, and 95 per cent of *them* have been black.

---

[8] Williams (1947), p. 97.

But why should I believe that the sample with which nature happens to have furnished me is a *representative* sample of the raven population?' To this question Williams, echoing Laplace, replies: 'Because it probably *is* a representative sample. It probably is, because most large samples are representative. And most large samples are, because most large samples arithmetically must be, representative ones.' This answer seemed to me, in 1955, to be supremely sane, right, and sufficient. In essence, though not in detail, it seems to me to be so now.

Between then and now, however, I completely lost my initial confidence in Williams's book. This was not owing to any of the published criticisms of it; for these, although numerous, and written in many cases by distinguished philosophers, have all along seemed to me to be entirely worthless. But I slowly became conscious of various distinctions, all of them essential to a defensible version of Williams's argument, which are entirely neglected in his book. (The distinction between logical and factual probability, and the distinction between assessments and principles of probability, are two of them.) These were faults of omission, of course, and therefore not incurable. But finally I did find in the central argument of his book a fault of commission, and one which seemed to me incurable and mortal. As this fault was one which is very far from being peculiar to Williams, I will say what it was.

We often express an assessment of factual probability by saying something of this form: 'The probability of an *F* being *G* is such-and-such'. Here we use the indefinite article 'an' or 'a', not as a universal quantifier, nor yet as an existential quantifier, but in a way which is—well, a way peculiar to assessments of factual probability! But often, too, we express an assessment of factual probability by using instead a universal quantifier, and ascribing the probability to each of the individual *F*'s: 'Any *F* has a probability such-and-such of being *G*'. Thus where we might have said, for example, that the probability of an *F* being *G* is 0·9, or is high, or is close to certainty, we often say instead that:

$$(77) \quad \text{Any } F \left\{ \begin{array}{l} \text{has a probability 0·9 of being} \\ \text{has a high probability of being} \\ \text{is very probably a} \\ \text{is almost certainly} \\ \text{is almost certain to be} \end{array} \right\} \quad G.$$

Analogous schemas exist, of course, whatever may be the value ascribed to the probability: '0·2', 'low', or whatever.

It is from instances of schemas like (77), I may observe, that what is called the 'propensity-interpretation' of factual probability draws all its sustenance. And such instances, it must be admitted, abound in science, in everyday life, and in writings about probability, including the preceding pages of this section. They are everywhere, and no statements could appear more innocent. But this appearance, like that of so much else that we say about probability, is deceptive.

One instance of the schema (77) is the generalization, with which biologists have made us all familiar, that

(78) Any mutation is almost certain to be harmful.

This, conjoined with

(79) *M* is a mutation,

entails that

(80) *M* is almost certain to be harmful.

Indeed, how could it not? What is 'any' in (78), if it is not a universal quantifier? And what is a universal quantifier, if it does not have syllogistic force? But if 'any' in (78) does have syllogistic force, then (78), conjoined, as it consistently can be, with what might perfectly well be true,

(81) *M* is a beneficial mutation,

entails that

(82) *M* is beneficial and almost certain to be harmful.

And (82), unfortunately, either makes no sense at all or is necessarily false.

Now the central argument of Williams's book fairly swarms with instances of the schema (77). (For example: '. . . any sizable sample very probably matches its population in any specifiable respect'.[9]) And I thought for some time that such statements are actually indispensable to his argument. I therefore thought that I had detected in that argument a fatal defect: that it could not

---

[9]   Ibid., p. 100.

dispense with statements which, conjoined with truths, can generate necessary falsities or nonsense.

I tried to prove this in a paper which I gave (in a departmental seminar) about five years ago. But in the ensuing discussion Mr R. M. Kuhn (then an undergraduate) convinced me that I was mistaken, not as to the philosophy of the matter, but as to the fact: that Williams's argument *could* be so reconstructed as to be free from any instance of the fatal schema (77).

Soon afterwards Mr Kuhn wrote out at my request his version of Williams's argument. This was the immediate predecessor of my version in (iii) below. Kuhn's version still had, in my opinion, a number of defects. All of these, I think, I have removed. Whether I have not, in this process, introduced new defects of my own into the argument—as I have often done before— remains to be seen.

(ii)

As it is usually formulated, the law of large numbers contains (as we have seen) not just one but two occurrences of the word 'probability' or some synonym of it. But it is possible to formulate the law in a way which does not contain any occurrence of any such word, but is purely mathematical. (Perhaps this is why Keynes said that Bernoulli's law 'exhibits algebraical rather than logical insight'.[10]) It was just such a purely mathematical law of large numbers, as I have said, that Williams invoked in the second version of his central argument.

What corresponds to Williams's law of large numbers in my version of his argument will likewise be a purely mathematical proposition. But my premiss will be far less general than his was, and the amount of 'algebraical insight' required of the reader in order to see that it is true will be much less than that which Williams's argument demanded. Indeed, the mathematics which my argument requires is, in principle, entirely elementary.

But philosophers are very unused to having any mathematics at all made an essential part of a philosophical argument. There is therefore a serious danger that the mathematical part of my argument, despite its being in principle elementary, will present

---

[10] Keynes (1921), p. 341.

an obstacle to the philosophical reader. The present section is an attempt to circumvent this danger, by allaying in advance any doubts that a philosopher might have about the one mathematical premiss that I do employ.

Consider, then, a population consisting of just one million ravens, and the large samples of ravens which this population contains.

It is not, of course, meant here, by calling a sample 'large', that it is large in relation to the size of the population. 'Large' is used here in an absolute, though indefinite, sense. For example, it is a sufficient condition of a sample of our population being a large one, that it contain 3000 ravens.

In this population there must be some particular proportion, either 0 or 1 or something between, of black ravens. On the value of this proportion will depend the value of certain other proportions. One of these is, the proportion of 3000-fold samples which do not differ by more than 3 per cent, in the proportion of black ravens they contain, from the proportion of black ravens in the population itself.

Evidently, this proportion will be a maximum, that is, 1, if the proportion of black ravens in the population is 1; in other words, if all ravens in the population are black. It will be a maximum, similarly, if the proportion of black ravens in the population is 0; that is, if none of them is black. For in either of these cases, no large sample (or any sample) can diverge at all, in its proportion of black ravens, from the proportion of black ravens in the population.

This proportion falls below the maximum, of course, as soon as the proportion of black ravens in the population departs from the extreme cases of 1 and 0. If just 99 per cent of the million ravens are black then 'the chance' (to speak loosely) of a 3000-fold sample diverging by more than 3 per cent in its blackness-frequency from 99 per cent is positive, though small. Similarly if just 1 per cent of the population is black. The proportion (to speak accurately), among the 3000-fold samples, of samples which are thus non-divergent or near-matching, though close to 1, is less than 1 in either of these cases. For in either of these cases the materials from which *not*-near-matching samples can be assembled do exist, though they are not abundant.

This proportion falls still further, obviously, as the blackness-frequency in the population departs still further from the extremes of 1 and 0. The number of 3000-fold samples whose blackness-frequency departs by more than 3 per cent from the blackness-frequency of the population will obviously be far greater, if just 75 per cent of the population is black, for example, than it will be if just 99 per cent of the population is black. For the materials from which such divergent samples can be assembled are far more abundant in the former case than in the latter; while of course the total number of 3000-fold samples included in the population is fixed.

It is clear, therefore, that the 'worst case' for a 3000-fold sample of our population being one which is a near-matcher of the blackness-frequency in the population, is the case in which the latter is just 50 per cent. It is just then that 'the chance' (as we say) of such a sample departing by more than 3 per cent from the blackness-frequency in the population is at its maximum. Or, to speak accurately, it is just then that the proportion of near-population-matching 3000-fold samples, to all 3000-fold samples, is at its lowest.

All of this is very obvious. What is not obvious, but in fact surprising, is this: that even this worst case is still a very good one. That is, the proportion, among 3000-fold samples, of those which do not diverge by more than 3 per cent in their blackness-frequency from the blackness-frequency in the population, is still very high even when the population-frequency is 50 per cent.

What *is* that proportion in this case?

The number of 3000-fold samples which a population of a million ravens contains is, of course, simply the number of different combinations, each of 3000 individuals, which can be formed from among a million individuals. The number of different combinations of n individuals which can be formed from m individuals is

$$\frac{m!}{n!\,(m-n)!}$$

('$m!$' is short for 'factorial m', which in turn means the product of the numbers m, $m-1$, $m-2$ . . ., $m-(m-1)$.) So the number of 3000-fold samples in a population of a million is

$$\frac{1,000,000!}{3000!\,997,000!} \ .$$

This, then, is the denominator of the fraction we are seeking.

The numerator is, the number of 3000-fold samples in our population which do not diverge in blackness-frequency by more than 3 per cent from 50 per cent.

This number will evidently be the sum of: the number of 3000-fold samples which contains exactly 47 per cent black ones (that is, 1410 black ones); the number which contains exactly 48 per cent black ones (that is, 1440 black ones); and so on, up to the number which contains exactly 53 per cent (that is, 1590) black ones; as well as the number of 3000-fold samples which contain some non-integral percentage of black ravens between these limits of 47 and 53 per cent (such as 1414 black ones).

How is each of these numbers to be arrived at? Well, take for example the number of 3000-fold samples which contain exactly 47 per cent black ones. That number must be the product of: the number of different combinations of 1410 individuals that could be drawn from the 500,000 black ravens; and the number of different combinations of 1590 individuals that could be drawn from the 500,000 non-black ones in the population. That is,

$$\frac{500,000!}{1410!\,498590!} \times \frac{500,000!}{1590!\,498410!}.$$

This, then, is the first of the numbers which are to be summed in the numerator of the fraction we are seeking.

It will be evident to the reader that both the denominator of our fraction, and each of the numbers to be summed in its numerator, is a number so enormous that to calculate its value exactly is in practice out of the question, here or in any other context. But methods of closely approximating such values have been known for a long time.

When these methods of approximation are applied, the denominator of the fraction we seek, that is, the number of 3000-fold samples in a population of a million, turns out to be approximately $10^{8867.9}$. The first of the numbers to be summed in the numerator, that is, the number of 3000-fold samples which contain just 47 per cent black ones, turns out to be approximately $10^{8864.2}$. The sum of all the terms to be summed in the numerator, that is, the number of 3000-fold samples containing between 47 and 53 per cent black ones, turns out to be approximately $10^{8867.9-0.00087}$.

That is, in a population of a million ravens just 50 per cent of which are black, the proportion of 3000-fold samples which match within 3 per cent the blackness-frequency in the population is:

$$\frac{10^{8867.9-0.00087}}{10^{8867.9}} \, .$$

But this is very high: in fact more than 99 per cent.

This means that even when the blackness-frequency in the population has that value which makes the proportion of near-matchers among 3000-fold samples the lowest it can be, that proportion is still more than 90 per cent. In other words, *whatever the proportion of black ravens may be in a population of a million, at least nine out of ten 3000-fold samples of that population do not diverge from that proportion by more than 3 per cent in the proportion of black ravens they contain.*

This is, for my purposes, the all-important result. And as the reader has seen, nothing more is *in principle* required to reach it than the elementary theory of combinations. It is true that the mathematics required by the methods of approximation are not elementary; but everything else is.

The result which is italicized above also holds if, with the sample size still fixed at 3000, we consider instead a population of two million, or of three million. In fact it holds independently of any increase in the population-size beyond a million.

The same result will obviously hold *a fortiori* if we consider instead samples which are larger than 3000-fold. (For such samples actually improve the 'chance' of a match.) Hence, with a population of a million or more, at least nine out of ten 3000-or-more-fold samples will nearly match the blackness-frequency of the population.

Nor does the above result depend on the population being as *small* as one million. It holds, in fact, however small the population is, as long as it is of such size that it does contain ten 3000-fold samples. Suppose, for example, that the population contains only 3020 ravens. Then it remains true that at least nine out of ten 3000-fold samples are near-matching ones, and true *a fortiori* that at least nine out of ten 3000-or-more-fold samples are near-matchers. For in this case, of course, *all* 3000-or-more-fold samples are near-matching ones.

(iii)

Some abbreviations are needed.

'Pop' will be short for: 'the population of ravens, each at least 100 cc in volume and no two overlapping, on earth between 10,000 BC and AD 10,000'.

By calling a sample of Pop a '*near*-Pop-matcher with respect to the proportion of black ravens it contains', I mean (as in the preceding section) that the proportion of black ravens in that sample does not differ from the proportion of black ravens in Pop by more than 3 per cent. Similarly for 'near' in the proposition E below: 'near 95 per cent' means 'between 92 and 98 per cent'.

Certain propositions are abbreviated by capital letters, as follows:

A: S is a 3020-fold sample of Pop.

B: At least $\frac{9}{10}$ths of the 3000-or-more-fold samples in Pop are near-Pop-matchers with respect to the proportion of black ravens that they contain.

C: S is a near-Pop-matcher with respect to the proportion of black ravens it contains.

D: Just 95 per cent of the ravens in S are black.

E: The proportion of black ravens in Pop is near 95 per cent.

(The propositions A–E are all contingent, since each of them entails that Pop contains at least one raven. None of them, of course, is *asserted* in the argument below. They are simply *mentioned* in certain other propositions, principally assessments of logical probability.)

Hereafter I omit the cumbrous phrase, always intended to be understood after 'near-Pop-matcher(s)', 'with respect to the proportion of black ravens that they (it) contain(s)'.

The inference from the conjunction of A and D to E is an inductive one. It is also an inference which people who are not sceptics about the induction think has high probability: that is, they think that the conclusion has high probability in relation to the premisses. The following version of Williams's neo-

Laplacean argument is, I think, a proof that the non-sceptics are right in thinking so.

(83) For all x, all $\frac{m}{n}$, all $r > 3000$,
P(x is a near-Pop-matcher/x is an r-fold sample of Pop, and at least $\frac{m}{n}$ths of the 3000-or-more-fold samples in Pop are near-Pop-matchers) $\geq \frac{m}{n}$.

(This premiss is what corresponds in my version to Williams's premiss about the probability of proportional syllogisms: which was that P(x is G/x is F, and $\frac{m}{n}$ths of the F's are G) $=\frac{m}{n}$, for all x, all F, all G, all $\frac{m}{n}$. What (83) says is simply this. Take any inference which is an instance of the schema

(84) At least $\frac{m}{n}$ths of the 3000-fold samples in Pop are near-Pop-matchers
x is an r-fold sample of Pop
$\overline{x \text{ is a near-Pop-matcher;}}$

then, if $r > 3000$, this inference has probability $\geq \frac{m}{n}$.)
It follows from (83) that

(85) P(S is a near-Pop-matcher/S is a 3020-fold sample of Pop, and at least $\frac{9}{10}$ of the 3000-or-more-fold samples in Pop are near-Pop-matchers) $\geq 0\cdot9$.

That is, in virtue of the above abbreviations,

(86) P($C/A.B$) $\geq 0\cdot9$

Now,

(87) Necessarily, if Pop is finite, and large enough to contain ten 3000-or-more-fold samples, then at least $\frac{9}{10}$ of the 3000-or-more-fold samples in Pop are near-Pop-matchers.

(This premiss is what corresponds in my version to Williams's mathematical law of large numbers. Since (87) is entirely lacking in generality, it is, of course, no sort of *law*. But the conditional which it says is necessary is, if what was said in the preceding section is true, an arithmetical truth.)

(88) Necessarily, Pop is finite.

(The members of Pop, it will be recalled, are by definition confined to a finite region of space-time, and required to be of a specified minimum size, with no overlaps.)

From (87) and (88) it follows that

(89) Necessarily, if Pop is large enough to contain ten 3000-or-more-fold samples, then at least $\frac{9}{10}$ of the 3000-or-more-fold samples in Pop are near-Pop-matchers.

From the abbreviations above, it is obvious that

(90) Necessarily, if A then Pop is large enough to contain ten 3000-or-more-fold samples.

From (90) and (89) it follows that

(91) Necessarily, if A then at least $\frac{9}{10}$ of the 3000-or-more-fold samples in Pop are near-Pop-matchers.

That is, in virtue of the abbreviations above,

(92) Necessarily, if A then B.

It is a principle of logical probability, and in any case obvious, that

(93) If necessarily if p then r, $P(q/p.r) = P(q/p)$.

That is, r is irrelevant to q in relation to p, if it is necessarily true that if p then r.

It follows from (93), (92), and (86) that

(94) $P(C/A) \geq 0.9$.

Now,

(95) $P(C/A.D) \geq P(C/A)$.

That is, 'Just 95 per cent of the ravens in S are black' is not unfavourably relevant (in Keynes's sense) to 'S is a near-Pop-matcher', in relation to 'S is a 3020-fold sample of Pop'. This is obvious.

(If we let D' be short for 'Just 50 per cent of the ravens in S are black', then D' *is* unfavourably relevant to C in relation to A. That is, 'S is a near-Pop-matcher' is less probable, in relation to 'S is a 3020-fold sample of Pop and just 50 per cent of the ravens in S are black', than it is in relation to the first conjunct of that conjunction. Even this unfavourable relevance is slight in amount: for as we have seen, (94) $P(C/A) \geq 0.9$, and, as the consideration of the 'worst case' in the preceding section will have suggested to the reader, $P(C/A.D)$ is *also* ≥ 0.9. But in any case the unfavourable relevance of D' is of course entirely consistent with the not unfavourable relevance of D, which is all that my (95) asserts. To admit it is no more than to acknowledge what is obvious, that where one proposition is not unfavourably relevant, a contrary proposition may be. Indeed, the unfavourable relevance of D' would furnish us with one of the premises of a *proof* of the not-unfavourable relevance of D, that is, of (95), if it were worth while, as it is not, to prove (95), rather than to take it as a premiss. For it is a principle of logical probability that if $r, s, t,$ etc., are exhaustive and pairwise-exclusive alternatives, then if one of these alternatives is unfavourably relevant to q in relation to p, then at least one other alternative is not so. The possible blackness-frequencies in S are exhaustive and pairwise-exclusive alternatives. Whence if one of them is unfavourably relevant to C in relation to A, at least one other of them is not.)

From (95) and (94) it follows that

(96) $P(C/A.D) \geq 0.9$.

It is a principle of logical probability, and in any case obvious, that

(97) $P(q/p.r) = P(q.r/p.r)$.

That is, a premiss of an inference can always be conjoined with the conclusion *salva probabilitate.*

It follows from (97) that

(98) $P(C/A.D) = P(C.D/A.D)$.

Whence with (96) it follows that

(99) $P(C.D./A.D) \geq 0.9$.

It is obvious, from the abbreviations above, that

(100) Necessarily, if $C.D$ then E.

It is a principle of logical probability, and in any case obvious, that

(101) $P(r/p) \geq P(q/p)$, if necessarily if q then r.

(That is, the probability, in relation to p, of any r such that q necessitates r, cannot be less than the probability of q itself.)

It follows from (101), (100), and (99), that

(102) $P(E/A.D) \geq 0.9$.

(103) The inference from $A.D$ to E is inductive.

So

(104) The inductive inference from $A.D$ to E has high probability.

(iv)

The argument just completed, along with the two arguments of the preceding chapter, forms the core of the rest of this book. Everything that follows is either an extension of one of these three arguments, or a defence of one or more of these arguments or extensions.

While these three arguments are thus all-important for my purposes, they are not as easily surveyable as one would wish. It is not easy for a reader to remember all their premisses. For this reason I here collect, in a form which *is* easily surveyable, all the premisses of each of the three arguments.

To assist the reader further, I have in each case distinguished between those premisses which are principles of logical probability, those which are statements of logical probability, and those which are neither.

The premisses of the first argument of Chapter V:

Principles of logical probability: (27), (28).
Statements of logical probability: (44), (45), (46), (51).
Other premisses: (48).

The premisses of the second argument of Chapter V:

Principles of logical probability: (16), (27), (28).
Statements of logical probability: (46), (55), (59), (63).
Other premisses: (56).

The premisses of the argument of Chapter VI:

Principles of logical probability: (93), (97), (101).
Statements of logical probability: (83), (95).
Other premisses: (87), (88), (90), (100), (103).

VII

RESPONSES TO THESE ATTEMPTS; AND RESPONSES TO THEM

(i)

SUPPOSE some one were to object to the argument of Chapter VI by saying, 'That is not a proof that induction is justified; for it does not prove that an inductive inference with a *universal* conclusion is ever justified.' Or suppose some one objected to the arguments of Chapter V by saying, 'Neither of these arguments is a proof that induction is justified, for neither proves that an inductive inference to a *singular* conclusion, about a particular unobserved raven, is ever justified.'

Such objections would obviously be irrelevant. Of course it is true that the argument of Chapter VI does not prove that inductive inference to a universal conclusion is ever justified, and that the arguments of Chapter V do not prove that inductive inference to a conclusion about a particular unobserved raven is ever justified; but these facts are no criticisms of those arguments. As we saw in Chapters III and IV, the sceptical thesis that induction is unjustified is a universal proposition. Proof of a single counter-example to it is therefore sufficient to disprove it, and therefore sufficient to prove that induction is justified.

Objections of the kind just mentioned would be what I have elsewhere called 'Irish' ones.[1] According to the authors of *1066 and All That*, the Irish question has been kept alive for nearly a thousand years by means of the following simple but effective stratagem: whenever the British government seemed to be on the brink of finding the answer to the Irish question, the Irish *changed the question*. And whether or not this is true, it is certainly true that in philosophy 'objections' of this kind are sometimes made and mistaken for relevant criticism.

In fact the earlier versions of the arguments of Chapters V and VI above elicited a large number of Irish objections. The central

[1] Cf. Stove (1976a).

argument of Williams (1947) was set aside as of no interest by one writer, for example, on the ground that it did not touch the case of inductive inferences with *theoretical* conclusions.[2] It was ignored by others[3] because it did not touch the case of inductive inferences with *universal* conclusions. There were other 'objections' still more extravagantly Irish. (The unbeatable record is held by the philosopher[4] whose 'objection' was, in substance, that Williams had failed to prove any inductive inference *valid*.) And the version of the arguments of Chapter V which was given in Stove (1973) was found wanting on the ground that it did not touch the case of inductive inferences with conclusions *which do not entail the premisses*.[5]

These objections (other than the one just referred to in parentheses) would have been just, and would be just when directed against the arguments of Chapters V and VI here, if and only if what I have elsewhere called the master-axiom of Irish quantificational logic were true: that $\sim(x)Fx$ only if $(x)\sim Fx$. But it is not true.

That *all* inductive inferences are justified is false in any case (as I have said several times already). The inference from (2) to (8) is an obvious counter-example to it. A more famous counter-example is Goodman's:[6] the inference from

All the many emeralds observed before the year 2000 are grue

to

All the emeralds observed after 2000 are grue.

('Grue' means 'green if observed before 2000 or blue if observed after 2000'.)

Still other examples could be given, but all such examples are irrelevant where the question is, as it is here, just whether there is some inductive inference, or none, which is justified. Where what is in dispute is just whether some F are G, it is impertinent to

[2] See Barker (1957), pp. 97–101.
[3] Popper and his followers. See, e.g., the article by Lakatos in Lakatos (1968), *passim*.
[4] Cf. Wisdom (1952), pp. 217–18, especially the last two lines.
[5] Cf. Stove (1976a).
[6] Cf. Goodman (1954), ch. III.

mention examples which only prove, what is not in dispute, that some *F* are not *G*.

Inferences like the two just mentioned do, of course, show the falsity of something which has sometimes been believed: that non-deductive logic is (as deductive logic is supposed to be) purely *formal*. But it is only for someone who believes that, that such inferences pose any problem; and in particular (as we have just seen) they do not pose any problem for a philosopher just because he is not a sceptic about induction.

Yet nowadays non-sceptics constantly allude to 'the problem about grue', as though they had, simply as non-sceptics, an obligation to worry about such inferences. This is an instance of the tendency for imaginary obligations to multiply indefinitely in scrupulous consciences. If a scrupulous person undertakes an obligation which it is logically impossible for anyone to discharge, then (as the religious instances sufficiently illustrate) the anxiety arising from his failure to discharge this obligation is apt to conjure into existence further and equally imaginary obligations. Nor is there any logical, as distinct from biological, limit to this process. Now philosophers are scrupulous people, and the non-sceptical ones among them having taken upon themselves earlier in this century the impossible obligation to 'justify induction', it is not at all surprising to find them now admitting, or rather, anxiously insisting, that they have in addition an obligation to 'solve the problem about grue'.

(ii)

'But it is begging the question against the inductive sceptic, to take some principles of logical probability as premisses, as you have done in the arguments of Chapters V and VI.'

Such an objection was undoubtedly felt, though it was never very clearly expressed, by some readers of Stove (1973). And if the objection had been a just one there, it would be equally so here, since here as well as there some principles of logical probability are indeed taken as premisses. But in fact it is a complete mistake.

What is in dispute between the sceptic and the non-sceptic is a certain *assessment* of logical probability, and nothing else. But the *principles* of logical probability cannot beg the question against any assessment of logical probability, or in favour of the contradictory assessment: for they do not entail any assessment of logical probability at all. The principles leave you entirely free to make any assessment that you might want to of the value of any particular logical probability; just as the principles of a geometry leave you free to make any assessment you might want to of the length of any particular line. The principles of logical probability only tell you that *if* certain assessments of logical probability are true, then certain other assessments of logical probability are true.

It is exactly the same with any kind of probability, for example factual probability. The principles of probability$_2$ do not entail any assessment of probability$_2$. They only tell you that *if* certain assessments of probability$_2$ are true, then certain other assessments of probability$_2$ are true.

In the field of factual probability, an analogue of the inductive sceptic would be someone who maintained, for example, that the probability$_2$ of a female birth among humans is twice that of a male birth. Like the sceptic's assessment of the logical probability of inductive inferences, this assessment of the factual probability of a female birth is obviously false, and one which it would not be difficult to prove false. But the premisses of such a proof could not consist just of *principles* of probability$_2$, since *they* are all entirely consistent with this eccentric assessment of probability$_2$, as they are with every other. The premisses would have to include some *assessments* of probability$_2$ as well. Suppose then that some one attempted a proof of the falsity of this assessment of probability$_2$. It would evidently be ridiculous to object to this attempted proof, that it begged the question about the probability of a female birth, on the ground that there are principles of probability$_2$ among its premisses: propositions, that is, such as the negation principle, that the probability$_2$ of an *F* being *G*=1—the probability$_2$ of an *F* not being *G*. Yet the objection stated above, to the arguments of Chapters V and VI, is precisely parallel to this.

The principles of probability, while they never forbid any one assessment of probability, do of course forbid certain *conjunctions of* assessments. Thus the negation principle of factual probability forbids, for example, the conjunction of 'The probability$_2$ of a human birth being female is 0·7' with 'The probability$_2$ of a human birth not being female is 0·4', though it does not forbid either conjunct. In exactly the same way, the principles of logical probability forbid certain conjunctions of assessments of logical probability, without forbidding any one conjunct.

What the arguments of Chapters V and VI show is that, among the conjunctions of assessments of logical probability which are forbidden by the principles of logical probability, there are some which we would not have expected to be so forbidden. For example, the conjunction of the *sceptical* assessment (14) of inductive inference, with the *fallibilist* assessment (63) of a particular inductive inference; and the conjunction of the minimal sceptical assessment of induction, with the natural assessment (83) of a certain class of proportional syllogisms. But the principles do not forbid the sceptical assessment of induction, any more than they forbid any other conjunct of these conjunctions.

(iii)

'In his arguments against the sceptical thesis about induction, Stove uses the negation principle of logical probability (27), and the conjunction principle (28), as premises. These propositions imply that the values of logical probabilities are such as can be added to and multiplied by one another. And since these principles are perfectly general, ranging indifferently over all values of the variables *p, q, r*, etc., to use them as premises in an argument amounts to assuming that the probability of one proposition in relation to another always has a numerical value, whatever two propositions these may be. This assumption, however, has been expressly rejected by some philosophers, for example by Keynes; and Koopman, for another, published a set of principles of logical probability which are purely comparative in nature and which therefore avoid this assumption. The inductive sceptic is at liberty to join these philosophers in rejecting that assumption, and therefore in rejecting some of the premises of Stove's arguments against him.'

This objection is one which was made by Mr Michael Bradley[7]

---

[7] Bradley (1977).

to the central argument of Stove (1973), though I have put it here in my own words.

The same objection cannot be made to the argument of Chapter VI above. There were just three principles of logical probability among the premisses of that argument. They were: the principle that a premiss necessitated by another premiss is irrelevant, that is,

(93) If necessarily if p then r, $\mathrm{P}(q/p.r) = \mathrm{P}(q/p)$;

the principle that a premiss can always be conjoined with the conclusion *salva probabilitate*, that is,

(97) $\mathrm{P}(q/p.r) = \mathrm{P}(q.r/p.r)$;

and the principle that the probability of a proposition cannot exceed that of a proposition necessitated by it, that is,

(101) $\mathrm{P}(q/p) \leq \mathrm{P}(r/p)$, if necessarily if q then r.

These three principles, it will be evident, are all purely comparative. They say only that certain probabilities are equal in value, not that they have the same, or any, numerical value; or that one probability is less than another. *A fortiori* they do not, singly or in conjunction, imply that the logical probability of q in relation to p has a numerical value whatever p and q may be.

At the same time, these principles are so obviously true that any set of axioms for the principles of logical probability, even if it were only a set of axioms for purely comparative principles, would clearly be defective if it did not include all three among its axioms or theorems.

Mr Bradley's objection *can* be made, on the other hand, to both of the arguments of Chapter V above. For they both have among their premisses both the negation principle (27) and the conjunction principle (28).

But the first of those two arguments can easily be recast in such a way that it is no longer exposed to Mr Bradley's objection. (This was foreshadowed, in fact, by the short summary of that argument which I gave at the end of it.)

Any true instance of the schema $\mathrm{P}(q/r.p) = \mathrm{P}(q/r)$ asserts something which Keynes aptly called 'the irrelevance of p to q (in relation to r)'. It follows from the conjunction principle (28) that irrelevance, in *this* sense, has the property of symmetry. Hence follows as a special case the principle of the symmetry of initial irrelevance (37): that (where p and q are each initially possible) p is initially irrelevant to q (in relation to r) if and only if q is initially irrelevant to p (in relation to r). But (37) is not itself obviously true: we believe it, if we do, because we believe the conjunction principle (28) of which it is a consequence. In other words, not every relation among propositions for which 'the irrelevance of p to q' would be an apt name is symmetrical. There is nothing in the *concept* of the irrelevance of one proposition to another (in relation to a third) which requires this relation to be symmetrical.

There are other properties, however, which any relation among propositions, for which 'irrelevance' would be an apt name, *does* have to have. One of these is what I will call 'invariance under negation': I mean, for example, that if p is irrelevant to q (in relation to r), then not-p too is irrelevant to q (in relation to r). Some one could, as I have implied, perfectly well have the concept of irrelevance, without acknowledging, or even while denying, the symmetry of this relation. But some one who thought that irrelevance could vary under negation, so that for example p could be irrelevant to q while the negation of p was *relevant* to q, would not have grasped the concept of irrelevance at all. For the irrelevance of p to q is, whatever else it may be, its making no difference to q, whether p be supposed true, *or not-p be supposed true*, or neither.

It follows as a special case that initial irrelevance is invariant under negation in the respect just mentioned: that is, that (where p and not-p and q are each initially possible) p is initially irrelevant to q (in relation to r) if and only if not-p is initially irrelevant to q (in relation to r). And this property of initial irrelevance, unlike its symmetry, does not need to be inferred from the conjunction principle or from any other principles of logical probability, but is obvious in itself.

But the principle just stated is of course none other than (42) of the first argument of Chapter V. It is therefore easy to see how that argument can be recast if we wish to avoid Mr Bradley's objection to it. I there *derived* (42), partly *via* the symmetry of irrelevance (37), from the negation and conjunction principles (27) and (28). But suppose that Mr Bradley is right, and that the inductive sceptic is free to dissent from (27) and (28), as implying what some other philosophers have denied, that the probability of q given p has a numerical value for any p and q. Very well then: *begin* the argument with (42). Almost the whole argument will then be simply this: that 'Not all the observed Australian ravens have been black' is *not* initially irrelevant to 'All Australian ravens are black', whereas by (42) it would have to be so, if the sceptical thesis (14) were true. The *only* principle of logical probability then appealed to in the argument will be (42): a principle which is both obvious in itself, and purely comparative.

By way of a partial response to Mr Bradley's objection, Mr Chris Mortensen showed how Stove's (1973) argument against (14) could be reconstructed, using only principles which are theorems of Koopman's purely comparative axiom system for probability.[8] That argument, then, can be freed from its dependence on 'global-numerical' premisses such as (27) and (28). The same is true, we have now seen, of the first argument of Chapter V above. It will be worth while to point out in addition—(though it would take us too far afield to prove the point here)—that (42), the only principle which the first argument of Chapter V now employs, is also a theorem of Koopman's axiom-system.

It is not possible, as far as I have been able to discover, to do the same kind of thing for the *second* argument of Chapter V. To free that argument, that is, from its dependence on the symmetry of irrelevance (37), and from its dependence, therefore, on one of the principles which Mr Bradley thinks the inductive sceptic is free to reject, namely the conjunction principle (28).

If only for this reason, I ought to say that I do not concede to Mr Bradley that the inductive sceptic *is* free to reject any principles which imply that $P(q/p)$ has a numerical value whatever p and q may be; and do not concede, therefore, that an argument is not a disproof of inductive scepticism (14), if it depends on such 'global-numerical' premisses. Suppose, what is not the case, that all three of my attempts above, and suppose even that all possible attempts to disprove the sceptical thesis, depend on premisses which imply that $P(q/p)$ has a numerical value for all p and q. Would this fact, if it were a fact, be a defect in those attempts? Would it show, as Mr Bradley thinks, that those

[8] Mortensen (1977).

arguments have certain premisses which the inductive sceptic is free to reject?

It would not show anything of the sort. To see this, consider a parallel case. It will be advisable—since inductive inference is a subject on which philosophers' sympathies are by now hopelessly predisposed to the sceptical side of the question—to choose a case in which the inference being assessed is a non-inductive one. So let the inference in question be, say, the one from E, 'Just 95 per cent of all ravens are black and Abe is a raven', to H, 'Abe is black'. And now suppose that some one maintains that

(105) $\mathrm{P}(H/E) = 0.95$,

and also maintains that

(106) $\mathrm{P}(\sim H/E) = 0.4$.

This person need fear no criticism whatever, if Mr Bradley is right. The obvious and sufficient criticism of what this person maintains is, of course, this: that in view of the negation principle

(27) $\mathrm{P}(q/p) = 1 - \mathrm{P}(\sim q/p)$,

(105) and (106) cannot both be true. *No* criticism of the conjunction he maintains is possible, however, which does not take as a premiss either (27) or some consequence of it which, like

(107) $\mathrm{P}(q/p) + \mathrm{P}(\sim q/p) \leq 1$,

entails that $\mathrm{P}(q/p)$ has a numerical value for all p and q. So with Mr Bradley's help, the person we are imagining will find it easy to rebut all such criticisms. 'This is taking for granted that all logical probabilities have a numerical value: an assumption expressly denied by Keynes and others, and the denial of which is therefore open to me too.' (Compare the first paragraph of this section.)

Even against an argument like the second one of Chapter V, then, Mr Bradley's way of protecting the sceptical thesis (14) from disproof is (as I have described it elsewhere) a 'kamikaze' or scorched-earth defence. It protects (14) from disproof at the cost of protecting from disproof even such enormities as the conjunction of (105) and (106).

And in any case, as we have seen, to the argument of Chapter VI, and to the first argument of Chapter V as amended in this section, Mr Bradley's objection does not apply at all; since these two arguments do not have premisses which imply that for all p and q, $P(q/p)$ has a numerical value.

(iv)

Keynes thought not only that some logical probabilities do not have a numerical value, but that two logical probabilities need not even be comparable in value: that is, that one need not be equal to, or greater than, or less than, the other. Still further, he thought that for some p and q, the logical probability of q in relation to p simply does not exist.

(That $P(q/p)$ does not exist for *self-contradictory p* is, of course, not a minority opinion but on the contrary the standard one. The reason is that it is standard opinion that a self-contradiction entails every proposition; whence the negation principle (27) would fail, if $P(q/p)$ exists with p self-contradictory. But Keynes thought that even for some not-self-contradictory values of p, $P(q/p)$ does not exist, though he never offered to say just which cases these are.)

This fact suggests a new objection, on the lines of Mr Bradley's, to the arguments of the two preceding chapters. 'Those arguments have among their premisses propositions which imply that $P(q/p)$ exists for all p and q; but Keynes and others have expressly denied that assumption, and the inductive sceptic too is therefore free to deny any premisses which imply it.'

No one did in fact make this objection to the central argument of Stove (1973), but they could have, and I do not know why no one did. If good philosophers now set so high a value, as the example of Mr Bradley shows they do, on the sceptical thesis (14) about induction, that they would more willingly part instead with, say, the negation principle (27) of logical probability, then this way of objecting to my former attempted disproof of (14) was open to them, just as Mr Bradley's was.

But in the present context this objection would meet exactly the same fate as Mr Bradley's. The second argument of Chapter V, depending as it does (as far as I have been able to discover) on (27) and (28), does depend on premisses which imply that $P(q/p)$ has a numerical value, and *a fortiori* exists, for any p and q. But the same is not true of the argument of Chapter VI, or of the (amended) first argument of Chapter V. The only principles of logical probability there used as premisses were, to repeat:

(93)   If necessarily if p then r, $\mathrm{P}(q/p.r) = \mathrm{P}(q/p)$;
(97) $\mathrm{P}(q/p.r) = \mathrm{P}(q.r/p.r)$;
(101) If necessarily if q then r, $\mathrm{P}(q/p) \leq \mathrm{P}(r/p)$;

and

(42)   If $\mathrm{P}(p/T)$, $\mathrm{P}(\sim p/T)$, and $\mathrm{P}(q/T)$ are each > 0, then $\mathrm{P}(q/T.p) = \mathrm{P}(q/T)$ if and only if $\mathrm{P}(q/T.\sim p) = \mathrm{P}(q/T)$.

And it is evident that these principles do not imply, singly or in conjunction, that $\mathrm{P}(q/p)$ exists for all p and q. (97), for example, implies that $\mathrm{P}(H.E'/E.E')$ exists and is equal to $\mathrm{P}(H/E.E')$ if $\mathrm{P}(H/E.E')$ exists; but it does not imply the antecedent of this conditional.

(v)

The situation we have now reached, if we pause to reflect on it, must surely appear a little remarkable. The conclusion of any inductive inference, Hume said, is no more probable in relation to the premiss than it is *a priori*, or at least is never as probable as non-sceptics suppose. This assessment of logical probability is proved to be false, in the only way a proposition of that kind can be proved false. That is, assessments of logical probability inconsistent with it are validly inferred, *via* standard principles of probability, from obviously true assessments of the logical probability of certain non-inductive inferences. And what is the result? Nothing more than an outbreak of Irish and other evasive manoeuvres. 'Ah, but Hume's thesis concerned only inductive inferences which have *unrestrictedly universal* conclusions/ *singular* conclusions/conclusions which *do not entail the premiss*', etc. 'Ah, but Hume's principles of probability may have been *non*-standard ones', etc.

The fact is, scepticism about induction leads by now a charmed life. Nothing can discredit it, or so much as loosen the hold it has on philosophers' minds. A critic of it may choose what weapons he will, and employ them as he may—ordinary language, the arithmetic of large numbers, the logic of probability, the history of science, whatever—the result is still the

same. Not only are all actual known criticisms of inductive scepticism felt to be hopelessly beside the mark: not one philosopher
in a thousand can tell you what *possible* kind of criticism of it
would prove it false (supposing it to be false).

This *is* a remarkable situation. On the other hand, it cannot
surprise anyone who is acquainted with the apotheosis of Hume
which has taken place in the present century, especially though
not only in relation to his philosophy of induction. Hume's actual
achievements concerning induction wildly exaggerated; his
greatest achievements merely invented; his worst arguments
accorded a profound respect; a boundless indulgence extended
to other people's arguments, however bad, when they support his
sceptical conclusion; a standard of rigour which is applied
almost nowhere else (and least of all to Hume himself), applied
to arguments *against* that conclusion: such things as these nowadays form the background to any discussion of scepticism about
induction. I have given detailed instances of them elsewhere[9];
and Williams justly complained of some of the same things as
early as 1947.[10]

The sceptical thesis is immune to all actual criticisms that have
been made of it, because (as I have said) not one philosopher in
a thousand can say what kind of criticism of it would be possible,
(supposing it to be false); and that in turn is because not one in a
thousand can tell you what kind of proposition the sceptical
thesis itself *is*. What its modality is; what its quantification is:
these are vital matters concerning which philosophers' ideas (as I
have implied earlier) are utterly and fatally indistinct. But there
is nowadays also a most important confusion in philosophers'
minds concerning the very *subject* of the sceptical thesis. This is
due to a certain ambiguity which has overtaken the word 'inductive' itself in recent years.

During most of the last four hundred years, philosophers have
meant, when they spoke of *inductive* inference, inference from (a
premiss about) the observed to (a conclusion about) the unobserved, in which the conclusion says about the unobserved
something like what the premiss says about the observed. This
itself, of course, is not ideally precise, especially its second

---

[9] Cf. Stove (1965); Stove (1973), pp. 125–32; Stove (1976b); Stove (1976c).
[10] Williams (1947), p. 15.

clause. Nor have all philosophers without exception understood 'inductive' in just this sense. Still, this sense of the word undoubtedly deserves to be called the mainstream one. It is the sense in which most philosophers still use the word 'inductive' most of the time. (And it is, of course, the sense in which the word is used in this book.)

In the 1940s, however, Carnap, apparently without realizing that he was doing so, began to use the word in a new sense. An inference is inductive in Carnap's sense, if and only if it is not 'deductive', that is, not deductively valid: the conclusion does not follow from the premiss.[11] And by now this sense of 'inductive' has acquired considerable currency, though without driving out the mainstream sense, and without being at all widely recognized as being a different sense of the word from the mainstream one.

Yet it should be evident that the two senses are not only different, but logically independent of one another. Carnap's sense of 'inductive' is purely evaluative: it concerns the logical value of the inference in question, and nothing else. The mainstream sense, on the other hand, is purely descriptive: it concerns what kind of propositions the premiss and the conclusion of the inference are, and nothing else. It is *no* part of the mainstream sense of 'inductive', and still less is it the whole of that sense, that the inference in question be not deductively valid.

I have pointed out elsewhere the historical circumstances which made Carnap's neologism possible and even natural. I have also pointed out some intellectually disastrous consequences which it nevertheless has.[12] Here I intend to point out another such consequence: that to use 'inductive' in Carnap's sense suffices on its own to generate the illusion that it is impossible to disprove the sceptical thesis about induction.

This will be most easily seen if, rather than considering all possible attempts to disprove the sceptical thesis, we consider instead a typical example of such an attempt. The argument of Chapter VI above is such a typical example; so let us take that.

In that argument, we derived the conclusion that a certain inductive inference (in the mainstream sense) has high probability. Our premisses included (83). This proposition ascribes high

---

[11] See Carnap (1962), p. 580, glossary, s.v. 'inductive inference'.
[12] Cf. Stove (1973), pp. 22–3, 75, and 92.

probability to certain inferences. But there was no circularity in employing it as a premiss in the derivation of our anti-sceptical conclusion, because none of the inferences to which (83) ascribes any probability is an inductive one (in the mainstream sense). They are, rather, certain inferences of a (roughly) proportional syllogistic kind.

But of course those inferences *are*, in addition, ones which (except where $m = n$) are *not deductively valid*. They are, therefore, inferences which, in *Carnap's* sense, *are* inductive ones. The argument of Chapter VI is therefore exposed to the following easy rejoinder. 'You derive the conclusion that some inductive inferences have high probability, but you do so from premisses including (83), which already *asserts* that some inductive inferences have high probability. Your "proof" is therefore circular: you have simply begged the question against the inductive sceptic's thesis.' And if 'inductive' is taken, each time it occurs in this rejoinder, in Carnap's sense, then the rejoinder is entirely just. In short, if the word 'inductive' is used in Carnap's sense, then any proof that induction is justified, or any disproof of the sceptical thesis, *must* fail through circularity.

This effect is reinforced, of course, if you insist, as some writers now do, on miscalling logical probability, 'inductive probability'.[13] In fact the general confusion introduced by Carnap's neologism reaches its peak with this disastrous phrase. You might as well speak of 'cometary velocity' in mechanics, say, as though comets had a kind of velocity all their own, or introduce 'Mexican reproduction' as a fundamental concept in biology.

The distinction between the two senses of 'inductive' having gone generally unnoticed, many philosophers now move unconsciously from the one sense to the other. When the distinction is noticed, it is noticed only as a terminological point of no importance.[14] And certainly the distinction *seems* unimportant. Yet in fact it has this enormous importance: that neglect of it at once makes the inductive sceptic's position appear impregnable. (So easily, we thus see once again, are great effects in philosophy brought about by apparently contemptible verbal causes.)

The anti-sceptic's position must appear more hopeless still, of

---

[13] e.g. Burks (1977).
[14] Salmon (1982), p. 240.

course, if failure to adhere exclusively to the mainstream sense of 'inductive' is combined with the belief that the anti-sceptic has an obligation to 'justify induction'. And in fact, of course, these two things usually *are* combined.

(vi)

It must be admitted, in view of the preceding sections, that the arguments of Chapters V and VI, even if they are in fact proofs that induction is justified, are unlikely to carry much conviction. There are too many apparently possible ways of eluding them, and the desire to see them eluded is too strong. I have now tried to show that a number of the apparently possible ways of eluding them are not really possible. But somehow the arguments of Chapters V and VI do not seem well suited to bringing about real conviction of the falsity of the sceptical thesis.

Is there any way of making those arguments more convincing?

I said at the start of this chapter that one of the apparently possible ways of eluding those arguments is to object that none of them proves that an inductive inference with a *singular* conclusion is ever justified. This is, of course, a pure 'Irish' objection: simply an attempt to change the question. Now it is obviously unwise, in general, to yield to the temptation to pursue some new question, because even if we do succeed in answering the new question, the Irish critic is then almost certain to change the question yet again. On the other hand the anti-sceptic—the preceding sections show—cannot afford to neglect any opportunity he may have of making his arguments more convincing; and at the same time, inferences from the blackness of observed ravens to the blackness of a particular unobserved raven seem, to many philosophers, to be a peculiarly important sub-class of inductive inferences. For these reasons it may be worth while to show that the argument of Chapter VI can in fact be extended so as to prove that certain inductive inferences of this kind have high probability.

Here, to remind the reader, are certain abbreviations which were employed in Chapter VI.

A: *S* is a 3020-fold sample of Pop.
D: Just 95 per cent of the ravens in *S* are black.

E: The proportion of black ravens in Pop is near 95 per cent.

Here are two additional abbreviations.

F: Abe is a member of Pop and not a member of S.
G: Abe is black.

The extension of the argument of Chapter VI is as follows:

(108) $P(G/E.F) \geq 0.9$;
(109) $P(G/E.F.A.D) \geq P(G/E.F)$.

Neither of the inferences assessed by (108) or (109) is, of course, inductive. The inference from $E.F$ to G is of a (roughly) proportional syllogistic kind. Premiss (108) is an obviously true assessment of that inference. It is a premiss of essentially the same kind as (83) of Chapter VI, only much less general.

Premiss (109) simply says, what is equally obviously true, that the additional information $A.D$ is at least not unfavourably relevant to the proportional syllogistic inference from $E.F$ to G.

From (108) and (109) it follows that

(110) $P(G/E.F.A.D) \geq 0.9$.

Further

(111) $P(E/A.D.F) \geq P(E/A.D)$.

This premiss is also obviously true.

(Both the inferences compared in (111) are inductive ones, of course. But the premiss is not one to which the inductive sceptic can object. For (111) is a *consequence of* inductive scepticism (14), in view of the fact that

(112) The inference from $A.D$ to E, and the inference from $A.D.F$ to E, are both inductive.

For obviously,

(113) $P(h/e.e') = P(h/e)$ for all h, all e, and all tautological e';

whence from (112) and (14), where T is some tautology,

(114) $P(E/A.D.F) = P(E/T) = P(E/A.D)$.

Finally, it is also obviously true that

(115) $P(E/A.D.F.G) < 1$.

Now by the conjunction principle (28),

(116) $P(E.G/A.D.F) = P(E/A.D.F) \times P(G/A.D.F.E) = P(G/A.D.F) \times P(E/A.D.F.G)$.

Consider the four terms in the right-hand equality of (116). From (115) the fourth term is < 1. From

(102) $P(E/A.D) \geq 0.9$,

which was proved in Chapter VI, and (111), the first term is ≥ 0.9. From (110) the second term is ≥ 0.9. Whence the third term is ≥ 0.81. That is

(117) $P(G/A.D.F) > 0.81$.

Now

(118) The inference from $A.D.F$ to G is inductive.

Whence

(119) The inductive inference from $A.D.F$ to G has high probability.

And the inference from $A.D.F$ to G has, of course, a singular conclusion concerning a member of Pop which is not included in the sample S.

(vii)

Williams's 1947 argument, we saw, had as a premiss the natural assessment of the probability of proportional syllogisms. In other words, it was simply assumed in that argument that, for example,

(120) P(Abe is black/Abe is a raven and just 95 per cent of ravens are black) = 0.95.

Likewise my reconstruction of Williams's argument in Chapter VI depended on a similar premiss: it was (83). The same sort of assumption was made again, in the extension in the preceding section of the argument of Chapter VI: this was the premiss (108). (It is true that the inferences which are the subject of (83) or of (108) are not *precisely* proportional syllogistic in form, as the subject of (120) is; still, they are evidently of the same general character.)

It was perfectly proper to proceed in this way. For the premisses (83) and (108) are obviously true. And as the inferences which are their subjects are not inductive ones (in the mainstream sense), there was no circularity in using these propositions as premisses of an argument against scepticism about inductive inference (in the mainstream sense). But it is more than proper to proceed in this way: it is well advised. For it is true (as Williams believed) that philosophers, though they have had their natural assessments of inductive inference severely eroded in this century, have not undergone the same thing with respect to their natural assessments of proportional syllogistic inference. Perhaps they *ought*, in consistency, to have done so. The 'deductivism' which lies behind scepticism about inductive inference ought, one might think, to generate scepticism about proportional syllogistic inference too. But in fact this has not happened. While inductive scepticism is epidemic in the philosophical profession, statistical or proportional scepticism (as it might be called), is all but non-existent. Scarcely any philosopher, then, will withhold assent from (83), or (108). That is why it is well advised to use such propositions as premisses in arguing against something which many philosophers do believe, viz. inductive scepticism.

Still, perhaps Hume at least, as I suggested in Chapter VI, *would* deny (83) or (108) or both. And perhaps some other philosophers now, under pressure from the argument of Chapter VI and its extension in this chapter, will begin to favour this forthright way of eluding that argument.

For this reason it would be desirable, if it were possible, to show that the argument of Chapter VI, and its extension, do not *need* to take (83) or (108) as premisses: that those propositions, obviously true though they are, can in fact be derived from other propositions which are still more obviously true. If this could be done, then the Laplace–Williams argument, as reconstructed and extended above, would be freed from its present dependence on natural assessments of proportional syllogistic inference.

This can in fact be done. It will not be done here, because to prove (83) would take us an intolerably long way out of our way. Even to prove (120) would be exceedingly laborious. But it will suffice to indicate how the natural assessments of proportional syllogistic inferences *can* be proved, if I prove one which concerns a certain micro-instance of that kind of inference. To simplify the proof still further, I will choose an inference which has less 'subject–predicate' structure than paradigm proportional syllogistic inferences have. This simplification will do no harm: the proportional syllogistic character of the inference in question will still be manifest enough. (And the proof will be found tedious enough, even so.)

Consider, then, the inference from H, 'Just two of the individuals Abe, Bob, Charles, are black', to I, 'Abe is black'. The natural assessment of this inference is, of course,

(121) $P(I/H) = \frac{2}{3}$.

This is obviously true. But it can be derived from other assessments of probability which are still more obviously true, as follows.

Let T be some tautology.

By the conjunction principle (28),

(122) $P(H.I/T) = P(H/T) \times P(I/T.H)$;

whence

(123) $P(I/T.H) = \dfrac{P(H.I/T)}{P(H/T)}$.

Hence, by the irrelevance of tautological evidence (113),

(124) $P(I/H) = \dfrac{P(H.I/T)}{P(H/T)}$.

Abbreviate 'Abe is black' by 'Ba', and so on; abbreviate 'and' by '.', 'or' by 'v', 'It is not the case that' by '~', then

(125) H is logically equivalent to:
$(Ba.Bb.\sim Bc) \text{ v } (Ba.\sim Bb.Bc) \text{ v } (\sim Ba.Bb.Bc)$.

It is a principle of logical probability, and in any case obvious, that

(126) If p is logically equivalent to p', and q logically equivalent to q', then $P(q/p) = P(q'/p')$.

From (124), (125), (126) it follows that

(127) $P(I/H) =$
$$\frac{P(Ba.((Ba.Bb.\sim Bc) \text{ v } (Ba.\sim Bb.Bc) \text{ v } (\sim Ba.Bb.Bc))/ T)}{P((Ba.Bb.\sim Bc) \text{ v } (Ba.\sim Bb.Bc) \text{ v } (\sim Ba.Bb.Bc)/T)}$$

(128) The conjunction in (127) of Ba with the long disjunction is logically equivalent to: $(Ba.Ba.Bb.\sim Bc)$ v $(Ba.Ba.\sim Bb.Bc)$ v $(Ba.\sim Ba.Bb.Bc)$.

(129) The proposition after the colon in (128) is logically equivalent to: $(Ba.Bb.\sim B.c)$ v $(Ba.\sim Bb.Bc)$ v $(Ba.\sim Ba.Bb.Bc)$.

Hence by the equivalence principle (126),

(130) $P(I/H)=$
$$\frac{P(((Ba.Bb.\sim Bc) \text{ v } (Ba.\sim Bb.Bc) \text{ v } (\sim Ba.Ba.Bb.Bc)/T)}{P(((Ba.Bb.\sim Bc) \text{ v } (Ba.\sim Bb.Bc) \text{ v } (\sim Ba.Bb.Bc)/T)}.$$

It is a principle of logical probability, and in any case obvious, that

(131) If $P(q.r/p)=P(q.s/p)=P(r.s/p)=0$, then $P(qvrvs/p)=P(q/p)+P(r/p)+P(s/p)$; whence, if three propositions are pairwise-exclusive, then the probability of their disjunction is the sum of the probabilities of the disjuncts.

(132) All the disjuncts in each long disjunction in (130) are pairwise-exclusive.

Whence, with (131),

(133) $P(I/H)=$
$$\frac{P(Ba.Bb.\sim Bc/T)+P(Ba.\sim Bb.Bc/T)+P(\sim Ba.Ba.Bb.Bc/T)}{P(Ba.Bb.\sim Bc/T)+P(Ba.\sim Bb.Bc/T)+P(\sim Ba.Bb.Bc/T)}.$$

Obviously,

(134) $P(\sim Ba.Ba.Bb.Bc/T)=0.$

Whence

(135) $P(I/H)=$
$$\frac{P(Ba.Bb.\sim Bc/T)+P(Ba.\sim Bb.Bc/T)}{P(Ba.Bb.\sim Bc/T)+P(Ba.\sim Bb.Bc/T)+P(\sim Ba.Bb.Bc/T)}$$

Now,

(136) $P(Ba.Bb.\sim Bc/T)=P(Ba.\sim Bb.Bc/T)=P(\sim Ba.Bb.Bc/T).$

And

(137) $P(Ba.Bb.\sim Bc/T)>0.$

Therefore

> (138) All the probabilities mentioned in the right-hand side of
> (135) are > 0 and equal to one another.

Whence

> (121) $P(I/H) = \frac{2}{3}$.

Most of the premisses employed in this argument call for no
comment: viz. the irrelevance of tautological evidence (113); the
judgement (134) that a certain contradiction is initially impossible; certain judgements of the logical equivalence ((125), (128),
(129)), or of the logical exclusiveness (132), of propositions; and
certain principles ((28), (126), (131)) of logical probability. The
only other premisses, and therefore the all-important ones, are
(136) and (137).

Premiss (137) is, of course, a special case of 'regularity' in
Carnap's sense: that is, of the thesis that no non-quantified contingent proposition is initially impossible.[15] It is also a special
case of Hume's thesis, that 'there can be no demonstrative arguments for a matter of fact and existence'. It is also a special case
of Aristotle's thesis, that it is only necessary truths which are
certain in relation to necessary truths.[16] These are theses which,
as far as I know—contrary to the immemorial slander that every
proposition has been denied by some philosopher—no philosopher denies.

Of course I do not offer this 'universal assent' as an *argument
for* (137). I do not argue for (137) at all. Its truth is as obvious as
any premiss of any argument for it could be. I do not even *assert*
(it should be noticed) any of the general theses just mentioned:
only a single instance of all of them.

Premiss (136) is, of course, a special case of the 'symmetry of
individual constants', in Carnap's sense: that is, of the thesis that
mere replacement of one individual constant by another, ('Plato'
for 'Socrates', say), wherever it occurs in an inference, never
changes the probability of that inference.[17] This too is a thesis
which, as far as I know, no philosopher denies. But again I do not
offer this fact as an argument for (136). I do not argue for (136)

---

[15] Carnap (1962), ch. v.
[16] Aristotle, 34a, 22 ff.
[17] Carnap (1962), ch. VIII.

at all, its truth being as obvious as any premiss of any argument for it could be. Nor, again, do I even assert the symmetry of individual constants in general: only a single instance of it.

The natural assessment (121), of the proportional syllogistic inference from 'Just two of the individuals Abe, Bob, Charles, are black', to 'Abe is black', can therefore be derived from propositions even more obviously true than it itself is. The same thing can be done, at the cost of only a longer and more complicated derivation, for (83) of the argument of Chapter VI, and for (108) of the extension of that argument. The proof that induction is justified, therefore, while it can properly and well advisedly be begun from natural assessments of proportional syllogistic inferences, *can* be begun much further back; from an instance of the symmetry of individual constants, and the fact that a certain contingent proposition is not initially impossible.

(I owe to Carnap my knowledge of the possibility of the kind of derivation just given of (121). As far as I know, everyone else who knows of this possibility is likewise indebted to Carnap. The derivation of which the above is a micro-instance occurs as part of Carnap's proof[18] that any 'confirmation-function' which is 'symmetrical' (136-like) and 'regular' (137-like) makes Bernoulli's law of large numbers, or rather Carnap's version of it, true.)

(viii)

It was proved in section (vi) above that

(117) $P(G.A.D.F) > 0.81$

where G is 'Abe is black', and $A.D.F$ is 'S is a 3020-fold sample of Pop and just 95 per cent of the ravens in S are black, and Abe is a member of Pop and not a member of S'. Now, everyone will agree, that

(139) $P(G/T) \leqq 0.81$,

where T is some tautology. Whence with the irrelevance of tautological evidence (113), it follows that

(140) $P(G/A.D.F.T) > P(G/T)$.

---

[18] Ibid., ch. VIII.

This, then, is another proof, additional to those of Chapter V, of the falsity of the sceptical thesis in its strong version (14). A large sample of ravens, 95 per cent black, *is* initially favourably relevant to the prediction that a particular raven not in that sample is black. And we saw in the preceding section that the proof of (117) can be grounded, not on the natural assessment (108) of a certain proportional syllogistic inference, but on premisses, (136) and (137), even more obviously true than that one.

VIII

WHY THESE ARGUMENTS DO NOT CONVINCE

PHILOSOPHY never restores pre-philosophical innocence. A philosopher may try to prove the truth of something he believed before he was a philosopher, but even if he succeeds, his belief never regains the untroubled character, and the settled place in his mind, which it had at first. There is a sort of biological impossibility about such a thing. You might as well hope to restore to a man of sixty the feeling his limbs had when he was ten, as hope to restore by means of philosophy the very stuff of your early convictions. And if a philosopher cannot do this for himself, still less can he do it for others.

For this reason it is not to be expected that the arguments of Chapters V–VII, even if they really are (as I think they are) proofs that induction is justified, should restore anyone's belief in that proposition as it existed before philosophical reflection set in. In fact this belief is one which is especially easily unsettled: not only is philosophy fatal to its native vigour, but even self-consciousness is so. You can become conscious that you have, for example, mathematical beliefs, or moral ones, without this discovery at once and irreversibly weakening those beliefs; but once you realize that you believe induction is justified, it is far too late to revive the 'animal faith' which originally invested that proposition.

The arguments of Chapters V–VII, however, are unconvincing in another way as well: they have little or no tendency to produce even intellectual conviction among philosophers. I say this partly on the basis of the reception by philosophers of earlier arguments sufficiently like them, but even more on the basis of introspection. (I can consult introspection here, because nowadays, as I said earlier, even the anti-sceptical philosopher has enough inductive scepticism in his system to make it unnecessary for him to consult others on such a point.) The sole effect nowadays of arguments like those of Chapters V–VII is to produce in philosophers a certain short-lived uneasiness. (Exactly, I cannot resist pointing out, what Hume said was the sole effect of *sceptical* arguments!) Why is this so?

Well, let us consider what the *real* reaction is, to arguments like those above, in the mind of the average sceptical philosopher of the present time. At the risk of appearing more stupid than the average, I will say what my own reaction is, *qua* inductive sceptic. It might be expressed as follows.

'You are wasting your own and others' time. You may juggle probabilities as long as you like, but you will never get around the fact that the future is independent of the past, the unobserved independent of the observed.'

I think this is typical enough. It is certainly stupid enough. Everything turns, of course, on the meaning of the word 'independent'.

There are just two senses in which philosophers speak of independence. In one of them, *p* is independent of *q* if and only if the conjunctions *p.q*, *p.~q*, *~p.q*, *~p.~q*, are each not necessarily false. This is the more common of the two senses, and is often called 'logical independence'. In the other sense, *p* is independent of *q*, in relation to *r*, if and only if $P(q/r.p) = P(q/r)$, or, an important special case, this equality holds at least for *tautological r*. That is, 'independence' is sometimes used as a synonym for 'irrelevance' in Keynes's sense of that word, or more specifically, as a synonym for 'initial irrelevance' in Carnap's sense. Irrelevance, or initial irrelevance, is, as I said, a less common sense of 'independence' than logical independence is. But when Keynes in 1921 coined the name 'irrelevance' for the equality of $P(q/r.p)$ and $P(q/r)$, he seemed to hesitate[1] between that name and 'independence'. If so, that was no doubt partly because the established name of the *statistical counterpart* of this equality was already then, as it still is, 'independence'.

Now, logical independence and initial irrelevance do have some properties in common: for example, both relations are symmetrical. It is true, furthermore, that '*p* is logically independent of *q*', and '*p* is initially irrelevant to *q*', are not logically independent of each other. But there are plenty of cases in which *p* is logically independent of *q*, and yet *p* is not initially irrelevant

---

[1]   e.g. Keynes (1921), pp. 121 and 138.

to q: for example, if p is 'Abe is a raven and just 95 per cent of ravens are black', and q is 'Abe is black'.

There are other examples of the very same sort in which p is the premiss and q is the conclusion of an *inductive* inference. This was proved, among other things, in Chapters V–VII above: for example, where p is *A.D.F* ('*S* is a 3020-fold sample of Pop and just 95 per cent of the ravens in *S* are black, and Abe is a member of Pop and not a member of *S*'), and q is *G* ('Abe is black'). It was proved, that is, that a proposition about the observed is sometimes *not* independent of a proposition about the unobserved, if by 'independent of' is meant 'initially irrelevant to'. For it was proved, (142), that *A.D.F* is initially favourably relevant to *G*. Of course *A.D.F* *is* independent of *G*, in the sense of logical independence. No one has ever disputed *that*, or ever would dispute so obvious a truth. But this truth does nothing towards settling the question whether or not inductive scepticism is true.

The average sceptical philosopher, or at least the one in me, is inclined to reply: 'But even when you have proved your cases of favourable relevance, I don't really see how that helps: it's all so hopelessly impalpable. Favourable relevance is not a *real* connection, after all: it's not, for example, a relation between past and future *events*, and so it leaves them just as "loose and separate", in Hume's words, as ever. It is a relation which holds only between *propositions*, those impalpable entities so dear to philosophers' hearts. All your stuff is really just verbal, isn't it?'

D. C. S.: 'Honestly, I sometimes wonder why I bother. At this rate, even if I were to succeed in proving that some proposition about the observed actually *entails* some proposition about the unobserved, you would say that my stuff was just verbal, because entailment is a relation which holds only among propositions. But to come back to favourable relevance: it is just one of the contraries of your irrelevance, and if my relevance is "impalpable" then your *ir*relevance is equally so. Of course, if you *don't* maintain that the premiss of an inductive inference is initially irrelevant to the conclusion, then, in disproving that, I have not disproved what you maintain. But if you do, then what you maintain is precisely as "impalpable" as the denial of it which I maintain.'

A. S. P.: 'Notice how, with you, the question between us always gets turned into a question about relations between propositions. This tendency of yours to "propositionalize" everything is so pronounced that I think it must be, in some way I don't fully understand, an essential feature of your position. Anyway, it is peculiar to your side of the question. If you attended instead, as one obviously should, to the *actualities*, to the *truth-makers* of those ubiquitous "propositions" of yours, you would soon come round to the sceptical side. So try to put aside the veil of propositions for once: think instead of the actual universe, and of our actual epistemic situation in it. When we do that, what do we find? That whatever the past history of the universe has been, however extensive our experience has been of ravens as uniformly black, and however "probable" this makes the blackness of unobserved ravens, still, the *fact* is that some or all future ravens, from some cause or none, may perfectly well *not* be black. Indeed, there may be no ravens at all in the future, since cosmic catastrophe may extinguish all life at any moment. Or the universe might simply cease to exist. If I had the literary art, as I have not, to bring home *fully* to your mind such facts as these, which after all are all that the inductive sceptic contends for, our disagreement would quickly be at an end.

'They are, of course, *unnerving* facts. I suppose that is why you are so anxious to keep a veil of propositions constantly between them and yourself. But if you wish to see the world rightly, you must not deny them, or let your attention be diverted from them.'

D. C. S.: 'Such facts as you cite are *not* all that the inductive sceptic contends for. For all that you have just done, flowers of rhetoric aside, is to insist on something which is not in dispute between us, but which on the contrary I have maintained all along: the *fallibility* of inductive inference.

'Then, the facts you cite, although they are facts all right, are *not*, what you call them, "actualities". Far from that, they are nothing but logical possibilities: as you will see for yourself if you recall the tell-tale word "may", or "might", which occurred in every one of your assertions of a supposed actuality. Nor was this avoidable: since no sane person, and least of all an inductive sceptic, is going to take it on himself to assert that some unobserved ravens *are* green, or that there *are* no future ravens, or the like'.

'Consequently, you have not got beyond the "veil of propositions" yourself. All you asserted was that

(141) P(h/e) < 1, for all e, all h, such that the inference from e
to h is inductive;

the thesis of inductive fallibilism. So you yourself have done no
more than assess the probability of certain propositions in relation to others.'

'This was not an accident, either. Whatever else the sceptical
thesis says, it must say *something* about the relation between the
premises and conclusions of induction; and the premises and
conclusions of induction are propositions. So even if I have misrepresented the sceptical thesis in some other way, I can hardly
be wrong in thinking that that thesis implies something about
certain propositions and the relation between them. Therefore it
is quite impossible, when it is scepticism about induction that is
in question, to set aside what you call the veil of propositions.'

A. S. P.: 'To speak of a sceptical *thesis* at all is another example
of your determination to propositionalize everything, and it puts
the nature of our disagreement in a hopelessly wrong light from
the beginning. The sceptic does not really have a thesis. He just,
as I said, sees the world rightly. So do you, really. The only difference between you and me is that I recognize the essentially
verbal nature of the consolations which are all you have to offer.'

D. C. S.: 'Well, *I* have a thesis. It is that some inductive inferences are justified, or are such that the premiss is a reason to
believe the conclusion. Anyone who thinks that that is true, or
neither thinks it true nor thinks it false, is no sceptic about induction. To be a sceptic, a person has to think that that thesis of
mine is false; and in that case he has a thesis too.'

'You think it false, so you have a thesis all right. But perhaps I
have mis-identified it. So let me try again, and ask you: what is it
about inductive inference that offends you? What is the fault,
which sceptical eyes alone have detected, in inferring the blackness of unobserved ravens from the blackness of observed ones?'

A. S. P.: 'Just the utter lack of connection between the premiss
and the conclusion. Unless there is some connection between
premiss and conclusion, an inference is not justified.'

D. C. S.: 'Spare me! This "lack of connection" is just the

"independence" business over again. If you mean that in order for an inference from p to q to be justified, p and q must not be logically independent, then what you say is false of course. To repeat, "Abe is a raven and just 95 per cent of ravens are black" is logically independent of "Abe is black", but the inference from the first to the second is justified nevertheless; and I have shown that there are inductive inferences which are, in this respect, just like this proportional syllogistic one. If you mean, by "lack of connection", that the premiss is initially irrelevant to the conclusion, then I have shown you that this is *not* true of all inductive inferences. The "lack of connection" between the premiss and conclusion, which you think is fatal to induction, cannot, then, be logical independence, nor yet initial irrelevance. So what is it?'

A. S. P.: 'I may not be able to *say* what it is, precisely enough to satisfy you, but I'm sure that you, like any other philosopher nowadays, can *see* the complete lack of connection between the premiss and conclusion of an induction. And there must be *some* connection between p and q, in order for p to be a reason to believe q.'

D. C. S.: 'Your last sentence is a pure triviality. If p is a reason to believe q, that fact *constitutes* a connection of sorts between p and q. So part at least of what you must mean, by alleging a complete lack of connection between the premiss and conclusion of an induction, is that the premiss is not a reason to believe the conclusion. But then, of course, that allegation is not a *reason for* inductive scepticism: it is just a way of *asserting* inductive scepticism.'

A. S. P.: 'You know perfectly well that I meant that there must be a *real* connection between p and q, or rather between the facts they respectively state, in order for p to be a reason to believe q.'

D. C. S.: 'What is the difference between a connection and a real connection?'

A. S. P.: 'I meant, of course, that in order for p to be a reason to believe q, there must be a connection between p and q *additional to p's* being a reason to believe q; and that this connection must be *something in nature*. If p is a reason to believe q, this truth cannot just "float". There must be something, and something in the actual world, that *makes* it true.'

D. C. S.: '". . . makes it true"? You mean, is sufficient, as well as necessary, for its truth?'

A. S. P.: 'Yes.'

D. C. S.: 'Is this right?: p is a reason to believe q if and only if r, where r (as it expresses "something in nature", "something in the actual world") is contingent.'

A. S. P.: 'Right.'

D. C. S.: 'So in the special case of inductive inference, a proposition p about the observed is a reason to believe a proposition q about the unobserved, if and only if a certain contingent proposition r is true. Is this what you think?'

A. S. P.: 'Yes.'

D. C. S.: 'But a proposition which is true if and only if a contingent proposition is true, is contingent itself; and a proposition is contingent if and only if its negation is contingent. Now you say that a proposition about the observed is *not* a reason to believe a proposition about the unobserved. So you must regard this sceptical thesis of yours as a contingent proposition.'

A. S. P.: 'Right.'

D. C. S.: 'And since, again, a proposition is contingent if and only if its negation is contingent, you must regard the negation of inductive scepticism too as a contingent proposition.'

A. S. P.: 'Right.'

D. C. S.: 'I thank you. For now I do understand why it is that arguments like those of Chapters V–VII fail to produce conviction. All their premisses are obviously necessary truths, while their conclusion seems to you to be contingent. Now we all know, and do not need Hume to tell us, that "there can be no demonstrative arguments for a matter of fact and existence": that is, that necessary truths have no contingent consequences. So if in a particular argument they appear to do so, we know that there must have been some trick, even if we cannot put our finger on it, and the argument leaves us cold. (The ontological argument for the existence of God strikes many people as just such a case.) Since the negation of the sceptical thesis about induction seems to you contingent, arguments for it which are entirely *a priori must* strike you as altogether unconvincing.'

Philosophical dialogues, almost without exception, are what Samuel Butler called them: 'the most offensive form, except poetry and books of travel in supposed unknown countries, that even literature can assume.'[2] My only excuse for the foregoing is

---

[2] Butler (1923), p. viii.

that, at the point where I began it, it seemed the only natural way
to proceed. Anyway, the conclusion reached in the dialogue is, I
think, true as far as it goes: that the unconvincingness of arguments like those of Chapters V–VII is to be explained by the
apparent contingency of their conclusion, combined with the
manifestly *a priori* character of their premises.

But this explanation does not go far enough, and in particular
it is obviously too 'intellectualistic'. *Why* does the denial of the
sceptical thesis seem contingent? Or, what comes to the same
thing, why does the sceptical thesis seem contingent? It is not
contingent, of course. Indeed, the suggestion that the sceptical
thesis is contingent, as I said in Chapter IV, is too evidently nonsensical, once it is clearly expressed, to be defended by anyone.
Yet the implication that it is, is one which meets us wherever we
turn in the philosophy of induction: in the sceptics, in the anti-
sceptical 'presupposition-discoverers', in almost every philosopher. In fact this idea, that what is at issue between the inductive
sceptic and the rest is something contingent, is one which comes
so naturally to philosophers, that it is scarcely possible for any of
us to free his mind entirely from it. Why is this illusion so widespread and so strong among philosophers?

In summary the reason is that until a man *is* subject to this illusion, he is not yet a philosopher, or at least has not been initiated
into the philosophy of induction. But this needs explaining.

Scepticism about induction is undoubtedly a thesis, but as I
said in Chapter IV, it stems from a certain *feeling*: a diffused or
'cosmic' feeling of insecurity. The beginner in philosophy is, of
course, a stranger to this feeling, and he cannot for the life of him
'see what the problem is' about induction. To get him to do so,
you must, as every teacher of philosophy knows, *play on his
nerves.* You have to make the fallibility of induction a source of
anxiety to him. The logical possibility of the conclusion of any
induction being false though the premiss be true, although it is
no more than the most harmless necessary truth, must be
brought home to his mind as something unnerving. Then, and
only then, does he 'see the problem of induction'.

That sounds as though it might be rather hard to do. How is it
to be done? Well, it is not hard, and we should ask rather, how *is*
it done? For done it is, every time some one is initiated into the
philosophy of induction.

It is not done, as one might have expected it to be, or it is done to a slight extent only, by collecting cautionary examples, drawn from common life or the history of science, of inductive inferences from true premisses which *have* had false conclusions. It is done by literary art: for example, by the device to which I drew attention in Chapter I, of letting expressions evaluative of inductive inference undergo severity-shift. (For example, from 'invalid' to 'unreliable', to 'unjustified', etc.) In that way, the fallibilist thesis about induction is insensibly transformed into the sceptical one; and the sceptical thesis, of course, really *is* unnerving.

But severity-shift is not the only device for making the fallibility of induction a source of anxiety: there is another one, at least equally important. I omitted this device from Chapter I, partly because I wanted the portraits which make up the rogues' gallery there to be absolutely clear-cut; whereas the present device does not admit of very sharp delineation. I call it, for want of a better name, 'the rhetoric of independence'. The most striking of all examples of it, and also the most influential, is Hume's calling the observed and the unobserved, and indeed 'all events', '*entirely loose and separate*'.[3] But when Hume, or anyone else, speaks of the observed and the unobserved, or of the premisses and conclusions of induction, as being 'independent', or as having 'nothing to bind them together', or as 'utterly disjoint', or as 'lacking any connection', we have other specimens of the rhetoric of independence.

The rhetoric of independence does two things. First, it fuses the fallibilist thesis about induction with the sceptical one. No rational man is nervous about an inference just because he is truly told that it is a fallible one, or that it is logically possible for the premiss to be true and the conclusion false. But who, that is rational, is *not* nervous about inferring one proposition from another, if he is truly told that his premiss and conclusion *lack any connection*, are quite *independent*, or concern things *entirely loose and separate* from one another? The rhetoric of independence thus does at one stroke what is also done in stages by severity-shift: it invests the fallibility of induction with the unnervingness which properly belongs only to the sceptical thesis.

Second, the rhetoric of independence makes this amalgam of

[3] Hume (1748), p. 74.

fallibilism and scepticism *appear contingent.* Consider the proposition that all events are entirely loose and separate. It is hardly a
necessarily false proposition, is it? And it certainly *seems* to be a
proposition about the *actual* universe: Hume would say it
'concerns matter of fact and existence'. So it would have to be a
contingent truth, if it is true. And Hume certainly makes us think
it is true. By the time he has finished with us, the scales seem to
have fallen from our eyes. With his help we seem to have made a
discovery of an astounding kind, and an unnerving kind, about
the actual universe: that it contains 'no necessary connections
between distinct existences', or in other words really is all 'loose
and separate'.

Of course this is nonsense. The fallibility of inductive inference
is not contingent; and no one can even really believe, however
often they may imply, that if the world were different in a certain
way, inference from the blackness of observed ravens to the
blackness of unobserved ones would be valid. Nor is inductive
scepticism a contingent thesis. To put it mildly, Hume is *not* the
world's champion scientist, discoverer of a fundamental law,
which has stood the test of time so much better than anything of
Newton's or Einstein's, that there are no adhesives.

What I have just said will be admitted by everyone, so far as it
concerns Hume's phrase 'loose and separate'. No one will con-
tend for that phrase being anything more than a metaphor. But
hardly anyone realizes, what it is of the utmost importance to
realize, that the kindred phrases 'lack of connection', 'independence', 'disjointness', and all the other examples of the rhetoric of
independence, are not one whit better. Take for example the
average sceptical philosopher nowadays. He is haunted by this
conviction of the independence of the future and the past, the
independence of the observed and the unobserved. Nothing can
shake this conviction, and it is what he always falls back on in the
end, not only in his public disputations but in his private
thoughts. Only, he cannot tell you, or himself, what he means by
'independence'. It is not logical independence. Then, in the
irrevelance-sense of 'independence', it has been proved even to
his satisfaction that the observed and the unobserved are *not*
always independent. And neither he nor anyone else knows of
any third sense of 'independence'.

The rhetoric of independence has, then, two effects: it amalgamates the fallibilist and the sceptical theses, and it makes this amalgam appear contingent. By the first effect, it imparts to the fallibilist thesis just that touch of unnervingness which must be felt before there is any 'philosophical problem' about induction at all. By the second it generates the illusion, shared to some extent by all parties to this 'problem', that the sceptical thesis is contingent. It is that illusion, we saw earlier in this Chapter, which prevents arguments such as those of Chapters V–VII from carrying conviction to philosophers' minds. What is ultimately responsible for the unconvincingness of those arguments is, therefore, the rhetoric of independence.

PART TWO

PROBABILITY

INTRODUCTION

THE two topics, induction and probability, are nowadays so closely linked in philosophers' minds, that no explanation is felt to be needed why a book, for example, which is about induction, should also be about probability. Far from that, philosophers nowadays find a real difficulty in mentioning either topic without the other. 'Probability and induction', and 'induction and probability', have gone far towards becoming, in the philosophical profession, 'welded' conjunctions, like 'use and wont' or 'pith and substance'. This has happened only in the present century, and I have elsewhere tried to explain how it came about.[1] But however it came about, induction and probability are certainly by now *too* closely linked in philosophers' minds, and in fact are often inextricably confused.

This confusion is at its worst, somewhat surprisingly, among those philosophers who are especially interested in both induction and probability. It finds expression there, as I have indicated in Part One, in the currency of phrases like 'inductive probability', (where what is meant is logical probability), and 'inductive logic', (where what is meant is non-deductive logic). Such phrases put enormous obstacles in the path of clear thought, either about induction or about probability. They are especially injurious, (as was pointed out in chapter VII (v)), where what is in question is scepticism about induction: because that is a question about *the probability* of *induction*, and a question, therefore, where a failure to distinguish between two things must be absolutely fatal to clear treatment.

I need to explain, then—even though my profession is far from requiring from me any explanation—why this book, having been so far about induction, should have a second part, about probability. But the explanation is not hard to give. It is as follows.

It has been proved in Part One that there are inductive inferences the conclusions of which are more probable in relation to the premisses than they are *a priori*, and that the conclusions of

---

[1] Stove (1973), pp. 98–107.

some inductive inferences are as probable in relation to the premisses as non-sceptics think they are. But the premisses of my proofs were, principally, statements of logical probability; and propositions of this kind, or at least the published *systems* of propositions of this kind, lie under certain definite objections from philosophers, as well as under a less definite but even more damaging suspicion. So, although my purposes in this book are entirely polemical and critical, and I therefore neither have attempted nor will attempt anything systematic enough to be called a theory of logical probability, the arguments of Part One cannot possibly receive a fair hearing, unless I can show that the objections commonly entertained against the theory of logical probability are mistaken. This, and this alone, is the reason for the existence of Part Two.

The theory of logical probability is itself, however, only one form, though certainly the most ambitious form, that non-deductive logic has assumed; and some at least of the objections which have been made to it are equally objections to non-deductive logic in *any* form. In addition to that, even those objections which are peculiar to the theory of logical probability all stem, I believe, from mistakes about the relation between non-deductive and deductive logic, or from mistakes about deductive logic itself. For these two reasons, while my main object in this Part is to defend the arguments of Chapters V–VII, by defending the theory of logical probability, a considerable proportion of what follows is not about the theory of logical probability specifically, but about non-deductive logic in general; and this in turn required that considerable attention be devoted to deductive logic itself.

IX

THE MYTH OF FORMAL LOGIC

(i)

WHEN I mention logic in the first four sections of this chapter, I mean deductive logic; and, expressed in graffito style, what I believe about deductive logic is this: cases rule. I do not mean that there are no general truths at all in logic. I think there are plenty, and I will mention some in a minute. What I mean is that hardly any of the true propositions of logic are purely formal. But I need to explain what I mean by 'purely formal', and before that, what I count as a proposition of logic.

That 'All swans are black and Abe is a swan' entails 'Abe is black', or that it does not; that the argument from the former proposition to the latter is valid, or that it is invalid; that the latter is a logical consequence of the former, or that it is not: these I take to be different ways of saying the same thing, and I count any proposition of this kind as a proposition of logic. That is usual enough. What is less usual is this: I do not count anything as a proposition of logic *unless* it entails a proposition of this kind. Thus what I call propositions of logic are only a proper subset of what would usually be called so, though as against that, they are the propositions which are the *raison d'être* of logic, on almost any view of logic.

I will call propositions of this kind 'judgements of validity or of invalidity'. I count something as a proposition of logic, then, if and only if it is a judgement of validity or of invalidity; that is, if and only if it says categorically, of some concrete argument or other, that it is valid or that it is invalid, or that the conclusion is or is not entailed by, or a logical consequence of, the premiss.

A judgement of validity or of invalidity may be *singular*, like the example I just gave: that is, it may be about just one argument. But we also make *general* judgements of validity or of invalidity. We pick out a certain *class* of arguments, and say that *every* member of that class is valid, or that every member of it is invalid. A general judgement of validity or of invalidity entails singular ones. For example, the singular judgement of validity mentioned above is entailed by many general ones, including: '"All F are G and x is F" entails "x is G", for all x, all F, all G.'

This last statement is not only a general judgement of validity, but is one which is purely formal in my sense. For I call a general judgement of validity or of invalidity 'purely formal', if and only if, in order to pick out the class of arguments in question, it employs at least one individual variable, or predicate variable, or propositional variable, and places no restriction on the values that that variable can take: that is, any propositional constant whatever can replace the variable if it is a propositional variable, any predicate constant can replace it if the variable is a predicate variable, and any individual constant can replace the variable if it is an individual variable.

Formal logic aspires to find judgements of validity or of invalidity which are not only true and general, but also purely formal in *at least* my sense. My thesis is that, above a low level of generality, there are few or no such things to be found.

Outside the purely formal, though, I admit that true general propositions of logic are common enough. For example, 'For any necessarily true p, and any contingent q, "p" does not entail "q"'; or again, 'For any contingent p and any necessarily false q, "p" does not entail "q".' These are general judgements of invalidity, and I think that both of them are true. But they are not counter-examples to my thesis, of course, because they are not purely formal. They obviously do place restrictions on the values that can be taken by the propositional variables which they use to pick out the class of arguments in question.

Then again, there are plenty of true propositions of logic which *are* purely formal, once the name 'propositions of logic' is not confined, as I confine it, to judgements of validity or of invalidity. For example: 'If p entails q and q entails r then p entails r'; or, again, 'if p entails q then p-and-r entails q, for any r'. Here I have left the quantification mainly tacit, but everyone will 'read it in', and will then see that these truths are purely formal in my sense. For they allow any proposition at all as a value of any of the propositional variables. But then, these things are not propositions of logic in my sense, since they do not pronounce any categorical judgement of validity or of invalidity. They are only truths of (what I will call) *meta*logic. All they say is, that certain arguments are valid *if certain other arguments are.*

(ii)

I first consider purely formal judgements of invalidity.

Here is one which I think is true; and if it is, it will be obvious that there are many others like it. '"All swans are black and x is black" does not entail "x is a swan", for any x'.

This truth is, of course, of so low a degree of generality, and hence of formality, that most logicians would strenuously object to its being called a *purely formal* logical truth at all. But it *is* purely formal in my sense, obviously; and no apology is needed for that. It is a very humble fragment of formal logical truth, to be sure. Still, you might go farther and fare worse. In fact, if you go *much* farther, and allow *predicate* variables, or propositional ones, freely into your judgements of invalidity, you are *sure* to fare worse. For example, '"All F are G and x is G" does not entail "x is F", for any x, any F, any G', is false; and so is '"If p then q, and q" does not entail "p", for any p, any q'.

The argument

(a) Hume is a father

  Hume is a male parent

is valid. It is a logical consequence of the supposition that Hume is a father, that he is a male parent. And since if p entails q, then p-and-r entails q, for any r, the following two arguments are also valid.

(b) All male parents are fathers
  Hume is a father

  Hume is a male parent;

and

(c) If Hume is a male parent then Hume is a father
  Hume is a father

  Hume is a male parent.

Arguments (b) and (c) are instances respectively of the 'fallacy of the undistributed middle term', and of the 'fallacy of affirming the consequent'. As these arguments are valid, it is not true that every argument which is an instance of either of those forms is invalid.

Of course, *subject to certain restrictions*, all instances of those forms are invalid. For example, the following statement is true:

'"All *F* are *G* and *x* is *G*" does not entail "*x* is *F*", for any *x*, any *F*, any *G* *such that F and G are logically independent predicates*'. But then, this is not a purely formal judgement of invalidity, since it restricts the values admissible for the predicate variables. Indeed, because of the nature of the restriction here imposed, this statement happens not to be a judgement of invalidity at all. The logical independence of two predicates is simply the invalidity of certain arguments. Consequently this statement, although it looks like a judgement of invalidity, is no such thing: it does not pronounce *any* argument invalid. In fact it is only a metalogical truth. All it says is that certain arguments are invalid *if certain others are*.

It will be obvious that what has just been done for undistributed middle and affirming the consequent, can be done in the same way for all the other so-called formal fallacies. To pick out the 'form' called denying the antecedent, will require two propositional variables; to pick out the 'form' called illicit major will require three predicate variables, and so on. And then it will always be possible to choose values of these variables which yield a valid instance of the form in question. There is, in short, no such thing as a 'formal fallacy', as that phrase is usually understood.

As this fact is extremely obvious, it is to be presumed that all logicians know it. But if you publicize this fact, they regard you as not only a bore but a menace, and, for their own part, they certainly do not publicize it. I have seen a great many logic books, textbooks and other, and I have known of a great many logic courses, but never one which so much as mentioned the fact that all the so-called formal fallacies have valid cases.

In fact that is 'putting it mild'. In every logic textbook that I do know of, and every logic course, the opposite was either stated, or implied, or suggested. And that is *still* putting it mild. Countless thousands of students, over many generations, have in fact taken away from their logic courses *little except* the conviction that affirming the consequent, undistributed middle, etc., are invalid in every case. That, indeed, was the very point on which, it was supposed, their studies had raised them above the vulgar, and had armed them against unscrupulous rhetoricians. Even their teachers, I am ashamed to say, only a few decades ago regularly ridiculed the Un-American Activities Committee of the US

Senate precisely on the ground of its supposed addiction to the fallacy of affirming the consequent or undistributed middle.

Entire consistency on the matter, it must be admitted, was hardly ever achieved by anyone: students, teachers, or textbook writers. The same process of affirming the consequent, which in an early chapter of the textbook had been duly exposed as betraying logical ignorance or unscrupulousness, had a habit of turning up again in the last chapter, on scientific method, but this time as nothing less than the logical mainstay of the entire structure of empirical science. But then, no one is perfect.

Are these things of the past? Not in the least. Students of elementary logic, with no exception that I have heard of, are still being taught, or at least encouraged to believe, that every instance of, say, affirming the consequent, is invalid. The terminology is sometimes different, but the substance is the same. For example, students are still being taught, or encouraged to believe, that any argument of that form *can be proved invalid by a truth table.*

I. M. Copi says, in his widely used and justly respected text (Copi, 1954): 'We can establish the invalidity of an argument by using a truth table to show that its form is invalid'. He was thinking, of course, not exactly of 'If p then q, q, so p', say, but of '$p \supset q$, q, so p'. But that difference makes no difference here, and Copi's unmistakable teaching is, that any instance of the latter form can be proved invalid by a truth table; namely, of course, at that line in the table where p is false and q is true.

The sentence just quoted was from the first edition (1954) of Copi's textbook (p. 60). By the fourth edition of 1973, the sentence is interestingly different, and reads instead: 'We can establish the invalidity of an argument by using a truth table to show that *the specific form of that argument* is invalid' (p. 45, emphasis added). This suggests that, between those editions, someone had invited the author to try his skill, at proving invalidity by truth table, on a case like (c) above, or rather on its counterpart with the hook; and that he had, as a result, realized his mistake. But if he did realize it, he did not succeed in correcting it. Copi's notion of the specific form of an argument turns out to be signally unspecific; for 'the specific form' of any case of affirming the consequent, say, is none other than the familiar '$p \supset q$, q, so p'. And in the fourth edition, as in the first, the student is told that all he need do, to prove the invalidity of any argument of this form, is to prove the invalidity of this 'specific form'. So, although Copi must know perfectly well, for example, that the truth-functional counterpart of (c) above cannot be proved invalid by a truth table, or by anything else, for the simple reason that it is valid, he just cannot help himself: he must and will go on teaching students that it *can* be. In this way, and under a new terminology, the old illusion that there are invalid forms of argument is imparted to ever-new generations of students, apparently to be transmitted to the remotest posterity.

Perhaps I will be told that it is unfair to judge formal logic by its textbooks, even superior ones. It is not unfair, but I will let that pass. For the idea that every instance of an 'invalid form' is invalid has far better authority in its favour than textbooks of logic. It has, by implication at least, the unanimous endorsement of philosophers, in virtue of something that they do every day.

Philosophers proceed, and not just when they are teaching elementary logic, as though invalidity can be proved by means of a 'parallel argument': that is, as though it is enough to prove the invalidity of a given argument, if one can mention a second argument, which has the same logical form as the given one, and of which all the premisses are true and the conclusion false. Thus for example, the argument

All swans are black
Abe is black
Abe is a swan,

is supposed to be proved invalid by citing, for example, the argument

All persons now in this room are under 200 years old
Mr Hawke is under 200 years old
Mr Hawke is a person now in this room.

If there has been, in the entire history of the world, so much as one word published in criticism of this so-called method of proving invalidity, I have not had the good fortune to meet with it, though not for want of trying. On the contrary, this 'method' is constantly endorsed, as I have implied, by the practice of even good philosophers; and some philosophers of reputation (Popper for one)[1] have expressly endorsed it in print.

[1] See Popper (1968), p. 297.

It is illusory none the less; and in fact, of course, is essentially the same illusion as we have already met with in two other forms. The second argument's having true premisses and false conclusion proves, indeed, that *it* is invalid. But the invalidity of the given argument follows, from the invalidity of the second one, only if that is conjoined with the assumption that any argument which shares its logical form with an invalid argument is invalid itself. But that is precisely the assumption that all instances of a form which has invalid instances are invalid: the assumption which (b) and (c) suffice to show is false.

The mistakes I have been talking about, or rather the different forms of a single mistake, are made possible by not attending to arguments like (a), (b), and (c). (Or, of course, by not attending to the counterparts of (b) and (c) which contain ' ⊃ ': again, that difference makes no difference here.) Accordingly, when arguments like these *are* pressed on the attention of the formal logicians, their reaction is unfailingly instructive. This reaction is one of uneasy disapproval. And both the disapproval, and the unease, are very understandable.

The formal logician is profoundly reluctant to call argument (a), for example, valid. To call an argument valid is to attribute to it the highest possible degree of logical value. Now, it is the fundamental article of the formal logician's creed that logical value in general, or at least validity in particular, is *essentially formal*. 'Logical *form*' is the subject of all his professional care and study, as well as the source of his livelihood. But (a) is an argument whose logical value owes nothing, obviously, to its logical form, while it is, equally obviously, an argument of the highest possible logical value. For a formal logician to be asked to call (a) valid, therefore, is a torment to him, even though he knows it is so: it is asking him to discard the fundamental article of his professional creed. And arguments (b) and (c), of course, offer an even more gratuitous affront to that creed than (a) does.

But, alas, the formal logician is even more profoundly reluctant to call (a) invalid; indeed, he dares not call it so. For (a) can, of course, be turned into an argument which he *does* call valid, by the mere addition of a necessarily true premiss, 'All fathers are male parents', or 'If Hume is a father then Hume is a male parent'; while the formal logician holds—at least the vast majority of them do, and for very good reasons—that an argument which is valid with a necessary true premiss is valid without it. The same goes, of course, for arguments (b) and (c) as well.

Thus, the formal logician cannot call (a), (b), or (c) valid, consistently with his professional creed: hence his disapproval of them. But he dares not call them invalid either: hence his unease.

A situation so painful as this one is bound to produce distress signals, even if only half-conscious ones. Some of the commonest of these signals sound as follows. 'Argument (c) is *invalid in propositional logic*'; '(b) is *not valid in predicate calculus*'; '(a) is *neither quantificationally valid nor truth-functionally valid*'. You can easily see how suitable such phraseology is to the distressed logician's situation. A phrase like 'invalid in propositional logic', for example, by including the word 'invalid', has the effect of setting the desired *tone*, the tone of disapproval; while at the same time it is admirably non-committal, because after all—as the formal logician himself will hasten to assure you—'invalid in propositional logic' no more entails 'invalid', than (say) 'suspected murderer' entails 'murderer'.

Still, these phrases betray their painful birth, by being nonsensical. You might as well say of an argument that it is invalid in the spring, or in the south, as say of it that it is invalid 'in' predicate logic, or whatever. Arguments are not 'in' predicate logic, or 'in' any other artefact that logicians may happen to make. Still less is their invalidity or validity 'in' anything at all, except the arguments themselves.

Such phraseology is, of course, of extremely recent origin, and I think I understand what the linguistic route was which made it available to logicians in recent times. I take it that 'not valid in propositional logic', say, is actually a contraction of 'not able to be *proved* valid by the axioms of rules of any system of propositional logic'. Similarly, I suppose, 'not valid in predicate calculus', is a contraction of 'not able to be proved valid by the axioms or rules of any system of predicate logic'.

It is perfectly true, of course, that the arguments (a), (b), (c) are not able to be proved valid by any logical system, or at least by any existing one. No person of sense thinks one atom the worse of these arguments on that account, of course, or would consider them any the better, if a system were devised which *did* enable them to be proved valid. But if my historical suggestion is right, then the phraseology I am speaking of, as well as being nonsensical, is evidence of a tendency among logicians which is deplorable, and of which there is only too much other evidence: I mean, the tendency to identify an argument's *being* valid, with its being able to be *proved* valid by means of some system or other which logicians have devised.

It would not be surprising if logicians were tempted to make this identification, magnifying greatly as it does the importance of their profession. But the identification is ridiculous all the same. The valid arguments would be valid, and the invalid ones would be invalid, even if it were never possible to prove any of them so, and if there never had been, and never was to be, such a thing as a system of logic, or a logician, in the world. Nothing could be more obvious than that.

Formal logic aims at *high* generality: at a degree of generality so high, at the least, as to forbid the employment, in order to pick out a class of arguments, of any propositional constant, or predicate constant, or individual constant. Generality of this high degree is present in the judgement that all cases of undistributed middle, or of affirming the consequent, are invalid. But these judgements of invalidity, we have seen, are false. So are all the others which correspond to the other supposed formal fallacies.

Of course this does not *prove* that all judgements of invalidity, possessing this degree of generality, are false. Still, it is a good reason to believe that; and that is what I believe. That is, that all purely formal judgements of invalidity, which employ *no* propositional constant, predicate constant, or individual constant to pick out the class of arguments in question, are false.

But my thesis is rather stronger than that. It is that all purely formal judgements of invalidity which are not of *low* generality are false.

To make this thesis as testable as one would wish it to be, I should, of course, state exactly *how* low is 'low': exactly what, according to me, that level of generality is, above which purely formal judgements of invalidity are *without exception* false. But this is a point which I have not been able to settle to my own satisfaction.

Fortunately, however, my thesis is perfectly testable as it is. For, in the field of logic, philosophers and logicians possess a large fund of strong and virtually unanimous intuitions about generality. There is very little danger, consequently, of any test of my thesis petering out in disagreements as to whether a given judgement of invalidity is, or is not, of low generality.

(iii)

I turn now to purely formal judgements of validity.

As in the case of invalidity, there are plenty of these which are true, but of 'villainous low' generality. "'All swans are black and x is a swan" entails "x is black", for all x'; and so on.

But above that level, and in particular, again, once we allow predicate variables or propositional variables into our purely formal judgements of validity, falsity very soon sets in, just as it does with our judgements of invalidity. Purely formal judgements of validity, if they employ a predicate variable or a propositional variable to pick out the class of arguments in question, are all or almost all exposed to counter-examples, direct or indirect, or they generate paradoxes.

The class of invalid argument is so heterogeneous, and so vast—since after all, p does not entail q, for almost any p and almost any q—that no one should ever expect to be able to reduce all of *it* to a few simple types. But it seems, at least, to be different with the class of valid arguments. There, it does seem possible to bring nearly all cases under a few simple, very general, and even purely formal types. It seems possible, because it seems as though logicians have in fact done it.

But I think that this is only the official and daylight face, as it were, of logic. It is a different story outside, at night, and especially in the oral tradition. Why, the very same man who in print appeals, with apparently the most perfect confidence, to (say) hypothetical syllogism as a valid form, will in conversation with you cheerfully allow himself to cast the most scandalous aspersions on it. In fact there is nowadays scarcely a philosopher who cannot show you, in private and between consenting logic teachers, a collection of logical dirty pictures. Perverse counter-examples, paradoxes at once disgusting and tedious, dog our footsteps whenever we attempt to frame purely formal judgements of validity which are of high generality while being true. With whatever eugenic care we select the parents, monstrous offspring sooner or later ensue. The elephant man is not in it by comparison: this is a whole museum of pathology, or of porno-logy as you might say.

My own collection of these things is not a very large one. (A very large collection of them is a rather bad sign, humanly speak-ing; just as is the opposite but of course connected thing, the obsession with maintaining formal purity. Formal logic, Jowett said, is neither a science nor an art but a dodge; I say that, what-ever else it is, it is a character defect.) But, strictly in the interests of science, I must now expose a few of my specimens to view.

First, transposition: '"If *p* then *q*" entails "If not-*q* then not-*p*", for all *p*, all *q*.' That is a purely formal judgement of validity, and one which has as good a chance of being true as most. But 'If Baby cries then we beat him', does not entail 'If we do not beat Baby then he does not cry'. It may well be doubted whether parental severity is even a biological guarantee of a stoical infant; but a *logical* guarantee it certainly is not. (I owe this example to Mr Vic Dudman, of Macquarie University.)

Second, a syllogistic rule: '"All *F* are *G* and *x* is *F*" entails "*x* is *G*", for all *x*, all *F*, all *G*.' That is a purely formal judgement of validity with as good a claim on our belief as any. Here I offer, not a counter-example, but a counter-example-or-paradox, the paradox being an obvious relative of the Liar. (I owe this example to a first-year student of many years ago, Mr Peter Kintominas.)

(d) All arguments with true premisses and false conclusion are invalid

(d) is an argument with true premisses and false conclusion

(d) is invalid.

If (d) is invalid then our syllogistic rule is false straight off. If (d) is valid, then its conclusion is false, and so one of its premisses must be false. Then the problem is to find the false premiss. The first premiss is true. So is the second part (we are supposing) of the second premiss. The falsity must therefore be in the first part of the second premiss: but where? Indeed, since the conclusion, if false, is necessarily false, and since the first premiss is necessarily true, and since the second part of the second premiss is necessarily true: please find the *necessary* falsity which is asserted by the first part of the second premiss, (the part which says that both premisses are true).

Third, hypothetical syllogism, plus one kind of universal instantiation. (This example is due to Dr Paul Hyland.)

'All men are mortal' entails 'If Socrates is a man then Socrates is mortal'; which in turn entails 'If Socrates is a man then it is not the case that Socrates is an immortal man'. So, entailment being transitive, 'All men are mortal' entails 'If Socrates is a man then it is not the case that Socrates is an immortal man'. Conjoin that conditional with the necessarily true conditional, 'If Socrates is an immoral man then Socrates is a man'. Hypothetical syllogism then gives you, 'If Socrates is an immoral man then it is not the case that Socrates is an immortal man'. Entailment being transitive, and necessarily true premisses being dispensable, we now have that 'All men are mortal' entails 'If Socrates is an immoral man then it is not the case that Socrates is an immortal man'. And so it does: there is nothing untoward so far.

But if hypothetical syllogism and universal instantiation are valid in all cases, it likewise follows from 'All men are mortal' that 'If Socrates is an immortal man then it is not the case that Socrates is an immortal man'. And that is false. 'All men are mortal' is contingent. But 'If Socrates is an immortal man then it is not the case that Socrates is an immortal man', is necessarily false. And a contingent proposition cannot entail a necessary falsity.

This is an instance of what I meant by speaking earlier of *indirect* counter-examples. I call it indirect, because it makes use of metalogical truths: the transitivity of entailment, and the dispensability of necessarily true premisses. But, assuming those standard principles, what the case shows is this: purely formal judgements of validity, concerning hypothetical syllogism and universal instantiation, are inconsistent, not only with a certain true singular judgement of invalidity, but with the general non-formal judgement of invalidity, that contingents never entail necessary falsities. And which side of this inconsistency ought to be given up, is perfectly obvious.

But Hyland's example is more directly instructive as well. 'All men are mortal' really does entail 'If Socrates is an immoral man then it is not the case that Socrates is an immortal man', and really does not entail 'If Socrates is an immortal man then it is not the case that Socrates is an immortal man'. So the difference between a valid argument and an invalid one sometimes depends on the absence at one point of the letter '*t*'. Yet there actually are people who believe in the possibility of *formal* logic: a hopeful undertaking, indeed!

With this I return my specimens to their plain wrapper.

In the validity of those 'valid forms' which logicians have made familiar to us, most of us have at first a degree of confidence which, as it is peculiarly high, is also peculiarly fragile. To preserve that degree of confidence in a purely formal judgement of validity, is impossible for a rational person, once *even a reasonable suspicion* has been raised about it. With purely formal judgements of validity, it is as with female sexual purity under an extreme purist regimen: giving grounds for belief in a lapse, is itself one kind of lapse. Suppose, then, what as far as I can see is impossible: that my three specimens should be able to be somehow reconciled with the purely formal judgements of validity against which I advanced them. Still, as these specimens at least give *some* grounds for believing those judgements to be false, to have the perfect confidence we once had in the general validity of transposition, etc., will be impossible for us, if we are rational, *even now.* And then, it is to be remembered, there are plenty more where my three specimens came from.

The conclusion which I draw from this and the preceding section, even if it is not true, has at least the merit of being a natural one. There are no logical forms, above a low level of generality, of which every instance is invalid: every such supposed form has valid cases. There are few or no logical forms, above a low level of generality, of which every instance is valid: nearly every such supposed form has invalid cases or paradoxical cases. The natural conclusion to draw is that formal logic is a myth, and that over validity, as well as over invalidity, forms do *not* rule: cases do.

(iv)

I do not know of anyone except myself who believes or ever has believed this philosophy of logic. Nor do I expect it to make quick converts now. It is too complete an inversion of the common opinion. That opinion is, of course, that logic is essentially formal, that logic is nothing if not formal, that the very phrase 'formal logic' is pleonastic, etc. Something of logicians' snobbery contributes to this opinion, of course: think, for example, of the kind of distaste which most logicians feel for courses called 'informal logic'. But it is also a conviction deeply and widely held.

As this is the common opinion, anyone may be excused for thinking at first when he hears it said that formal logic is a myth, that he is hearing an attack on logic itself; some sort of scepticism about logical truth, and hence about the possibility of logical knowledge; some counsel of despair about logic. But this would be not only a mistake, but the very reverse of the truth. My philosophy of logic is so far from being sceptical that it is if anything indecently affirmative. Not only do I believe, as I have implied, that there *are* logical truths, true judgements of validity or of invalidity; I believe that every normal human being is, in the extent of his knowledge of such truths, a millionaire. Only, I hold, as I have implied, that almost every logical truth which anyone knows, or could know, is either not purely formal, or is singular or of low generality.

Of course to the *formalist*, anyone who generalizes less hastily than he does looks like a sceptic, just as the tortoise looks to the hare to be standing still. But we must simply disabuse the formalist of this error. I am perfectly entitled to say, for example, that argument (b) above is valid, but that I will judge the next case of undistributed middle that I meet on its merits. Indeed, since some cases of that form *are* valid, and some are not, it is absurd to say anything less. This is not sceptical refusal to generalize; it is merely respect for very obvious facts. Similarly in general: there is nothing in the least sceptical in saying, about one instance of a certain logical form, that it is valid, and saying, about another instance of it, that it is not. Such sayings jar on formalist ears, of course, but that counts for nothing.

But to satisfy the reader that my view of logic is dogmatic rather than sceptical, let me remind him: I denied that all instances of undistributed middle are invalid because *I claimed to know* of instances of it which are valid. And I denied that hypothetical syllogism and universal instantiation are valid in all cases, because *I claimed to know* that contingents never entail necessary falsities. These are claims to logical knowledge; even, in the second case, a claim to *general* logical knowledge. They may be mistaken claims, of course; but at any rate the making of them is not consistent with despairing of the possibility of logical knowledge.

Of course, I *do* counsel the *formal* logician to despair, since I have given reasons to believe that what he seeks is not to be found. But to despair of the possibility of formal logical knowledge does not at all require that we despair of the possibility of logical knowledge.

The formal logician, though perpetually drowning in an ocean of counter-examples, paradoxes, and the like, equally perpetually lives in hope. He is like Boxer in Orwell's *Animal Farm*, and repeats to himself, 'I must work harder'. 'I *may* finally arrive at purely formal judgements, of validity at least, which are of high generality, and free, now and for evermore, from every suspicion of falsity'.

Why, and so he *may*. Still, this hope of his is almost entirely groundless. Almost nothing in the historical record supports it, and almost everything points in fact the other way. Does anyone suppose that, in logic nowadays, weird counter-examples, para-doxes, etc., are a stationary population, or a species actually in danger of extinction? The fact, of course, is precisely the reverse: anomalies *increase* with increasing formality. This is known as the progress of formal logic, and is reckoned one of the glories of the twentieth century, by contrast with all of the earlier modern period, which logicians love to call 'the dark ages of logic'.[2]

And how, indeed, could things be otherwise? In natural science, our generalizations are mostly of low generality, and even then, before we can find a counter-example to any of them, nature itself must give us its co-operation. There are no such salutary impediments in the case of formal logic. There, the generalizations are of such boundless extent as to afford bound-less encouragement to the search for counter-examples; and to supply those, nothing more is required than the energies of men who are clever, leisured, and deeply contra-suggestible. The supply has been more than adequate in the past, as any rational person would expect from so fertile a source; and if you are rational, you will expect the supply to be kept up in future too.

But the aspiration to high generality in logic is not only groundless; it is a colossal nuisance, as causing endless waste of

[2] A. N. Prior; but I have been unable to rediscover where I read these words.

time and effort. For it invests the obstacles it encounters with an importance which is entirely illusory.

If, for example, the Dudman argument about Baby is invalid, as it is, this is a fact which, to put it mildly, is of little interest or importance in itself. It does not even mean, as I have stressed, that even a single other case of transposition is invalid. It is of interest or importance *solely* as refuting the claim of logicians that transposition is a valid form. Similarly with the Kintominas example, and with every other specimen in the museum of pornology. No one would need to devote a moment's thought to such silly things, nobody would care anything at all about them, if they, or things like them, were not needed for the job of knocking formalist hopes on the head. But since in fact those hopes, though groundless, are perpetually renewed, the tiresome but necessary work of extinguishing them is likewise always still to do.

It is the same all through the history of formal logic: with the Liar Paradox, with the class of all classes not members of themselves, etc., etc. What a chronicle of wasted time! What is there, what could there possibly be, in the statement 'This statement is false', to make it worth one-thousandth part of the attention which has been lavished on it during two thousand years? Actual mental disorder apart, nothing, it is evident, could ever have invested such a trifle with importance, and of course nothing did, except its being an obstacle to certain formalist expectations. But it is *those expectations which deserve critical scrutiny,* though they almost never get it—not the poor uninteresting Liar, which has had so much of it.

In logic what is needed is to mortify, not to inflame, the passion for high generality. It would help to this end if we sometimes asked ourselves the common-sense question, 'What do we want generality *for*?' Where natural science is concerned, this question is easily answered. We want generality because it is needed for prediction, for control, and for explanation, and not for any reason independent of these three. But none of these reasons is available, where it is logic that is in question. To talk of prediction or of control in connection with logic would be a poor joke enough. And whether or not explanation is as important even in natural science as many philosophers now suppose, it is not even a joke in logic. There are *no* explanations in logic.

Indeed, I do not think that anyone has ever claimed, for logic, that it *does* explain anything. There is, of course, a faint insinuation of some such claim, in certain neologistic phrases like 'quantification *theory*'. But such phrases are a mere abuse of the word 'theory' (and, I may add, a self-serving abuse, it being supposed nowadays to be *a good thing* to have a theory). For a theory is, whatever else it is, something true or false, something which someone might believe or disbelieve; but what logicians dignify with the name of 'quantification theory' is nothing of that sort. In any case, there are certainly no explanations in logic, in *my* sense of 'logic': one true judgement of validity or of invalidity can, of course, *entail* another and less general one, but even then it never *explains* it. The greatest logician in the world cannot explain, any more than the layman can, why 'All swans are black and Abe is a swan' entails 'Abe is black'.

As it is scarcely possible, after 2500 years of hoping and searching, to point to a single purely formal judgement of validity which is not false or paradoxical, it can hardly be said that formal logic has been rich in positive results. It must be confessed, on the other hand, that it has been singularly fruitful of other results, especially in the present century. The foundations of logic itself, and with them the foundations both of mathematical and of natural science, thrown into complete and irreversible confusion: these are not contemptible consequences of the search for high generality and pure formality in logic. We didn't get where we are today by adopting an unambitious, piecemeal approach to logic, no sir! And as for the stone age philosophy of 'cases rule': why, if we had been content to settle for that, we would probably still be judging each argument on its merits to this day.

(v)

Deductive logic, then, is not purely formal. But what has this got to do with the defence of the arguments in Chapters V–VII above?

The summary answer is this. Non-deductive logic in any form, and hence the theory of logical probability, is now thought by many philosophers to have been discredited once and for all by the problem about 'grue', first brought to light by Nelson

Goodman in 1954.[3] A reader of this book is therefore likely to
think that the arguments of Chapters V–VII are (somehow)
fatally exposed to the 'grue' problem. None of this is true. The
importance of 'grue' has been greatly exaggerated. In fact, 'grue'
is fatal only to the belief that non-deductive logic is *purely
formal*. But that is not something which the premises of my
arguments in Chapters V–VII commit me to, or even something
which influenced me in framing those arguments. And even those
philosophers who *did* believe that non-deductive logic is purely
formal, did so only because they believed that *deductive* logic is
purely formal. Once *that* illusion is dispelled, therefore, 'grue' is
not a fatal problem to anyone.

But this is far too summary. We need to consider just what the
case of 'grue' shows, and what it does not. To do this, we need
first to go back a little in history.

That all inductive inferences are fallible—that is to say, invalid,
'non-deductive'—is a truth which philosophers have been re-
markably slow to admit. Hume laboured long and hard to bring
it home to their minds, but in vain, until, long afterwards,
Einstein came to his assistance, and 'history teaching by example'
made it a truth impossible to resist any longer.[4] *Then*, indeed,
philosophers made up for lost time, and soon so changed the
meaning of the word 'inductive' as to make it *analytic* that inductive inference is fallible.[5] But never mind: one way or another, by
the mid-twentieth century at the latest, the fallibility of induction
was a truth fully absorbed by philosophers.

Once that happens, however, a philosopher faces a stern
dilemma. He must either embrace inductive scepticism, or
abandon deductivism. He must, that is, either affirm that a
proposition about the observed is never a reason to believe a
proposition about the unobserved; or he must admit that one
proposition can be a reason to believe another, without the inference from the one to the other being valid ('deductive').

As the former alternative is scarcely compatible with sanity,
most philosophers have sensibly preferred the latter. That is,
they have abandoned deductivism, even if they have done so, in
most cases, neither very consciously nor very enthusiastically.

---

[3] Goodman (1954), pp. 74–5.
[4] Stove (1973), pp. 98–104.
[5] See ch. VII (v), and Stove (1973), pp. 22–3 and 107–10.

But to abandon deductivism is to acknowledge the existence of non-deductive logic.

Logic, however, had always been supposed to be essentially formal; and, before this time, it had never been necessary to acknowledge the existence of non-deductive as well as of deductive logic. That having now become necessary, it was the most natural thing in the world for philosophers to assume that non-deductive logic, too, is essentially formal. And assume this they did.

This assumption was, I think, shared for several decades by *all* philosophers who had abandoned deductivism and thereby admitted the existence of non-deductive logic. But the assumption was most influential, naturally, in the work of those philosophers who set out to treat non-deductive logic *systematically*; most notably, therefore, in the work of Hempel and Carnap.

Hempel is perfectly explicit. He tells us that he aims 'to set up purely formal criteria of confirmation in a manner similar to that in which deductive logic provides purely formal criteria for the validity of deductive inference'.[6] He even entitled his basic contribution to non-deductive logic 'A Purely Syntactical Definition of Confirmation'.[7] Not everything that Hempel meant by calling his theory of confirmation 'purely syntactical' is relevant here. But part of what he meant, that is relevant here, and a respect in which Carnap's theory of logical probability (or 'degree of confirmation', as he called it) is also purely syntactical, can be explained as follows.

Deductive logic, when it is thought of in the usual formalist way, does not itself *contain* any of those propositions which, at the start of this chapter, I called judgements of validity. Such propositions are, indeed, the very *raison d'être* of deductive logic; but they are not delivered directly, so to speak, by deductive logic. Neither present-day 'quantification theory', nor traditional 'syllogistic', is supposed to have, as part of its content, the proposition, for example, that '(x) (Man $x \supset$ Mortal x) and Socrates is a man' entails 'Socrates is mortal'. What deductive logic does deliver directly are only certain *schemas* or *forms* for judgements of validity: for example, that '(x) ($Fx \supset Gx$) and x is F' entails 'x

---

[6] Hempel (1965), p. 10.
[7] Hempel (1943).

is G'. Of course this statement, and every other like it, is strictly false, or rather senseless, because of its dummy constants: '(x) $(Fx \supset Gx)$ and x is F' is not a kind of thing, obviously, which *could* really entail anything. Still, everyone knows what is meant: namely, the kind of proposition discussed in section (iii) above, with 'F', 'x', etc. as *variables*, bound by universal quantifiers. And a judgement of validity, for example about the above argument concerning Socrates' humanity etc., is reached, by simply substituting individual constants and predicate constants for the variables or dummy constants of this form or schema. The freedom to make such substitutions is supposed to be unrestricted, though falsely supposed if section (iii) above is right; and it is in this that the *formal* character of deductive logic consists.

Non-deductive logic, then, set out to be formal in the same way. 'The criteria of confirmation' Hempel writes, 'should contain no reference to the specific subject matter of the hypothesis or of the evidence in question.'[8] Accordingly, Hempel's theory of confirmation does not itself contain any concrete 'judgements of confirmation', as I will call them: propositions such as '"Abe is black" confirms "(x) Black x"'. Such propositions are, indeed, the *raison d'être* of the theory; but they are not delivered directly by the theory. The theory directly delivers only schemas or forms for judgements of confirmation: for example, '"x is F" confirms "(x) Fx"'. An actual judgement of confirmation, such as the one just mentioned about Abe, is reached by simply substituting individual constants and predicate constants for the variables or dummy constants of the form or schema. And the analogy with deductive logic, which was guiding Hempel's enterprise, required that the freedom to make such substitutions be unrestricted here too. In this respect, Carnap's theory of logical probability is likewise purely formal. What Carnap calls 'the sentences of the languages L' are, of course, not sentences at all in fact: only sentence-schemas. His statements of logical probability, which mention two such sentence-schemas, therefore inherit this schematic character themselves. And no restriction is placed on the individual constants or predicate constants which may be substituted for the variables or dummy constants in the sentence-schemas.

---

[8] Hempel (1965), p. 10.

Non-deductive logic, then, as Hempel and Carnap conceived it, was purely formal. In particular, it placed no restriction on the predicates substitutable into a schema for judgements of confirmation or for statements of logical probability.

Yet one has only to say this, to realize at once that these writers did not at all consistently adhere to their conception of non-deductive logic as purely formal. This is especially obvious in the case of Hempel. For his theory *does* in fact, and expressly, place restrictions on the predicates substitutable into confirmation-schemas: they must, among other things, be *observational.*[9] Nor, of course, was this an accident. Hempel was a logical positivist, and regarded confirmability as a peculiarity which *distinguishes* empirical hypotheses both from the propositions of mathematics and logic, and from the 'pseudo-propositions' of metaphysics.[10]

An insoluble problem was posed for Hempel, therefore, by a judgement of confirmation such as ' "The number three is prime" confirms "All numbers are prime" ', or ' "Socrates is predestined by God to eternal torment" confirms "Everyone is predestined by God to eternal torment." ' The corresponding judgements of initial favourable relevance pose a similar insoluble problem for Carnap. As consistent logical positivists, Hempel and Carnap must have called these propositions false. As *formal* non-deductive logicians they must, if consistent, have called them true.[11]

Still, if Hempel and Carnap, under pressure from their other philosophical commitments, could not consistently adhere to the belief that non-deductive logic is purely formal, that is no more than an historical accident. Perhaps some one else could. But that is precisely the hope which 'grue', when it came along, extinguished.

It is obviously true that 'All the emeralds observed before AD 2000 are green' confirms 'Any emerald observed after AD 2000 will be green'. A systematic theory of confirmation, if it is any good, will deliver this judgement of confirmation, among many others. If 'green', at its last occurrence here, is replaced by 'blue', an obviously false judgement of confirmation results: a judge-

---

[9] See Ibid., (1965) pp. 22, third paragraph, and Hempel (1943), p. 22.
[10] Hempel (1965), p. 3.
[11] Cf. Stove (1966).

ment which no systematic theory of confirmation, that was any good, would deliver.

But now, as we have seen, a theory of confirmation, if as well as being systematic it is purely formal, will deliver the above true judgement of confirmation only *indirectly*: only, that is, as an instance of some *schema* for judgements of confirmation. As an instance, for example, of the schema: "'All the F observed before t are G" confirms "Any F observed after t is G"'. And Goodman's objection is, that there are predicate constants which, substituted into this or any similar schema, yield *false* judgements of confirmation.

Now let me introduce another predicate less familiar than 'green'. It is the predicate 'grue' and it applies to all things examined before t just in case they are green but to other things just in case they are blue. Then at time t we have, for each evidence statement asserting that a given emerald is green, a parallel evidence statement asserting that that emerald is grue. And the statements that emerald a is grue, that emerald b is grue, and so on, will each confirm the general hypothesis that all emeralds are grue. Thus according to our definition, the prediction that all emeralds subsequently examined will be green and the prediction that all will be grue are alike confirmed by evidence statements describing the same observations. But if an emerald subsequently examined is grue, it is blue and hence not green. Thus although we are well aware which of the two incompatible predictions is genuinely confirmed, they are equally well confirmed according to our present definition.[12]

In other words:

(142) 'All the emeralds observed before AD 2000 are grue' confirms 'Any emerald observed after AD 2000 is grue',

is a false judgement of confirmation. For, given the definition of 'grue', it entails the obviously false:

(143) 'All the emeralds observed before AD 2000 are green' confirms 'Any emerald observed after AD 2000 is blue'.

Yet (142) is an instance of the schema:

(144) 'All the F observed before t are G' confirms 'Any F observed after t is G'.

---

[12] Goodman (1954), pp. 74–5.

And (144) is a schema which, in virtue of its many true instances, and in every other respect, has as good a claim on our acceptance as any schema for judgements of confirmation.

Assuming that, given the definition of 'grue', (142) really does entail (143), then the case of 'grue' shows what Goodman claimed it shows: that 'confirmation . . . depends rather heavily upon features . . . other than . . . syntactical form'.[13] It therefore shows that non-deductive logic is not purely formal. For, just as the cases mentioned in sections (ii) and (iii) above showed that deductive logic is not purely formal, by showing that typical purely formal judgements of validity or of invalidity have false instances as well as true ones; so the case of 'grue' shows that a typical purely formal judgement of confirmation, such as (144), has false instances as well as true ones.

We saw in section (iv) above, that the admission that deductive logic is not purely formal, is not at all sceptical: it is no bar whatever to the possibility of deductive logical truth, or of knowledge of such truth. Similarly, the admission that non-deductive logic is not purely formal, is not sceptical: it is no bar whatever to the possibility of non-deductive logical truth, or of knowledge of such truth. On the contrary, and just as in the deductive case: it is precisely our claims to know non-deductive logical truths, such as that (142) is *false*, and that some other instances of (144) are *true*, which compel us to say that non-deductive logic is not purely formal. Yet scepticism about non-deductive logic has in fact been greatly encouraged by the case of 'grue'. Indeed, 'grue' has been thought to prove all sorts of things which it does not prove at all.

It is widely supposed, for example, that the 'grue' case is an objection or counter-example *to Hempel's definition of confirmation itself*; or in other words that the outrageous (143), or what is supposed to entail it, (142), or at the very least (144), is a consequence rigorously derivable from Hempel's definition. Several things Goodman says, including the last five words of the quotation above,[14] suggest that he believed this. Hempel himself has never, to my knowledge, denied that (143) is a consequence of his definition; which has helped to spread the belief that it is. But it is not. Not that Hempel saw 'grue' coming, and provided

[13] Ibid., pp. 73.
[14] Ibid., pp. 73, 75, and 76.

against it: it is well known that he did not. But as it happens, various provisions, inserted in his definition for other reasons, make it impossible for (143), or (142), or even (144), to be rigorously derived from that definition.

I will not attempt to prove this. (Strictly, indeed, it is impossible to prove such a thing.) Even to state in detail my reasons for believing it, would take us much too far out of our way. But anyone who supposes that (143), (142), or even (144), *can* be rigorously derived from Hempel's definition, should try to derive it rigorously. He will find the experiment instructive.

If Goodman did think that his case directly hit Hempel's definition, then he was still wider of the mark in saying (in the passage quoted above) that, given green emeralds before the year 2000, the 'green' prediction and the 'grue' or the 'blue' prediction, 'are *equally well* confirmed *according to our present definition*'. Hempel's definition cannot possibly have any consequences about two hypotheses being *equally well* confirmed. As is well known, his definition was just of the classificatory concept, 'confirms', and says nothing whatever about the comparative concept, 'confirms . . . as well as . . .'. Indeed, whether or not it was Hempel's definition that Goodman meant when he refers, as he constantly does, to 'our definition', he was at fault here. For he evidently drew his conclusion about *equal* confirmation, from premises which are judgements of *confirmation*, and nothing more.

It is widely supposed, similarly, that the case of 'grue' is an objection or counter-example to *Carnap's theory of logical probability*. What corresponds there to (142)–(144) are the following judgements of favourable relevance:

(142′) 'All the emeralds observed before 2000 are grue' is initially favourably relevant to 'Any emerald observed after 2000 is grue';

(143′) 'All the emeralds observed before 2000 are green' is initially favourably relevant to 'Any emerald observed after 2000 is blue';

(144′) 'All the F observed before t are G' is initially favourably relevant to 'Any F observed after t is G'.

The supposition is, therefore, that (143′), or (142′), or at least (144′), is a consequence rigorously derivable from Carnap's theory of logical probability. But it is not so. Again, it is out of the question to do more here than to *state* this fact, and invite anyone who thinks otherwise to try to produce such a rigorous derivation.

It is not true, then, that either Hempel's theory of confirmation, or Carnap's theory of logical probability, is itself hit by the problem of 'grue'. What grue *does* hit is a belief without which those theories would never have been constructed: that non-deductive logic is purely formal. But that is not at all the same thing.

If even the systematic constructions of Carnap and Hempel are not refuted by the case of 'grue', then that case cannot possibly hit the few tiny fragments of non-deductive logic which I used as the premisses of my arguments in Chapters V–VII. Still, those arguments will be thought by many philosophers to be exposed to the following objection, which is an adaptation of the 'grue' case. It has been made to the arguments of Williams (1947) and Stove (1973), out of which the arguments of Chapters V–VII have grown.

The difficulty is that an argument from logical probability is of a purely formal sort. As a result, it cannot differentiate between more and less 'natural' classes. The fact that all hitherto observed emeralds are green might be taken to bestow a probability upon the hypothesis that all other emeralds are also green. But what of the hypothesis that all emeralds are green up to AD 2000 but blue thereafter? That is to say, what of the hypothesis that emeralds are grue? If the evidence we have now (before AD 2000) bestows a certain logical probability on the hypothesis that all emeralds are green, why will it not bestow the same logical probability upon the hypothesis that all emeralds are grue?[15]

It is not obvious, and Armstrong says nothing to explain, what he means by calling the arguments of Williams (1947) or Stove (1973), 'purely formal'. Nor is it easy to be sure what his objection is supposed to prove. If it is supposed to be a proof of the invalidity of Williams's argument, or of mine, it can safely be rejected out of hand. For on that supposition it would be a 'proof of invalidity by a parallel argument'; and we saw in section (ii) above that there is no such thing. But I take it that the objection is supposed to be a proof, not of the invalidity, but of the 'non-proof-hood' of

[15] Armstrong (1983), pp. 57–8.

Williams's (1947) and Stove's (1973) argument. And I think that, by calling those arguments 'purely formal', Armstrong meant at least this: that those arguments have predicate variables or dummy constants in them, and that, as a result, a predicate like 'grue', as well as 'decent' predicates like 'black', or 'Australian swan', can be substituted into them.

When, making those assumptions, I try to re-formulate Armstrong's objection to my own satisfaction, the best I can do is the following. 'To "prove" in the way Stove (1973) did, or Williams (1947) did, that (for example) "All the many observed Australian swans have been black" is initially favourably relevant to "All Australian swans are black", cannot really be a proof of that proposition. For at that point in such a "proof" at which "black" and "Australian swans" were substituted for certain predicate variables or dummy constants, we were equally entitled to substitute instead "grue" and "emeralds". And then the argument would be a "proof" of the false proposition, that "All the emeralds observed before 2000 are green" is initially favourably relevant to "Any emerald observed after 2000 is blue".'

It is not easy to be sure that the objection, even in this version, is free from the reproach of trying to prove invalidity by a parallel argument. But I believe that it is, and that it is in fact a just objection to my (1973) arguments and those of Williams (1947). Or rather, I believe it is, *if (142') does entail (143')*; (and as to that, see below). Williams's version of his argument was certainly of the most unqualified, and quite unnecessary, generality. He was always enunciating his 'law of large numbers' for *any* attribute, any population, any large sample.[16] With 'grue' behind us, we can easily see that there was a standing invitation, in this generality, to an adaptation of the 'grue' case to his argument. (And Williams in fact acknowledged, in a letter to the present writer, that his argument needed 'some repair to cope with [grue]'.) Similarly, I believe, my argument (1973), by a piece of carelessness far less historically excusable than Williams's, is exposed to the adaptation of the 'grue' case formulated above.

But the arguments of Chapter V–VII are not. There is no way that anyone will ever be able to substitute 'grue' for any predicate variable or dummy constant in any of those arguments. The

---

[16] See Ibid., Williams (1947), ch. 4 *passim*.

simple reason is: *there are no predicate variables or dummy predicate constants in them.* Those arguments are, as the reader can easily check, from start to finish about the logical probability of certain concrete arguments. They are *never* about any argument-form or argument-schema which contains a predicate variable or a dummy predicate constant.

I adopted this course partly, of course, because I wished to prevent any possible adaptation of the 'grue' case to my arguments; but equally because I did not *need* to adopt any other. My purpose in Chapters V–VII was purely polemical: simply to prove the falsity of the sceptical thesis about induction. That thesis is a *universal* proposition. All I needed to do, therefore, was to prove a judgement of initial favourable relevance about, or an ascription of high logical probability to, *one concrete* inductive inference. That I could do. And prudence enjoined that I attempt to do no more.

The case would have been quite different, if I had undertaken some *systematic* work on logical probability; not a purely formal theory (for that is out of the question), but something of high generality: something, say, which would deliver numerical values of '$P(q/p)$' for a wide range of values of the two propositional variables. After Goodman, anyone who undertakes such work as that will indeed need to impose restrictions on the range of his predicate variables, so as to exclude 'grue' if he wishes to admit 'green' and 'blue'. (At least, he will, if (142') does entail (143').) But I was attempting no such thing, and I had no such need. All I did was to assert a few statements of logical probability, almost every one of which was free from all generality; and the few which do have some generality (such as (83)) still have none whatever in the predicate dimension. As a result, there is no predicate hole of any kind in the arguments of Chapter V–VII. So there is no hole into which anyone can plug 'grue'.

It is true, as I know from *expériences nombreuses et funestes,* that you cannot make the simplest and most specific assessment of logical probability, without some people supposing that you are thereby committed to so-and-so's *system* of logical probability, with all the attendant difficulties, however peculiar to it. You need only say that 'Abe is black' has probability 0·9 in relation to 'Abe is a raven and just 90 percent of ravens are black', and some philosophers will at once start talking to you about . . . *Carnap!*

About Carnap and 'the zero-probability of laws'; Carnap and 'grue'; Carnap and 'c-star' *versus* 'c-dagger'; and so on, and on. But this is no less ridiculous than it is vexatious. You might as well suppose that a man cannot say that 'All ravens are black and Abe is a raven' entails 'Abe is black', without his being thereby obliged to defend Aristotelian logic, or the system of *Principia Mathematica*, or Quine. This nuisance is, of course, another facet of something noticed in section (ii) above: the tendency to mistake system-makers, mere organizers of logical knowledge, for *sole proprietors* of it.

What, then, does 'grue' matter to the arguments of Chapters V–VII above? Nothing at all. Suppose, with Goodman, that (142) and (142′) do respectively entail the obviously false (143) and (143′), and hence are false themselves; or, suppose with Goodman, that 'All the emeralds observed before 2000 are grue' is *not* a reason to believe 'Any emerald observed after 2000 is grue.' What does that prove? Only that some inductive inferences are not rational, or, in Goodman's terminology, that some empirical predicates are not projectible. Well, what is that to my arguments? I only contended, in Chapters V–VII, against the inductive sceptic, and therefore contended only for the thesis that some inductive inferences *are* rational, or that some empirical predicates *are* projectible.

That some are *not*, we knew, in any case, long before. *Everyone* knows, as I said at the start of this book, that

(2) All the many ravens observed so far have been black,

while it is reason to believe

(3) All ravens are black,

is not a reason to believe

(8) All ravens are observed.

Or again, everyone knows, without needing Goodman to tell them, that 'All the emeralds observed before 2000 are emeralds which are green and which exist before 2000', though it is a reason to believe 'All emeralds are green', is not a reason to believe 'All emeralds are emeralds which exist before 2000'. In short, no one should have had to wait for 'grue', to learn that non-deductive logic is not purely formal. And the arguments of

Chapters V–VII, in particular, have nothing more to fear from the case of 'grue', than from the two cases just mentioned.

But 'grue' should not matter much even to *systematic* writers on non-deductive logic. It shows that they need to impose, on the range of their predicate variables, one more restriction than they had previously been aware of needing. But that is all it shows.

As to the would-be-*formal* non-deductive logicians, 'grue' shows, indeed, that *they* cannot have what they want. But why was *that* ever supposed, even by those philosophers themselves, to matter much? Well, because of the belief, of course, which they shared with all other philosophers, that *deductive* logic *is* purely formal. But that belief is not only false; it is one which, as there is nothing in sections (ii)–(iii) above which is not well known to philosophers, no one should ever have held in the first place.

But I think that the importance which was at first, and still is, attached to 'grue', has even less foundation than I have so far suggested. For I think that, given the definition of 'grue', (142) does *not* entail (143), and that (142′) does not entail (143′). I do not mean only that (142) does not entail (143) *given Hempel's theory of confirmation*, or only that (142′) does not entail (143′) given *Carnap's theory of logical probability.* I mean that (143) cannot be rigorously derived from (142), or (143′) from (142′), *via any* meta-principles of confirmation, or *via* any principles of logical probability, not able to be shown on other grounds to be false. The kind of things that would be needed to effect such a derivation are, of course, true propositions of the kind which Hempel sought under the names of 'equivalence conditions' on confirmation, 'consequence condition', and the like; or true principles of logical probability, and especially principles of relevance. But I do not believe that there are any such principles as will permit the derivation of (143) from (142), or of (143′) from (142′). In other words, I do not think that, even given the definition of 'grue', it is possible, without drawing on false premises, to get the 'green confirms blue' result from the supposition that 'grue confirms grue', or to get 'green favourably relevant to blue' from 'grue favourably relevant to grue'.

I cannot prove that this is so. I believe it, because I have never been able, despite many attempts, either to produce these rigorous derivations myself, or to meet with them in other writers.

Goodman's own 'derivation', quoted earlier in this section, is a model of non-rigour: a fact of which I have furnished some evidence above, and which is well-enough known—again!—in the *oral* tradition. But I do not know of any published discussion of 'grue' which either makes the required derivations rigorous, or says outright that they cannot be made so. There is, therefore, some reason to believe that they cannot be made so.

If (143′) *cannot* be rigorously derived from (142′), then, as I indicated earlier, 'grue' would be no problem even for the arguments of my (1973) or Williams's (1947). Those arguments would still, indeed, be imprudently and unnecessarily *general*, and would contain predicate variables which would allow 'grue' as a value. But there is no harm in licensing 'grue-to-grue' inductive inference, if that does not license 'green-to-blue' inductive inference.

But even if this last 'sceptical doubt' is misplaced, it is, for the reasons given earlier in this section, not easy to account entirely for the prodigious importance which has been attached to 'grue'. The main villain of the piece is undoubtedly the immemorial illusion that logic is nothing if not formal; but I suspect that the spirit of the age has also had a hand in the affair. If (142) does entail (143), or (142′) does entail (143′), then, as (143) and (143′) are obviously false, (142) and (142′) are false too, and if that is so then Goodman has added a new class of cases to the stock of inductive inferences which are not rational. As we had a sufficient stock of such cases before, this cannot possibly matter very much. But then, the spirit of the age is greedy of anything, however small, which strengthens the sceptical side of the question about induction. Speaking of the philosophical climate of 1947, Donald Williams truly said, what is even truer now, that our philosophy of induction,

in its dread of superstition and dogmatic reaction, has been orientated purposely toward scepticism; that a conclusion is admired in proportion as it is sceptical; that a jejune argument for scepticism will be admitted where a scrupulous defence of knowledge is derided or ignored; that an affirmative theory is a mere annoyance, to be stamped down as quickly as possible to the normal level of denial and defeat.[17]

----

[17] Ibid., p. 15.

X

IS DEDUCTIVE LOGIC EMPIRICAL?

(i)

Our knowledge of logical probability, Carnap said, is intuitive, not empirical.[1] Take regularity, for example, or any special case of it such as (137) above; or a simpler instance of it still, such as

(145) $P(\text{Abe is black}/T) < 1$.

If a person could not simply see this truth for himself, then there would be nothing anyone could do to enable him to learn it. In particular, it is not a truth of a kind which could be learnt from experience. Or again, take the symmetry of individual constants, or any special case of it such as (136) above; or a simpler instance of it still, such as

(146) $P(\text{Abe is black}/T) = P(\text{Bob is black}/T)$.

If some one does not know the truth of this *a priori*, then there is no way in which he could learn its truth *a posteriori*.

Someone who lacked all such 'probabilistic intuitions', or was 'inductively blind', Carnap says, could never learn any 'inductive logic' at all. (He means, of course, '*non-deductively* blind', and '*non-deductive* logic'; obviously, the arguments assessed by (145) or by (146) are not *inductive* ones.) The theory of logical probability, Carnap therefore concludes, rests on intuition.

He uses the word 'intuition' reluctantly, because, as he says, people are apt to think that, if logical probability rests on intuition, it follows that the theory of logical probability is as ill-founded as the claims of gypsies, mystics, and the like. But, Carnap says, this does not follow, and we will see that it does not, once we realize that *deductive* logic, which no one thinks ill-founded, *also rests on intuition.*

---

[1] What follows is a summary of Carnap (1968).

Thus, take simplification for example, or any special case of it; say

(147) 'Abe is black and Bob is black' entails 'Abe is black'.

If a person could not simply see this truth for himself, then there would be nothing anyone could do to enable him to learn it. In particular, it is not a truth of a kind which could be learnt from experience. Or take syllogism, or any special case of it, say:

(148) 'Abe is a raven and all ravens are black' entails 'Abe is black'.

If some one does not know this *a priori*, he cannot possibly learn it *a posteriori*.

It is no reproach to our knowledge of non-deductive logic, then, Carnap concludes, that it rests on intuition; for the same is true of our knowledge of deductive logic.

Here is an expression of the opposite view of our knowledge of deductive logic (and of mathematics).

I do not wish to deny that the indicated sciences have a marked advantage over others in the reliability of their doctrines. But nobody who has accepted even the larger part of the foregoing arguments can hold that the reasons for this are to be found in the circumstances cited by Kant. Indeed, I see no reason why we should forsake the explanation which was given long before Kant. It has always been maintained that these sciences enjoy such a high degree of certainty only because they have the advantage that their most important doctrines can be easily and variously tested by experience, and have been so tested, and that those doctrines which cannot be immediately tested are deducible by arguments which have been tested many times and have always been found valid, and finally, that the results which are obtained in these sciences do not infringe upon the human passions; hence most of these investigations were begun and finished without bias, and with suitable leisure and peace. The only reason why we are so certain that the rules *barbara, celarent,* etc. are valid is because they have been confirmed in thousands of arguments in which we have applied them. This also is the true reason why we are so confident, in mathematics, that factors in a different order give the same product, or that the sum of the angles in a triangle is equal to two right angles, or that the forces on a lever are in equilibrium when they stand in the inverse relation of their distances from the fulcrum, etc. But that $\sqrt{2} = 1.414 \ldots$, that the content of a sphere is exactly two-thirds of the circumscribed cylinder, that in each body there are three free axes of revolution, etc., we assert mainly because they follow from propositions of the first kind by arguments which others have conducted hundreds of times and have found valid; an additional factor is that in all these matters we do not have the slightest advantage if the thing turns out to be otherwise. That the reason for our confidence really lies in these circumstances can be seen most clearly from the fact that our confidence rises and falls as these circumstances dictate. If we have not tested the truth of a proposition either by experiment, or by repeated checking of its derivation, we do not give it unqualified assent, if we are at all sensible, no matter what Critical Philosophy may say about the infallibility of pure intuition . . . Does not experience teach us that we make mistakes in mathematical judgments, and that we make these mistakes more easily the more we trust what that philosophy calls by the high-sounding name of pure intuition? The geometrician who thought that a pair of solids have the same content if they are bounded by similar and equal sides made such a gross mistake certainly only because he trusted his intuition, i.e. mere appearance, too much . . .[2]

Bolzano, or his translator, here uses some turns of phrase which are at odds with the passage as a whole. They suggest that we learn a general judgement of validity from *singular* judgements *of validity.* That we learn, for example, the validity of *barbara,* that is, the truth of

(149) '*x* is *F* and all *F* are *G*' entails '*x* is *G*', for all *x*, all *F*, all *G*.

from *instances of it,* such as

(150) 'Abe is a person now in this room and all persons now in this room are black' entails 'Abe is black'.

But from the passage as a whole it is evident enough that this is not at all what Bolzano means, but is, rather, opposite to it. He means that we learn (149) by finding by experience that the premiss of instances of the *barbara* form *are true, and* that the conclusion is true, and by not finding, in all our experience, any instance of that form of which the premisses are true and the conclusion is false. According to Bolzano, then, it is not from propositions like (150), which are judgements of validity themselves (even if only 'little ones'), that we learn (149). It is from

² Bolzano (1837), pp. 345–5.

conjunctions, and conjunctions not only of a contingent, but specifically of an *observational* kind: propositions such as

(151) Abe is black and Abe is a person now in this room and all persons now in this room are black.

A philosophy of deductive logic which is at least very like Bolzano's was implied by Popper in some comments on the article of Carnap which was summarized above. Popper, of course, has always denied the existence of non-deductive logic, and he thinks that intuition ought not to be relied on anywhere. He therefore does not deny that *non*-deductive logic, or that the theory of logical probability, rests on intuition; indeed, he hastens to agree with this part of Carnap's thesis. What he does deny is the other part: that deductive logic is in the same epistemic boat as non-deductive logic.

Carnap says that deductive logic is based on deductive intuition. I contest this claim. Any rule of inference can be criticized by trying to find a *counter-example*—that is to say, an instance of the rule with *true* premises and a *false* conclusion.

The main argument against the parallelism, defended by Carnap, between deductive and the so-called inductive logic, is that while deductive logic can be rationally criticized by the search for counter examples, there is no such criterion for the invalidity of any alleged rule of inductive logic.

(a) It is interesting that Carnap gives an example of a deductive inference (whose validity, he holds, must be accepted intuitively) but no corresponding example of an inductive inference.

The reason is, I suppose, that no convincing example of any similar inductive rule of inference exists.

(b) I have had students who thought that 'All men are mortal; Socrates is mortal; thus Socrates is a man' was a valid inference. Yet they realized the invalidity of this rule when I discussed with them a counter example (arising from calling my cat 'Socrates').

My point is that there is no similar rule of inductive logic which is either intuitively valid or which stands up to criticism in the light of the history of science.[3]

Whereas Bolzano explicitly says that we learn deductive logic

---

[3] Popper (1968), pp. 296–7. Italics in text. The same things are said in Popper (1974), pp. 114–15.

from experience, Popper is not so explicit. He does not say that the counter-examples, for which we should and do search when a general judgement of validity is in question, must be ones which could be discovered by experience: *observable* counter-examples. Still, I think that that is what he must mean. The phrase 'intuitive knowledge', whatever exactly it means, at least means '*non-empirical* knowledge'; hence to deny that our knowledge of deductive logic is intuitive must at least be to say that it is empirical. In fact, the disagreement between Popper and Carnap would be entirely verbal, unless Popper does mean, by 'counter-examples', 'observable counter-examples'. A counter-example, at least a counter-example to a general judgement of validity, is a conjunction of the premisses of an argument with the negation of its conclusion. But if such a conjunction is not of a kind which could be discovered by experience, then it could be discovered only non-empirically. And if it were once admitted that knowledge of deductive logic can be acquired non-empirically, it would be mere quarrelling with a word, to deny that it can be acquired intuitively.

The limitation of counter-examples to observable ones necessitates, however, a further limitation. There can be observation, or experience, only of what is actual. We can, of course, *imagine* unrealized possibilities; but it is impossible that we should observe or experience them. (We might imagine we observe them, of course.) A counter-example, to a general judgement of validity, must therefore be a case in which the premisses *really are* true and the conclusion *really is* false. A *merely possible* counter-example, like an actual but unobservable counter-example, could be discovered only by an exercise of precisely that 'intuition' which Popper and Bolzano are concerned to deny.

I ascribe to Popper, then, an account of our knowledge of deductive logic which is essentially the same as Bolzano's. We discover invalidity by the successful search for counter-examples to general judgements of validity: we 'discover' validity by an extensive experience of examples in which both the premisses and conclusion are true, and an unsuccessful search for counter-examples; any counter-examples, and all the 'examples', alike being observable, hence actual, ones. If this is a misinterpretation of Popper, then that is unfortunate but not important. For it is no more than ascribing to him an unqualifiedly empiricist account of our knowledge of deductive logic; and if he does not subscribe to that, there are plenty of others who do, either expressly or by implication. In the nineteenth century there are Mill and all his followers; in the present century there are Quine and his followers, 'as the sands of the sea for multitude'; then there is, as we have seen—a better authority than any of these—Bolzano.

Here, as in the preceding chapter, when I speak of propositions of deductive logic, I mean only judgements of validity or of invalidity. Of these, however, every normal human being has an immense amount of knowledge: knowledge of what does, and what does not, follow from what. The question is whether, or how much of, this knowledge could have been acquired from experience?

This question is best broken up into two. How much of our knowledge of *invalidity* could have been acquired from experience? I will answer this first, and in connection with the quotation from Popper given above. Then, in connection with the quotation given above from Bolzano, I will answer the second question: how much of our knowledge of *validity* could have been acquired from experience?

(ii)

(A) As the above quotation shows, Popper expressly identifies a counter-example with 'an instance . . . with true premisses and a false conclusion'.

This identification is the basis of his objection to non-deductive logic, that 'while [propositions of] deductive logic can be rationally criticized by the search for counter examples, there is no such criterion for the invalidity of any [typical statement of logical probability]'.

The contrast which Popper intends here is, of course, perfectly real. *Barbara*, i.e. (149) above, would be refuted by a case in which the premisses were true and the conclusion false. But a typical statement of logical probability, say

(152) $P(x \text{ is } G/x \text{ is } F \text{ and just } \frac{m}{n} \text{ths of } F\text{'s are } G) = \frac{m}{n}$, for all $n > m > 0$, all x, all F, all G,

is not refuted by, for example, the conjunction:

(153) Abe is not black and Abe is a person now in this room
and just $\frac{3}{5}$ of persons now in this room are black.

Of course it is not. Who could ever have supposed it was?

But the basis of this 'objection', the identification of counter-
examples with conjunctions of true premisses and false conclusion, is simply absurd. It is only where a judgement of *validity* is
in question, that a counter-example must be a proposition of that
kind.

It is not even necessary to go outside the propositions of
deductive logic in order to see that counter-examples are not
always propositions of that kind. Suppose that what is in question is some general judgement of *invalidity*: say,

(154) For any contingent p and any necessarily true q, p does
not entail q.

A counter-example to *this*, evidently, will need to be a judgement
of *validity*. It will need also to be true, singular, and inconsistent
with (154); but a judgement of validity it must be. No mere
conjunction will do; least of all a *contingent* conjunction, such as
could be a counter-example to, say, *Barbara* (149). (I hope it is
unnecessary to say that in fact counter-examples to (154) are
easily found: substitute 'Abe is black' for p, and for q, 'If Abe is
black then Abe is black.')

Once the absurdity of Popper's initial identification is realized,
we see that, contrary to what he says, it is perfectly possible to
criticize a typical statement of logical probability, such as (152),
by trying to find a counter-example to it. Only, a counter-
example to (152) would evidently be *a statement of logical
probability itself*. It must also be true, singular, and inconsistent
with (152); but a statement of logical probability it must be.
Neither (153) nor any other conjunction, least of all a contingent
conjunction, would do.

(B) Popper says that 'Carnap gives an example of a deductive
inference (whose validity, he holds, must be accepted intuitively)
but no corresponding example of an inductive inference. The
reason is, I suppose, that no convincing example of any similar
inductive rule of inference exists.'

But Carnap *had* given examples of non-deductive counterparts of basic deductive 'rules'! In fact he gave two; the very two,

indeed, which above I reported him as giving, viz. regularity, and the symmetry of individual constants. That is, Carnap had mentioned, as examples of truths of non-deductive logic which could only be learnt intuitively, both

(155) $P(h/e) < 1 > 0$, for all tautological e, and all contingent non-quantified h;

and

(156) $P(h/e) = P(h'/e')$, for all e, e', h, h', such that e' can be generated from e, and h' from h, by mere uniform replacement of one individual constant for another.

He did not give these examples in just the form I have given them here: there are fifty different ways in which such propositions can be expressed. But he did give them, as anyone who consults the relevant page can see.[4]

Of course, there is nothing properly called *inductive* about (155) or (156). (The class of inferences assessed by (155) actually excludes the class of inductive inferences, and (156) includes inductive inferences indifferently among *all* inferences which satisfy the restrictions it places on values of the propositional variables.) But this counts for nothing: Popper was only following Carnap's own bad terminology according to which 'inductive' means 'non-deductive'. Equally of course, neither (155) nor (156) is properly called a 'rule'. But this too is trivial. A statement of logical probability *can* be expressed as a rule; and a rule of deductive logic *can* be expressed as a statement (and even as a statement of logical probability). There is nothing in the word 'inductive', then, or in the word 'rule', to excuse the remarkable instance which we have just witnessed of Popper's capabilities as a controversialist.

(C) Regularity (155), and the symmetry of individual constants (156), are very *general* statements of logical probability. It follows as a special case of (A) above that, contrary to what Popper says, they *can* be 'rationally criticized by the search for counter-examples'.

Of course, a counter-example to either of them will not be a mere conjunction of any kind, and least of all a contingent con-

---

[4] See Carnap (1968), p. 262.

junction. It will be a statement of logical probability itself. A counter-example to (155) would be a judgement of validity, or a statement of logical probability $= 1$. A counter-example to (156) would be a 'comparative inequality', that is, a statement of logical probability of the '$P(H/E) > P(H'/E')$' kind.

(D) It is ridiculous (as well as ungrammatical) to speak of a 'rule of inference', or of any generalization, being 'criticized by trying to find a counter-example'; still worse, to say that the generalizations of deductive logic, or that any generalization, 'can be *rationally* criticized by the search for counter-examples'.

Rational criticism, and even criticism, is hardly so easy as that! A person who is engaged in trying to find, or in searching for, a counter-example to a generalization, is *trying to find* a criticism of it. He is not *criticizing* it.

(E) 'I have had students who thought that "All men are mortal; Socrates is mortal; thus Socrates is a man" was a valid inference. Yet they realized the invalidity of this rule when I discussed with them a counter-example (arising from calling my cat "Socrates").'

We learn from this vignette that Popper was accustomed to teaching his students what is false (cf. Chapter IX (ii)): that the invalidity of an argument can be proved by a 'parallel argument'.

(F) In the above quotation, the words 'this rule' are baffling at first. What rule? Popper had not referred to any *rule*. The only thing he had referred to was a *case* of undistributed middle term: a case which is invalid.

But the explanation, I fear, is obvious. It is that Popper believes, and taught his students, that *every* case of undistributed middle is invalid: that is, that

(157) 'All *F* are *G* and *x* is *G*' does not entail '*x* is *F*', for any *x*, any *F*, any *G*.

If so, then again (in view of Chapter IX (ii)), he taught them what is false.

(G) Though (157) is false, its special case,

(158) 'All men are mortal and *x* is mortal' does not entail '*x* is a man', for any *x*,

might still be true. I believe, as I implied in Chapter IX (ii), that it *is* true. But it is important to realize that the truth of (158) does not follow from, say,

(159) Popper's cat 'Socrates' is not a man and Popper's cat 'Socrates' is mortal and all men are mortal.

Nor does (158) follow from any other counter-example to the general validity of undistributed middle. In fact, our knowledge even of the humble (158) cannot possibly have been acquired from experience.

Suppose that we learn (159) by experience. The general (158) follows, only if (159) is conjoined with the assumption that the substitution of any other individual constant for 'Popper's cat "Socrates"' would yield a syllogism no more valid than the one about Popper's cat. But this assumption is a special case of *the symmetry of individual constants* (156), and is by no means something which could be learnt from experience.

Suppose you met some one who was 'blind' to the symmetry of individual constants. He admits, say, that

All men are mortal
Socrates is mortal
Socrates is a man

is invalid; but he insists that

All men are mortal
Plato is mortal
Plato is a man

is valid. How could he learn of his error *from experience*? What *actual observable case* would prove him wrong? To ask these questions is to see that they cannot be answered. There is, then —just as Carnap implied—no way of learning from experience the symmetry of individual constants, or even so much of it as would enable us to infer, from (159) even the humble (158).

(Of course, we do not in fact meet with people who are blind to the symmetry of individual constants. But that is only a reminder that every normal person possesses an enormous amount of logical knowledge, and even some *formal* logical knowledge.)

(H) The invalidity of an argument from P to Q is just the logical possibility of P being true and Q being false. What are the most favourable circumstances which experience could afford us, for acquiring knowledge of this possibility? Evidently, just these, that P is actually true, that Q is actually false, and that the conjunction *P*-and-not-*Q*, as well as being true, is something which we could discover by experience: an observation-statement.

And what is the *most* that could be learnt, in these most favourable circumstances, about logical possibility and hence about invalidity? Evidently just this, that as *P*-and-not-*Q* is true, it is logically possible. In other words that

(160) '*P*' does not entail '*Q*'.

More information than that, about invalidity, could not be extracted, from the observable fact that *P*-and-not-*Q*, by omnipotence itself.

But this means that no *general* judgement of invalidity at all can be learnt from experience; only singular ones can.

(I) From the experience (159), therefore, the most that could be learnt in the way of invalidity is the singular judgement that

(161) 'Popper's cat "Socrates" is mortal and all men are mortal' does not entail 'Popper's cat "Socrates" is a man.'

In fact, however, *even this* singular judgement of invalidity is not one which could be learnt from experience. It can be learnt, indeed, from (159). But (159) *is not,* and anything else from which (161) could be learnt is not, *an observation-statement or report of a possible experience.*

The reason is, of course, that the third conjunct of (159) is a contingent proposition of unrestricted universality; and therefore neither it, nor any conjunction of which it is a conjunct, is a report of a possible, let alone of an actual, observation.

Ironically, therefore, the invalidity of the argument about the cat can not only not be used, as Popper thought it could, to prove the invalidity of the argument about Socrates: it could never have been discovered *itself* by the only means, namely experience, which Popper's philosophy allows for the discovery of invalidity.

The overall result is this. If an argument from *P* to *Q* is invalid, then its invalidity can be learnt from experience if, but also only if, *P* is true and *Q* is false in fact, and the conjunction *P*-and-not-*Q*, as well as being true, is observational. This has the consequence, first, that only singular judgements of invalidity can be learnt from experience; and second, that very few even of them can be so learnt. If the premiss *P* should happen to be false; or if the conclusion Q should be true; or if the conjunction P-and-not-Q is not observational but entails some metaphysical proposition, or some scientific-theoretical one, or even a mere universal contingent like 'All men are mortal': then it will *not* be possible to learn, by experience, the invalidity of *even this particular argument.*

It can hardly be necessary for me to enlarge on how insignificant a proportion it is, of the arguments known to be invalid, in which the conjunction of the premisses with the negation of the conclusion is both true and observational. In other words, scarcely any of the vast fund of knowledge of invalidity which every normal human being possesses can have been acquired from experience.

But it may be worth while to point out a few special consequences. One is, that we cannot learn from experience the invalidity of even so grossly invalid an argument as, say,

The sun rises in the west
Socrates is mortal.

Indeed, we cannot learn from experience the invalidity of *any* argument which either has 'The sun rises in the west' as its premiss, or has 'Socrates is mortal' as its conclusion: the former being false, and the latter true.

A special consequence of that, in turn, is this: that we cannot learn from experience the invalidity of even so slenderly based an *inductive* inference as, say,

Plato is mortal
Socrates is mortal

To learn from experience so immense a generalization as that *all* inductive inferences are invalid—to learn, that is, the supposedly trivial truth of the fallibility of all induction—is, of course, entirely out of the question: no general judgements of invalidity whatever being learnable from experience.

Nor is it from experience that anyone could ever learn *even the invalidity*, which is the least of the defects, of an argument such as:

God predestines 90% of the righteous to eternal torment
I am one of the righteous
God does not predestine me to eternal torment.

Even if some one found out by experience that P-and-not-Q, he could not *from this alone* learn that it is possible that P-and-not-Q. He must *also* have acquired, at the same time or earlier, the knowledge that

(162) 'p' entails 'It is possible that p', for all p;

or at least the knowledge that

(163) 'P-and-not-Q' entails 'It is possible that P-and-not-Q'.

Of course, he need not *know* that he knows (162) or (163); still, he does need to know at least (163). But to know (162) or (163) is to possess some logical knowledge, since these are judgements of validity (one general and one singular). Even the small part, then, of our knowledge of invalidity, which could be learnt from experience, could not be learnt without the assistance of some knowledge of validity. And *this* knowledge too, according to the Bolzano–Popper philosophy of logic, must also have been acquired from experience.

It is likely to be thought, from the preceding paragraph, that I am taking Bolzano and Popper unfairly literally. And certainly, ignorance of (163), if it is possible at all, is a most prodigious height of logical ignorance. It is so prodigious in fact, that to ascribe it to anyone is not only never justified in practice, but is scarcely intelligible even in principle. And yet I refuse to credit our putative learner of logic with even so small a piece of logical knowledge, prior to experience, as (163): is this not making a straw man of my opponent's position?

Not at all. The empirical account of our knowledge of logic must not be allowed to be eked out, as the need for plausibility arises, by crediting the putative logic learner with a fund of logical knowledge prior to experience. For if this were allowed, then the disagreement between the empirical account of our logical knowledge, and the intuitive one, would be either altogether imaginary, or so small as to be not worth bothering about.

(iii)

Of our knowledge of invalidity, then, a small part at most could have been acquired by experience. How much, now, of our knowledge of validity could have been acquired in that way?

None. If any judgement of validity could be learnt from experience, it would be a singular, rather than a general, one. So let us consider a (dummy) singular judgement of validity: that the argument from P to Q is valid. The validity of the argument from P to Q is the logical impossibility of P being true and Q being false. But that the conjunction P-and-not-Q is logically impossible, is not something which could be learnt from experience. Unless both its conjuncts are observation-statements, there could not be any question of learning *from experience* anything whatever about this conjunction. But even if both the conjuncts *are* observational, the nearest thing, that experience could afford us, to knowledge of the impossibility of their conjunction, is the knowledge that the conjunction is *false* in fact: that is, that P is false or Q is true. But the falsity of P-and-not-Q falls a long way short of the logical impossibility of P-and-not-Q. No singular judgement of validity, therefore, can be learnt from experience. And *a fortiori* no general one can.

As always, however, it is better to rely on concrete cases rather than general arguments. The question before us is really quite simple: could we ever learn, by observation or experience, that a particular argument is valid? Could we, for example, learn by experience the truth of the following?

(150) 'Abe is a person now in this room and all persons now in this room are black' entails 'Abe is black'.

Well, what kind of thing *can* we learn by experience? Why, propositions such as

(151) Abe is black and Abe is a person now in this room and all persons now in this room are black:

things like that, and nothing more than things like that. But knowledge of (151) is not a possible source of knowledge of (150). The two things are in fact utterly disparate. That Abe is a person now in the room, and that all the persons now in the room are black, in short, the truth of (151), we can *find out just by using our eyes*. But no one will seriously maintain that we can find out the truth of (150) just by using our eyes.

These considerations are so very obvious, and yet so inconsistent with the empirical account of our logical knowledge implied in the passage from Bolzano quoted above, that there must be some very basic point at which my ideas about deductive logic diverge from Bolzano's. It will be worthwhile to identify what this basic point of divergence is, and to consider how satisfactory, even given his own starting point, Bolzano's account of our logical knowledge is.

The basic divergence is as follows. I set out from the consideration of concrete arguments. Concerning them, I admit singular judgements of validity: that is, I allow that judgements of validity can really be, as many of them certainly appear to be, about a single concrete argument and no more. And my notion of validity is an undisguisedly *modal* one: the *impossibility* of the premiss *P* being true and the conclusion *Q* false. Bolzano, on the other hand, has a notion of validity which is purely extensional. He considers, never the concrete propositions *P* and *Q*, but always certain propositional *forms* or *schemas,* which result when concrete expressions in *P* and *Q* are replaced by schematic ones; and his notion of validity is essentially just this: that every uniform substitution, of concrete expressions for those schematic ones, which makes the premiss *P* true, makes the conclusion *Q* true too.[5]

According to Bolzano, therefore, there is really no such thing as a *singular* judgement of validity. A proposition may appear to ascribe validity just to a single concrete argument, but in reality this proposition has a universal quantifier 'buried' in it. ('Valid' is thus like 'solitary' and unlike 'surly', say, or like 'leafless' and unlike 'leafy'.) *All* judgements of validity, then, are really general; because all are, essentially, *formal.*

No starting-point for a philosophy of logic could well be less promising than this, if what was said in Chapter IX is true. But even apart from that, it is surely very implausible. Cannot a man know that

(148) 'Abe is a raven and all ravens are black' entails 'Abe is black',

without knowing that *barbara* is valid? Without knowing that is, that

(149) '*x* is *F* and all *F* are *G*' entails '*x* is *G*', for all *x*, all *F*, all *G*.

---

[5] Bolzano (1837), p. 209 ff.

Obviously he can: since most men do. Any suggestion to the contrary could only be explained, in fact, by referring once again to the tendency of formal logicians to confuse their own systematizations of logical knowledge, with logical knowlege itself.

But not only does Bolzano have nothing corresponding to what I call singular judgements of validity: he has nothing corresponding to my *general* judgements of validity either. What I call such are things like (149), or, otherwise worded,

(164) For all x, all F, all G, an argument from 'x is F and all F are G' to 'x is G' is valid.

But (149) and (164) essentially contain a modal element, 'valid', or 'entails', to which nothing corresponds in Bolzano. There, since he has replaced those modal notions by non-modal ones, the nearest thing to (149) or (164) would be:

(165) For all x, all F, all G, it is not the case that 'x is F and all F are G' is true and 'x is G' is false;

or in other words,

(166) For all x, all F, all G, either 'x is F and all F are G' is false or 'x is G' is true.

While, then, what I call a general judgement of validity is a proposition which ascribes validity to every concrete member of a certain class of arguments—and may be one which picks out that class of arguments is a purely formal way—Bolzano never ascribes *validity* to anything at all. His *subjects* are always argument-forms or schemas, never concrete arguments; and the predicate he ascribes to these schemas is, not validity, but only *always-preserving-truth*, or *freedom from any counter-example*.

Once we realize this, Bolzano's account of our knowledge of deductive logic, which at first reading is so implausibly 'inductive', becomes entirely natural. Indeed, the quotation marks just used are quite out of place. Deductive logic, Bolzano implies, simply *is* a *branch of inductive science*. Its generalizations are simply universally quantified contingent propositions, indeed empirical ones, just like the generalizations of natural science. The only reason we can have for believing them are, just as elsewhere in science, true observation-statements. The inference, from these observation-statements to the generalizations, is *inductive* inference; not just in the 'structural' or formal sense, in which, for example, Newton may be said to have arrived at the binominal theorem inductively. It is inductive inference in the full, mainstream sense: inference from *observed cases which contain no counter-example* to the schema hypothesized, to the conclusion, and to no more than the conclusion, that *there is no counter-example* to this schema.

Moreover, Bolzano is, as the quotation shows, an emphatic fallibilist about inductive inference. So if I were to say to him, as I have said earlier in this section, that no judgement of validity can be learnt from experience, he would have an easy rejoinder. 'Of course not', he would say, 'not what *you* would call "learnt from experience"; by which you appear to mean something like "directly discovered to be true". But there is no harm in logical generalizations not being learnable from experience in *that* sense: for the laws of nature are not learnable from experience in *that* sense, either. And as I am no sceptic about inductive inference, and hold that a hypothesized law of nature can nevertheless be *reasonably inferred* from experience, so I can and do hold that those generalizations of deductive logic, which we have reason to believe, have just this kind of evidence in their favour, and can have no other.'

Of course this position is not one which *Popper* could embrace. He *is* a sceptic about induction. But he is no sceptic (to say the least) about the commonly accepted generalizations of deductive logic. He therefore could not allow that deductive logic, which he prizes so much, has no more claim on our belief than is bestowed on it by that inductive inference which he despises so much.

But Bolzano can. Quine too can (if I understand him), and even must. And when 'validity' is understood in the extensional way explained above, and when 'learnt from experience' is understood in the fallibilist way explained above, the thesis that judgements of validity *can* be learnt from experience is not without a certain attractiveness. It has the merit of economy, as allowing us to dispense with any supposed faculty for 'intuiting' true judgements of validity. And it is agreeably down-to-earth.

It has a further great merit: it inevitably suggests a *unified* account of deductive and of non-deductive logic, and one which is attractively simple. Validity, according to this philosophy, is just always-preserving-truth. Validity is also the highest degree of logical probability, = 1. What, then, could logical probability *less than* 1 be, except preserving-truth-less-than-always? In other words, logical probability = $\frac{m}{n}$ is *relative-truth-frequency* = $\frac{m}{n}$; and we have arrived, it would seem, at a point of view which at once acknowledges the continuity between deductive and non-deductive logic, and respects the distinction between them.

Our knowledge of logical probability, on this view, would be empirical, just as our knowledge of validity is. Carnap would be right in maintaining that deductive logic and non-deductive logic are in the *same* epistemic boat. He would be wrong only in maintaining that the boat is not an empirical one.

Despite its attractiveness, this account of our logical knowledge is hopelessly false.

(iv)

First, as to our knowledge of validity. Bolzano says that the validity of *barbara,* or rather, that the *barbara* schema always preserves truth, is a hypothesis reasonably believed by us, just because of the extensive experience we have had of never finding any counter-example to it. That is, our grounds for believing (149), or rather, for believing

(166) For all *x*, all *F*, all *G*, either '*x* is *F* and all *F* are *G*' is false, or '*x* is *G*' is true,

consist just of observations we have made, such as

(151) Abe is black and Abe is a person now in this room and all persons now in this room are black.

That is putting it starkly; still it is, in essence, what Bolzano believes. We learn deductive logic by inductive inference.

But now, this is tacitly to concede, to certain propositions of *non*-deductive logic, precisely the intuitive status which Bolzano expressly denies to any proposition of deductive logic. Our putative logic learner is supposed to be devoid of all intuitive logical knowledge. Yet Bolzano is evidently crediting him with knowing, straight off, *at least this much*: that

(167): (151) confirms (149).

Of course, he need not be supposed to *know* that he knows (167); still, he is evidently being supposed to know it. But to know (167) is to have some logical knowledge, even if only non-deductive logical knowledge.

And Bolzano must suppose that (167) is known by our logic learner intuitively. Otherwise he would have to have learnt it, as he is supposed to be learning (166), by experience. And how would he accomplish this?

It must at any rate be from some observation-statements. I do not know what kind of observations Bolzano would regard as confirming (167): let us just call these observation-statements

(168) O_1.

But even if our logic learner *has* found by experience that O_1 he will be no further advanced. To learn (167), he needs to know, not only that O_1, but that

(169):(168) confirms (167).

But this is a proposition of logic too. If he does not know (169) intuitively, as by hypothesis he does not, then he will have to learn it, too, from experience. No doubt from some observations

(170) O_2.

But that is not enough. He will also need to know that

(171): (170) confirms (169);

and so on.

Obviously, he is never going to make it. Experience is *not* enough.

(v)

In other words, we could not learn, even in Bolzano's fallibilist sense of 'learn', any judgement of validity at all, even in Bolzano's extensionalist sense of 'validity', *unless we had some intuitive knowledge of non-deductive logic.* But if intuitive knowledge of non-deductive logic must be admitted, why resist the idea of intuitive knowledge of deductive logic?

Second, even if experience could account, as we have just seen that it cannot, for our knowledge of a schema's always preserving truth, it would not thereby account for our knowledge of *validity*. For validity is not at all the same thing as always-preserving-truth.

I will now try to show this. But I intend to try to show, at the same time, the falsity of its natural extension (mentioned above) to logical probability in general: the idea that logical probability $\frac{m}{n}$ is relative-truth-frequency $\frac{m}{n}$.

That validity is a schema's always preserving truth (or having relative-truth-frequency = 1), is a belief now widely, one might almost say universally, adopted by philosophers; though it is from Tarski,[6] rather than from Bolzano, that they have adopted it. But the identification of logical probability $= \frac{m}{n}$ with relative-truth-frequency $= \frac{m}{n}$ is also a belief very widely diffused. It is not made explicit as often as the corresponding belief about validity is; but it is, I fear, what is believed about logical probability by most philosophers who do not think much about logical probability at all; which is to say, by most philosophers. It has never, to my knowledge, been criticized at all. And it has the express endorsement of some philosophers of reputation.

C. S. Peirce says that in 'a logical mind, an argument is always conceived as a member of a *genus* of arguments all constructed in the same way, and such that, when the premises are real facts, their conclusions are so also. If the argument is demonstrative, then this is always so; if it is only probable, then it is for the most part so.' Again, 'we may . . . define the probability of a mode of argument as the proportion of cases in which it carries truth with it.'[7] Cohen and Nagel say that 'an inference is probable . . . if it is one of a *class* of arguments such that the conclusions are true with a certain relative frequency when the premises are true.'[8] Exactly the same is said by N. R. Hanson.[9] (This last, though, is hardly an independent testimony. Hanson (1969) is a posthumously published collection which contains extensive unacknowledged borrowings from Cohen and Nagel (1934).[10])

---

  [6] Tarski (1956), XVI.
  [7] Peirce (1932), vol. 2, para. 649 and 650.
  [8] Cohen and Nagel (1934), p. 151. Italics in text.
  [9] Hanson (1969), p. 368.
  [10] Cf. e.g. Cohen and Nagel (1934), pp. 13–14 with Hanson (1969), pp. 364–5; p. 155 of the former with pp. 369–70 of the latter; p. 159 with pp. 373–4; p. 168 with pp. 389–90; pp. 302–3 with pp. 392–3; pp. 306–7 with pp. 396–7.

Cohen and Nagel's reference to 'a class of arguments', it can hardly be necessary to say, was excessively loose. *Classes* we can form at will: any argument, consequently, could be given almost any logical probability we liked, just by our including it in some class of arguments which has, overall, the desired relative-truth-frequency. Peirce's phrase, 'a *genus* of arguments *all constructed in the same way*', indicates the necessary qualification. The class of arguments in question must be the class of *instances of the same schema,* before the relative-truth-frequency in the class can be identified with the logical probability of a concrete argument which is a member of that class.

An identification so natural as that of logical probability with relative-truth-frequency must have, one would think, at least a considerable fund of instances in its favour; and so it does. For example, the argument

Abe is a male parent

Abe is a parent

is valid, hence the conclusion has logical probability$=1$ in relation to the premiss. And the schema of which it is an instance,

x is a male parent
----
x is a parent,

also has relative-truth-frequency$=1$. For its relative-truth-frequency is evidently just the number of individuals which are both male parents and parents, divided by the number of individuals which are male parents. And these two numbers are evidently the same. Again, the argument,

Just 90% of ravens are black
Abe is a raven

Abe is black,

has logical probability$=0.9$; and the schema of which it is an instance,

Just 90% of ravens are black
x is a raven
----
x is black,

has relative-truth-frequency$=0.9$. And there are many other such cases.

But there are also countless cases in which the logical probability of an argument does *not* coincide with the relative-truth-frequency of its schema.

(A) The argument

Bob is a winged horse
_____
Bob is a horse,

is valid, hence the conclusion has logical probability=1 in relation to the premiss. But the schema

x is a winged horse
_____
x is a horse,

does not have relative-truth-frequency=1. Indeed it has no relative-truth-frequency at all. The number of individuals which are both winged horses and horses, divided by the number of winged horses, is a fraction of which the denominator (since there are no winged horses) is 0. But there is no such fraction.

(B) The argument,

Bob is a horse
_____
Bob is a winged horse,

has at least greater logical probability than the argument

Bob is a horse
_____
It is not the case that Bob is a horse.

The latter has logical probability=0. So the former has logical probability $>$ 0. But the schema for the former argument,

x is a horse
_____
x is a winged horse,

has relative-truth-frequency=0. For the number of winged horses divided by the number of horses $= \frac{0}{n}$, for some positive n.

(C) If all ravens are in fact black, then the schema

x is a raven
_____
x is black

has relative-truth-frequency=1. Suppose the relative-truth-frequency of a schema is identical with the logical probability of any instance of it. Then, if all ravens are black, the logical probability of the argument

Abe is a raven
Abe is black

must also be= 1. But the logical probability of the argument

All ravens are black
Abe is a raven
Abe is black

is undoubtedly= 1. Whence, on the above supposition,

(172) If all ravens are black, then P(Abe is black/Abe is a raven)=P(Abe is black/Abe is a raven. All ravens are black).

But this is obviously false. On the contrary, the following judgement of favourable relevance,

(173) P(Abe is black/Abe is a raven. All ravens are black) > P(Abe is black/Abe is a raven),

is obviously true: *whether or not* all ravens are black, whether the sun rises in the east or west, and whatever the price of fish may be.

Indeed, any truth is irrelevant (in Keynes's sense) to 'Abe is black' given 'Abe is a raven', if the logical probability of an argument is the relative-truth-frequency of that argument's schema. For the relative-truth-frequency of the schema,

x is a raven
x is black,

is a fraction of which the denominator is the number of individuals which satisfy the propositional function '*x* is a raven'; but that is necessarily the same as the number of individuals which satisfy the propositional function '*x* is a raven and *T*', where *T* is a truth. The same will evidently hold for any argument which is an instance of a schema that has a relative-truth-frequency. Hence if logical probability is identified with relative-truth-frequency, true additional premisses will *always* be irrelevant. But while this is, of course, true of *necessarily* true additional premisses, it is grotesquely false of truths in general.

(D) Similarly, any true proposition, conjoined with the conclusion of the argument

> Abe is a raven
> Abe is black,

will yield an argument with the same logical probability as that one, if the logical probability of an argument is the relative-truth-frequency of its schema. The schema

> x is a raven
> x is black

has a relative-truth-frequency which is a fraction of which the numerator is the number of individuals that satisfy the propositional function 'x is a raven and x is black'; but that is necessarily the same as the number of individuals which satisfy the propositional function 'x is a raven and x is black and T', where T is a truth.

Hence if all ravens are black, the above schema, and the schema,

> x is a raven
> x is black and all ravens are black,

have the same relative-truth-frequency. Suppose that the relative-truth-frequency of a schema is identical with the logical probability of any instance of it. Then if all ravens are black, the argument,

> Abe is a raven
> Abe is black and all ravens are black,

has the same logical probability as the argument

> Abe is a raven
> Abe is black.

But this judgement of indifference (in Keynes's sense) is obviously false. On the contrary, the following,

(174) P(Abe is black and all ravens are black/Abe is a raven)
       <P(Abe is black/Abe is a raven),

is obviously true: whether or not all ravens are black, wherever the sun rises, etc.

The same will evidently hold for any argument which is an instance of a schema that has a relative-truth-frequency. Hence, if logical probability were relative-truth-frequency, the conjunction of the conclusion of an argument with a truth would *never* lower the logical probability of the argument. But while this is, of course, true of *necessarily* true additional conclusions, it is grotesquely false of true additional conclusions in general.

(E) We have seen so far that, where a schema contains one dummy individual constant, the relative-truth-frequency of the schema need not coincide in value with the logical probability of an instance of the schema, and, indeed, need not exist at all. But where a schema contains two or more dummy individual constants, the one argument may instantiate two or more schemas having different relative-truth-frequencies.

The argument,

William Hazlitt loved Sarah Walker
Sarah Walker loved William Hazlitt,

instantiates the schema

(a) x loved S. W.
    S. W. loved x;

it also instantiates the schema

(b) W. H. loved y
    y loved W. H.;

and the schema

(c) x loved y
    y loved x.

The biographical literature about Hazlitt suggests that the relative-truth-frequency of schema (b) is actually $=0$, and it is certainly less than the relative-truth-frequency of (c); probably, therefore, also less than that of (a). Hazlitt was (as they say) unlucky in love. But now, the logical probability of the argument cannot be identical with two or more different relative-truth-frequencies. On the other hand, none of the three schemas has any more claim than the others to be regarded as *the* schema, the relative-truth-frequency of which is to be identified with the logical probability of the argument.

(Dr G. Priest of the University of Western Australia, and Dr L. O'Neill of the University of Melbourne, independently pointed out to me this objection to identifying logical probability with relative-truth-frequency.)

The objection could, of course, be avoided by saying that the argument about Hazlitt has no logical probability at all. But this would be painfully *ad hoc*. There is no more reason to deny logical probability to that argument, than to the argument

Abe is a raven
<u>Abe is black;</u>

which is the very kind of argument for which the identification of logical probability with relative-truth-frequency is *most* plausible. Why should an argument's containing more than one individual constant prevent it having logical probability? And in fact, of course, it does not: the argument

Just 90% of living ravens are descended from Abe
<u>Bob is a living raven</u>
Bob is descended from Abe

has a logical probability, just as a *one*-individual proportional syllogism has.

(F) Most arguments, however, contain no individual constants at all; and wherever this is so, while there will be a schema (or more than one) of which the argument is an instance, *no such schema has a relative-truth-frequency.* Yet the argument may unmistakably have a logical probability.

The argument,

All ravens are black birds
<u>All black birds are cunning,</u>
All ravens are cunning,

is valid, and hence has logical probability $= 1$. It is an instance of the schema

All F are G
<u>All G are H</u>
All F are H

But this schema has no relative-truth-frequency.

I cannot prove this last statement. But if the reader thinks it is false, he should try to say what the relative-truth-frequency of this schema consists in: the number of *what,* divided by the number of *what*? Where individuals, and only individuals, are concerned, nothing is easier than to answer this question. The relative-truth-frequency, for example, of the schema,

> *x* is a raven
> *x* is black,

is simply the number of black ravens divided by the number of ravens. But for a *no*-individual schema, such as the one above, the reader will find that it is simply impossible to say what might be meant by speaking of the relative-truth-frequency of the schema.

The fact is that, once a schema contains a dummy *predicate* constant, or *a fortiori* a propositional one, it no longer makes sense to ascribe a relative-truth-frequency to the schema. The best case to illustrate this is, not a comparatively complicated schema like the above syllogistic one, but for example

> Abe is *F*
> Abe is *G.*

This is, like

> *x* is a raven
> *x* is black,

a schema of which

> Abe is a raven
> Abe is black

is an instance. But it is quite impossible to answer the question, what the relative-truth-frequency of the schema

> Abe is *F*
> Abe is *G*

consists in. The reader should try the experiment himself. There *is* no relative-truth-frequency of this schema.

And this is just as well for the identification of logical probability with relative-truth-frequency. For, as will be obvious, different instances of the schema,

> Abe is F
> ‾‾‾‾‾‾‾
> Abe is G,

have *different* logical probabilities. Whence, if this schema *did* have a relative-truth-frequency, its value could not be identical with the logical probability of its instances.

(G)   A purely propositional schema such as

> P
> ‾
> Q

is degenerate, just because every argument whatever is trivially an instance of it. But, if we disregard such degenerate schemas, then there are many arguments which have a logical probability although they are not instances of *any schema at all*. They instantiate no schema, because they do not contain any non-logical constants to begin with, and therefore contain nothing which could be replaced by a schematic expression.

Examples are the argument

> Nothing at all exists
> ‾‾‾‾‾‾‾‾‾‾‾‾‾‾‾‾‾‾‾‾
> Something exists;

the argument

> Nothing at all exists
> ‾‾‾‾‾‾‾‾‾‾‾‾‾‾‾‾‾‾‾‾
> No individual exists;

the argument

> At most one thing exists
> ‾‾‾‾‾‾‾‾‾‾‾‾‾‾‾‾‾‾‾‾‾‾
> Nothing exists.

These arguments have logical probabilities. The first has logical probability $=0$; the second has logical probability $=1$; the third has logical probability $>0<1$. But as they contain no non-logical constants, they cannot have such constants replaced to yield a schema which they instantiate.

(These arguments, as well as being constant-free, are also, of course, non-formal, in the sense in which, for example,

> Abe is a raven
> ‾‾‾‾‾‾‾‾‾‾‾‾
> Abe is a bird

is non-formal. But this example will suffice to show that non-formality is not to be confused with constant-freeness.)

The class of constant-free arguments may perhaps seem odd or unimportant. For this reason I should point out that it includes most of the arguments which philosophers and logicians themselves *employ,* as distinct from those which they have principally *studied.* A superficial reader might suppose that philosophers and logicians are interested, and even interested to an inexplicable degree, in Socrates, or in his humanity or mortality, or in the mortality of all men. But in fact, of course, they are not in the least interested in any of those things. What they are interested in is, rather, individuals, properties, existence, universality, necessity, possibility—and probability and relative-truth-frequency! It is these things which their arguments are really about.

Thus the Humean argues, for example,

Whatever *is,* might *not be*
Nothing exists necessarily.

The Spinozist argues, on the other hand,

Unrealized possibilities are not among the things that exist
Whatever does exist, exists necessarily.

The Platonist argues

It is possible for something to be a certain way, and something else to be the same way
There are universals.

The Kantian argues

A non-existent thing can have any property that a thing which exists can have
Existence is not a property.

These are very paradigms of philosophers' arguments; and there is not a non-logical constant in any one of them.

The same is true of Bolzano himself, or of Tarski, or of any formal logician, when he argues about what constitutes validity: his own arguments, mere illustrations aside, will be constant free. This is simply a consequence of the immense generality to which formal logicians aspire. An interesting further consequence is this: that since the formal logician's account of validity *is* in terms of schemas or logical forms, his own arguments about validity, being themselves constant-free, cannot satisfy the requirements which he himself lays down for valid argument.

To sum up what has been said in this section. The validity of an argument is not to be identified with its schema always pre-serving truth, and more generally, the logical probability $\frac{m}{n}$ of an argument is not to be identified with its schema having relative-truth-frequency $\frac{m}{n}$. For (A) an argument can be valid, yet its schema have no relative-truth-frequency; (B) an argument can have logical probability > 0, yet its schema have relative-truth-frequency 0; (C) the two arguments

> Abe is a raven
> ‾‾‾‾‾‾‾‾‾‾‾‾‾‾
> Abe is black,

and

> All ravens are black
> Abe is a raven
> ‾‾‾‾‾‾‾‾‾‾‾‾‾‾
> Abe is black,

cannot have the same logical probability; yet the two schemas,

> x is a raven
> ‾‾‾‾‾‾‾‾‾‾‾‾
> x is black,

and

> All ravens are black
> x is a raven
> ‾‾‾‾‾‾‾‾‾‾‾‾
> x is black,

could easily have the same relative-truth-frequency (just by all ravens being black); (D) the two arguments

> Abe is a raven
> ‾‾‾‾‾‾‾‾‾‾‾‾‾‾
> Abe is black,

and

> Abe is a raven
> ‾‾‾‾‾‾‾‾‾‾‾‾‾‾‾‾‾‾‾‾‾‾‾‾‾‾‾‾
> Abe is black and all ravens are black,

cannot have the same logical probability; yet the two schemas,

$$\frac{x \text{ is a raven}}{x \text{ is black,}}$$

and

$$\frac{x \text{ is a raven}}{x \text{ is black and all ravens are black,}}$$

could easily have the same relative-truth-frequency, just by all ravens being black; (E) an argument can have at most one logical probability, but it can easily instantiate two or more schemas having different relative-truth-frequencies; (F) if an argument contains no individual constant, then no schema of which it is an instance has *any* relative-truth-frequency, although such an argument can be valid, or have any other logical probability; (G) arguments can be valid, or have other logical probabilities, and yet not be instances of *any* schema.

(vi)

The question at the beginning of section (iii) above was, how much of our knowledge of judgements of validity could have been acquired from experience? If one assumes, as I did, that the validity of an argument from P to Q is the impossibility of P being true and Q false, then the answer is easy—none; and all our knowledge of validity would then have to be ascribed to intuition.

But a thorough going empiricist philosophy of logic, such as Bolzano's, will try (in the familiar empiricist way) to replace this modal notion of validity by an extensional one. Bolzano's idea is that when we ascribe validity to an argument, we are really saying only that it is an instance of a schema which always preserves truth. Judgements of validity, then, are simply universal generalizations of an ordinary contingent, and even empirical kind. They *can* be learnt (in a suitably fallibilist sense) from experience, just as other propositions of this kind can be; and they cannot be learnt in any other way. There is no need, in trying to account for our knowledge of deductive logic, to bring in any reference to supposed intuitions.

But judgements of validity, we have now seen (section (v)), are *not* propositions to the effect that a certain schema has relative-truth-frequency $= 1$. And even if they were, we saw earlier (section (iv)), they could be learnt (even fallibly) from experience, only by some one who possessed intuitive knowledge of some other logical truths.

Our knowledge of judgements of validity, then, is not knowledge of empirical propositions; and none of it could have been acquired without at least some reliance on intuition.

Still earlier, in section (ii), we saw that, with trifling exceptions, our knowledge of *invalidity* could not have been acquired from experience, either.

We also saw, in section (v), that statements of logical probability $= \frac{m}{n}$ are not empirical hypotheses to the effect that a certain schema preserves truth with relative frequency $= \frac{m}{n}$. They too, then, where known, are not known from experience.

The upshot is, that Carnap was right both times. First, our knowledge of logical probability *is* in the same boat as our knowledge of validity or of invalidity; and second, that boat *is* an intuitive one. Bolzano was right the first time, wrong the second. Popper was wrong both times.

Keynes, writing in 1921, refers to 'the suspicion of quackery' which had all along adhered to the theory of probability, and had prevented it 'from becoming, in the scientific salon, perfectly respectable. There is still about it . . . a smack of astrology, of alchemy.'[11] This was certainly true of the 'classical' theory of probability, and it remains true to this day concerning the theory of *logical* probability, in the *philosophical* 'salon'. Philosophers themselves are not very good at making clear what specific objections it is that they have to the theory of logical probability. But one which is certainly widely felt, and has been often enough espoused, is this: the undisguised *a priori* character of the theory, its shameless lack of *empirical* foundations.

If this is a defect of the theory of logical probability in general, it is, of course, a defect of the fragments of that theory which are the premisses of my arguments in Chapters V–VII. That it is such a defect, I have neither denied nor affirmed. What I do claim to have shown is this: that if a lack of empirical foundations is a defect of the theory of logical probability, it is also a defect of deductive logic.

---

[11] Keynes (1921), p. 335.

One slight concession, we saw in section (ii) above, has to be made to empiricist philosophies of deductive logic. There *is* one small class of judgements of invalidity which *can* in principle be learnt from experience. These are *singular* judgements, of the invalidity of the argument from P to Q, where P-and-not-Q is an *observation*-statement and is *true*. Even where these conditions are satisfied, the invalidity of the argument *need* not be learnt from the experience of P-and-not-Q; and in fact, in most cases, it is not learnt in that way, but in the usual intuitive way. It is not from experience that most of us learn, for example, the invalidity of the argument

The sun rises in the east
Socrates is immortal.

Still, its invalidity *could* be so learnt.

This is a *trifling* exception to the non-empirical character of deductive logic. First, because it is peculiar to our knowledge of *invalidity,* having no counterpart at all on the side of validity. Second, because it comprehends so little of our knowledge even of invalidity: omitting, as it does, not only all *general* judgements of invalidity, but even all singular judgements of invalidity which concern arguments from P to Q where P is false, or Q is true, or P-and-not-Q is not an observation-statement. Still, it is an exception, and when I say that our knowledge of deductive logic is not empirical, I intend this minor qualification to be understood.

The same class of cases necessitates a corresponding minor qualification when I say that the theory of logical probability too is non-empirical. If the argument from P to Q is invalid, then the logical probability of Q in relation to P is less than 1. There *is*, therefore, also a small class of statements of logical probability of which the truth can in principle be learnt from experience. Namely, of course, the singular '$P(Q/P) < 1$', where P-and-not-Q is both observational and true. The exception, again, is trifling, because propositions of this kind make up so small a part of the knowledge of logical probability that everyone possesses. Still, it is an exception, and I intend this minor qualification to be understood when I say that statements of logical probability, like judgements of validity or of invalidity, are not empirical propositions and cannot be learnt from experience.

XI

IS THE THEORY OF LOGICAL
PROBABILITY GROUNDLESS?

(i)

I have now identified two specific objections to the theory of logical probability, and tried to meet them. One was the objection arising from 'grue', that the theory of logical probability, being a form of non-deductive logic, is not formal. The other was that the theory of logical probability is not empirical.

But these objections, even taken together, do not make up the main component of that general 'suspicion of quackery' under which, with most philosophers, the theory of logical probability labours. What this main component is, is not very easy to say. It is an objection at once more damning, and less definite, than the two I have considered so far. It is, accordingly, more often met with in the oral tradition than in print. The best summary I can give of it is as follows. 'The theory of logical probability has not merely no empirical foundations, but no foundations of any kind: it is a completely arbitrary, groundless, free-floating intellectual construction. There is no reason to believe a word of it.'

This is not a very definite objection. But it is none-the-less very important that I should attempt to answer it, because it is an objection which most philosophers *really* feel to the theory of logical probability. They do not often let this feeling emerge fully in print, as I have said. Still, they sometimes do. Thus for example Professor I. Hacking says, in direct reference to theories of logical probability like Carnap's, that they are 'theories . . . which *have no foundation at all*'.[1] And Professor T. S. Kuhn, without direct reference to Carnap's theory but undoubtedly intending to refer to it, says that such theories 'open the door to Cloud-cuckoo-land'.[2]

As this objection to the theory of logical probability is so strongly and so widely felt, I must do my best, despite its indefiniteness, to show that it is wrong. First, however, I should

---

[1] Hacking (1975), p. 143. Italics in text.
[2] Kuhn (1970), p. 264.

make it clear that in a certain sense I believe it is *right*, only not an objection.

I maintained in the preceding chapter, with Carnap, that our knowledge of logical probability 'rest on intuition'. Now this may suggest that I regard *our intuitions* as reasons to believe statements of logical probability. It may suggest, for example, that if I were challenged to give a reason to believe the thesis of regularity (155), or a reason to believe an instance of it such as

(145) $P(\text{Abe is black}/T) < 1,$

I might offer, say,

(174) *Intuition tells us that* (145).

And it may suggest that if I were asked to give a reason to believe the symmetry of individual constants (156), or to believe an instance of it such as

(146) $P(\text{Abe is black}/T) = P(\text{Bob is black}/T),$

I might reply:

(175) *Everyone knows that* (146).

But I would not. I believe, indeed, that (174) and (175) are *true*; and more generally (as I have earlier said), I believe that every normal human being possesses an enormous amount of logical knowledge, non-deductive as well as deductive. But I would not dream of giving (174) as *a reason to believe* (145), or (175) as a reason to believe (146). Universal assent to a logical truth is not among the reasons that anyone can have for believing it; and neither is its being known intuitively a reason anyone can have to believe it.

My position is, rather, as I indicated in Chapter VII (vii) above: that *no* reason can be given for believing an instance of regularity such as (145), or for believing an instance of the symmetry of individual constants such as (146). A reason to believe (145), or (146), would have to be a proposition the truth of which is more obvious than the truth of (145), or of (146). But as there is no such proposition, there is no such reason.

Propositions like (145) or (146) can be, of course, and are, reasons to believe *other* statements of logical probability. For example, (145) is a reason to believe the general thesis of regularity (155), of which it is an instance; though not, of course, a completely conclusive reason to believe it. Likewise (146) is a reason, though not a completely conclusive one, to believe the general thesis of the symmetry of individual constants (156), of which it is an instance. Again, as we saw in Chapter VII (vii), other instances of regularity and of the symmetry of individual constants, (136) and (137), are, when conjoined with certain other statements of logical probability, a reason, and even a completely conclusive reason, to believe

(121) P(Abe is black/Just two of the individuals Abe, Bob, Charles are black)$=\frac{2}{3}$.

But when it comes to giving reasons for believing (145) or (146) themselves, or (137) or (136): well, that simply cannot be done.

In some cases, then, a reason can be given for believing a certain statement of logical probability. But even in these cases–with the trifling exception noticed at the end of the preceding chapter–*the reasons are always statements of logical probability themselves*. And in all other cases, nothing at all can be given as a reason for believing a statement of logical probability.

Is *this* all that is meant by the vague objection that the theory of logical probability 'floats'? If it is, then I not only admit, but insist, that the theory of logical probability floats; and floats not only with respect to any possible anchorage *in experience*, but floats absolutely, or with respect to *any* epistemic anchorage.

But what, then, is the *objection*? It does not follow, I hope that it is unnecessary to say, because no reason can be given to believe *p*, that it is unreasonable to believe *p*, or that belief in *p* is *groundless*. Unless some propositions were known directly or without benefit or reasons for believing them, none could be known directly or by means of reasons. So from the theory of logical probability's floating, in the sense just admitted, it certainly does not follow that it is groundless, or that to believe it is unreasonable.

Perhaps it does follow, though, at least that the theory of logical probability is *arbitrary*? If so, that would be a definite enough objection to it.

(ii)

If the suspicion which the theory of logical probability arouses in philosophers can be traced back to one definite source, it is *the numbers*. Or at least, it is the numbers between 0 and 1. Philosophers are by now accustomed, or resigned, to hearing logical probability$=1$ assigned to Q in relation to P, where the argument from P to Q is valid, and to hearing logical probability$=0$ assigned, in the same case, to not-Q in relation to P. What the philosopher in the street *cannot* stomach is the suggestion that a number between these limits, such as 0·9 or $\frac{2}{3}$, can be assigned to the probability of one proposition in relation to another, without the help of a large infusion of arbitrariness. If you imply that a *logical* relation between two propositions can be expressed by a number like $\frac{2}{3}$ *not arbitrarily chosen*, the philosopher in the street is not only incredulous and suspicious: he is embarrassed. To him this is worse than 'smacking of astrology': it stinks of numerology.

It must be admitted that the theory of probability, in its 'classical' period, exhibited an enthusiasm for precise numbers which was strong enough to embarrass even its warmest admirers at the present day. The probability of testimony to a miracle being false; of a jury of optimal size convicting wrongly; of there being iron on Sirius; on belief in 'revelation' expiring by a certain date; of the sun rising tomorrow; all these probabilities calculated to as many decimal places as you like: such things have long been, and rightly been, a byword for the excessive optimism of the Enlightenment. (Some examples are mentioned by Keynes.[3]) Not one in a hundred, I may observe, of all the readers who have smiled over such things, could tell you precisely what it is that is wrong with them. Still, *one* of the things that is wrong with them is undoubtedly this: that numbers were sometimes assigned to probabilities *arbitrarily.*

But this historical fact, it can hardly be necessary to say, will not help anyone withhold assent from the premises of my arguments in Chapters V–VII. Among the premises of the arguments in Chapter V, there were no non-extreme numerical equalities at all: that is, no statements of logical probability of the

---

[3] Keynes (1921), pp. 171 and 184.

'P(H/E)=r' kind, where r is $> 0 < 1$. I showed in Chapter VII section (vii) that the argument of Chapter VI can be given *ultimate* premises which include no non-extreme numerical equalities at all. And even as the argument stands in Chapter VI itself, the only non-extreme numerical equality among the premises is (83), which is simply a slightly generalized version of statements like

(120) P(Abe is black/Abe is a raven and just 95% of ravens are black)=0·95,

and there is nothing arbitrary about *them*.

Still, it is, as I have said, widely felt that all non-extreme numerical equalities *are* arbitrary. And some philosophers have said as much in print.

My usage of the term 'logical probability' commits me, like Carnap, to ascribing to certain statements the *numerical* probabilities 1 and 0. But any other specific *numerical* values such as $\frac{1}{2}$ or $\frac{2}{3}$, transcend, in my usage of the term, both pure logic and 'logical probability'.

Referring to Carnap's present paper, I should accept the *term* 'strictly coherent credence function' (as long as it is *not linked with 'degrees of belief')* as falling into the field of 'logical probability'; but I should not call every instance of a 'strictly coherent credence function' a 'logical probability', because *according to my terminology,* the ascription of a numerical probability value such as $\frac{1}{2}$ to a statement carries us beyond logic.

What I call the theory of logical probability may be compared with metrical geometry such as, say, Euclidean geometry. In Euclidean geometry, the only distance (or area or volume) whose numerical measure is defined by the theory itself is the zero distance (or area or volume). Other ascriptions of specific numerical values are extra-theoretical: they are not introduced by the theory, but by arbitrarily defining a yardstick. (If the theory is the geometry of the real world these ascriptions may be part of the physical theory, provided it contains a fundamental constant of length; but the choice of the Paris metre is not like this.) In the theory of logical probability we have not only 0 but also 1; all other ascriptions of specific numerical values are, in my terminology, extra-logical applications; although there may be, in the objective or physical interpretations of probability, ascriptions which are part of physical theory.[4]

---

[4] Popper (1968), pp. 286–7.

Popper here allows as non-arbitrary, we see, only two kinds of statements of logical probability: the extreme numerical equalities, '$P(H/E)=1$', '$P(H'/E')=0$', etc. In fact, however, non-arbitrariness cannot possibly be confined to these. For *conjunctions* of propositions of these kinds entail some *comparative* equalities and inequalities, '$P(H/E) > P(H'/E')$', etc., which must therefore be non-arbitrary too. Again, if P is non-arbitrarily true or false, then so is its contradictory. Whence if '$P(H/E)=1$' is non-arbitrary, so is '$P(H/E) < 1$'; and if '$P(H'/E')=0$' is non-arbitrary, so is '$P(H'/E') > 0$'. Still, it is clear enough what Popper meant. He was evidently thinking only of the non-extreme numerical *equalities,* and his thesis was only that all of *these* are arbitrary.

But even that is false. There is nothing *arbitrary* about the instance of regularity

(137) $P(Ba.Bb.\sim Bc/T) > 0$,

in which the conjuncts abbreviate 'Abe is black', etc. On the contrary it is just obviously true. There is nothing arbitrary about the instance of the symmetry of individual constants

(136) $P(Ba.Bb.\sim Bc/T) = P(Ba.\sim Bb.Bc/T) = (\sim Ba.Bb.Bc/T)$.

It is just obviously true. There is nothing arbitrary, either, about the *principles* of logical probability. But, we saw in Chapter VII (vii), from (136), (137), and some of those principles (plus some other statements of logical probability all of the most impeccable non-arbitrariness, indeed triviality), it follows that

(121) $P(Ba/$Just two of the individuals a,b,c, are $B)=\frac{2}{3}$.

What follows from the non-arbitrary cannot be arbitrary. Yet (121) is a non-extreme numerical equality.

The assignment of a non-extreme number to a logical probability, then, is *not* always arbitrary. For we are *constrained* to some such assignments, if we believe two things: that a contingent non-quantified proposition is never certain or impossible in relation to a tautology; and that the logical probability of an argument is never changed by mere uniform exchange of one individual constant for another. And *these* beliefs are not arbitrary ones.

Regularity and the symmetry of individual constants do not

suffice, of course, to fix the numerical value of all logical probabilities. The argument above does not show, therefore, that a numerical value can *always* be assigned non-arbitrarily to P(*H/E*). But it does show that it sometimes can, and hence that the nearly universal conviction to the contrary is false. It therefore also shows, I may add, that it is sometimes entirely out of place, on account of its voluntaristic overtones, to speak of 'assigning' a number to a logical probability.

(iii)

'But what in the world are the *truth-makers* for statements of logical probability? Perhaps you are right, and even some of the non-extreme numerical equalities are non-arbitrarily true or false. And of course you are able to prove, supposing some such statements to be true, that certain others are too: the principles of logical probability make sure of that. But *in virtue of what* is any of them true in the first place? The theory of logical probability really is a Laputan floating island, unless this question can be answered.'

Here I am trying once more to give a definite shape to the vague objection stated in the second paragraph of this chapter; and I am drawing, now, entirely on the oral tradition. The above is not one of the happier deliverances of that tradition.

It is a sufficient reason for being intensely suspicious of the 'truth-maker' terminology, that while being a brand-new piece of philosophical language, it is already found, by those who use it, virtually indispensable, and is thought by them to do great things. But there is also a much better reason for being suspicious of it. 'What is the truth-maker of *p*?', 'What makes it true that *p*?', or 'In virtue of what is *p* true?', is *always* a pseudo-question. For in every case the true answer to it, the whole truth, and nothing but the truth, is simply: the fact that *p*. But that, of course, is too transparently trivial to satisfy anyone, and the philosopher who asked the question demands some other answer. That only shows, however, that he ought to have asked some other questions. If he cannot frame another and more sensible question—if he finds the 'truth-maker' terminology nearly or absolutely indispensible—then he should conclude that he did not have a sensible question to ask in the first place.

But I do not need to insist on this, or to repudiate altogether our present version of the 'groundlessness' or 'no-foundations' objection. I can perfectly well afford to adopt for a while the vicious terminology of 'truth-makers', and I will do so for the rest of this section. For my answer to the present objection lies quite elsewhere.

I am asked what are the truth-makers for statements of logical probability; and I must confess that I cannot answer this question at once. I expect soon to be able to do so, however. For all I need to know first is, what the truth-makers are for the true propositions of *deductive* logic. Of course the two things will not be exactly the same: still, we know from Chapter X that deductive logic and the theory of logical probability are in the same epistemic boat. The answer to my question will therefore be a sufficient general guide to me in framing the answer to the question I am asked. I therefore ask my question: what are the truth-makers for *judgements of validity or of invalidity*?

I am asked, what in the world is the truth-maker for, for example,

(120) P(Abe is black/Abe is a raven and just 95% of ravens are black) = 0·95.

I reply that, as (120) is not a contingent proposition, and still less an empirical one, there is, *in the world,* nothing which makes it true. If I am then asked what, even out of the world, makes (120) true, I promise to reply the moment my questioner tells me what, in the world or out of it, makes it true that an instance of *barbara* is valid: what makes it true, for example, that

(148) 'Abe is a raven and all ravens are black' entails 'Abe is black'.

(There might be some slight delay.)

I am asked, what makes it true that

(145) P(Abe is black/T) < 1.

I cannot reply, but promise to do so, as soon as my questioner tells me, what makes it true that the argument,

$$\frac{T}{\text{Abe is black}}$$

is *invalid*. (After all, the thesis of regularity, (155), is only a certain general judgement of invalidity.)

I am asked, in virtue of *what* is it true that

(146) P(Abe is black/T)=P(Bob is black/T).

I cannot yet tell, but I will know as soon as I learn in virtue of what it is true that the two arguments.

All men are mortal
Socrates is mortal
Socrates is a man,

and

All men are mortal
Plato is mortal
Plato is a man,

are *both invalid or both valid*. (After all, even deductive logic cannot get along without a little help from the symmetry of individual constants.)

The reader will easily recognize that we are dealing here with a generalization of something which occupied us repeatedly in Part One. That statements of logical probability require 'truthmakers', is just a generalized version of the idea that the rationality of inductive inference requires a 'ground': a ground *in nature*, according to the less sophisticated versions, but at any rate some ground or other. The idea is 'mere foolery' in the general case, as it is in the special case of induction. Still I fear, as I indicated in Part One, that nothing can loosen the grip which it has on philosopher's minds, at least as far as induction is concerned. But if anything can do so, it is the following simple stratagem (already recommended in Part One). When someone asks you, what *makes* (some) inductive inferences rational, or what makes their conclusions probable in relation to the premises, do not quarrel with his language or logic: do not complain, for example, about misconditionalization. Instead, *close with his offer*. Pretend that his question is not a pseudo-question, and promise to answer it the moment he tells you what it is, in nature or out of it, that *makes* (all) inductive inferences *invalid*. If your logical *probability* requires a ground, his logical *possibility* requires a ground no less; and if he finds, as he will, that he must be content to let the fallibility of induction 'float', he cannot object if you let its rationality float too.

Those philosophers who ask to be told what are the 'truth-makers' for statements of logical probability say that their interest in the matter is an ontological one. But, partly because they evince no more interest than any other sensible person does in the 'ontology' of *deductive* logic, I believe that it is nothing of the kind. It is rather, I believe, purely epistemic, and even philosophical in the worst and most familiar sense. The man who asks the new-fangled question, 'what is the truth-maker?' for, say,

(120) P(Abe is black/Abe is a raven and just 95% of ravens are black) = 0·95,

really means to ask the old-fashioned, philosophico-infantile, question,

(176) *How do you know* that (120)?

But, such 'how do you know?' questions being in considerable disrepute, he has been obliged to find a new and more respectable way of asking it.

The question, 'How do you know that *p*?', ordinarily carries with it no suggestion that the person addressed does *not* know that *p*: quite the contrary, obviously. But the philosophico-infantile 'How do you know that *p*?' emphatically does carry that suggestion with it. Accordingly, if someone asks us (176), the first part of our reply to him should be: (a) 'I do know that (120)'. The rest of it should be as follows. '(b) You too know that (120). (c) So does everyone else. (d) I do not know *how* I know that (120), though I can tell you this much, that it is in essentially the same way as I know (140). (e) I do not care how I know that (120). (f) Neither do you care about that, despite your question. For if I *did* know how I know that (120), and told you, my answer being

(177) ....,

your apparent interest in the question (176) would vanish on the instant to be instantly replaced, in the philosophico-infantile way, by an apparent interest in the question

(178) How do you know that (177)?'

No person of sense would allow himself to be detained for long over the question, how he knows that (120). No person of sense, *a fortiori*, would allow himself to be detained for long over the still worse question, which is a surrogate of that one, what is the 'truth maker' of (120).

(iv)

Reasons to believe a proposition of deductive logic, if they exist at all, are other propositions of deductive logic; and reasons to believe a statement of logical probability, if they exist at all, are other statements of logic probability. The only exceptions to this (noticed in Chapter X) are trivial in either case. Our logical knowledge, then, our knowledge of deductive as well as of non-deductive logic, really does float, in the sense that there is no epistemic anchorage for it *outside* logic.

This is apt to seem intolerable when one first thinks of it. The mass of our logical knowledge is certainly immense. It seems contrary to all physical analogy, to say nothing of biological common sense, to suppose that this whole huge mass is anchored only (and then only in parts) by itself: which is to say, is not anchored at all. Surely this 'floating island' picture of our logical knowledge cannot be right? It *must* be possible in principle, one feels, at least to *diminish* the number of logical truths which float: that is, for believing which there are either no reasons, or only reasons which are other logical truths.

But I believe that this is impossible, for a reason which was foreshadowed in Chapter X (ii) and (iv). This reason might be called 'the spaghetti effect', from its resemblance to the way in which an inexperienced spaghetti-eater, when he tries to get a pendant string of the stuff into his mouth, is always *too* successful.

Suppose (what I believe is impossible) that you *did* find out a non-logical truth *P* which is in fact a reason to believe the logical truth *Q*. You will not, even so, have found a reason to believe *Q*, unless, when you come to know that *P*, or earlier, you come to know that

(*R*) *P* is a reason to believe *Q*.

Of course you would not need to *know* that you know that (*R*); but you would need to know it. (Otherwise it might even happen, say, that you positively believe (*R*) to be false; in which case you would certainly not have come to know a reason to believe *Q*, by coming to know that *P*.) And now the trouble is that (*R*), if it is true (as we are supposing), is itself a truth *of logic*. It will be a truth of deductive or of non-deductive logic, according as *P* is or is not a *completely* conclusive reason to believe *Q*; but in either case it will be a logical truth.

So if we *did* succeed, by finding a non-logical reason *P* to believe the logical truth *Q*, in diminishing by one, *Q*, the number of logical truths which float, we would also have *added* one logical truth (*R*), to the mass of those which still float. For the rope by which we attempt to connect our logical knowledge to a non-logical anchor, is always and instantly sucked up, like beginner's spaghetti, and added to the very body of logical knowledge which we are trying to anchor. The attempt, therefore, to modify the floating-island picture of our logical knowledge, or to find, outside logical truths, reasons for believing logical truths, is a mere labour of Sisyphus.

XII

PROBABILITY AND TRUTH

(i)

THERE is an objection to the theory of logical probability, or at least to that theory's being of any intellectual or practical use, which concerns the lack of connection between the probability of an inference, where this is less than 1, and the truth of the conclusion of the inference. The objection, as well as I can express it, is as follows.

'It is rational to rely on *valid* inference from what we know or think we know, because the purpose of inference is to arrive at truths, and valid inference always preserves truth. So, if E is my total evidence, that is, all I know or think I know, and E entails a contingent proposition H, then the question 'Why should I believe H?' is easily answered. The answer is, 'Because there is a necessary connection between validity and preserving-truth', or 'Because if E is true then, necessarily, H is true.' But the case is very different where H is not entailed by my total evidence E, but is only highly probable in relation to it. There, the question 'Why should I believe H?' cannot be answered at all. Any such H *may* be false though E be true; the inference being only a probable one. There is no necessary connection between high probability and truth, or in general (as we saw in Chapter X) between logical probability $= \frac{m}{n}$, and truth being preserved with relative frequency $= \frac{m}{n}$. That $P(H/E)$ is high, or that $P(H/E) = 0.9$, cannot *itself* be a reason to believe H; for H is contingent, whereas these statements of logical probability, if they are true (as we are supposing), are *necessary* truths. We cannot even infer from them the conditional, 'If E, then the probability that H is high (or 0.9)'. For there may be other evidence E', perfectly consistent with E, such that $P(H/E') = 0.2$, say; in which case inference of the same kind would entitle us to infer, disastrously, 'If E and E', then the probability that H is high and low (or 0.9 and 0.2).' *No* reason can be given, then, why I should believe a proposition H which is merely probable in relation to my total evidence E. Bishop

Butler's dictum, that to us probability is the very guide of life, may be true in some sense; but it is *not* true of *logical* probability.'

This is the objection to which the present chapter is addressed. I will refer to it as 'Salmon's problem', although this is to risk *suggestio falsi* in two respects. First, Professor W. C. Salmon is not the only one to have posed the problem: many others have made what appears to be essentially the same objection to the theory of logical probability (for example Kneale[1] and Blackburn[2]). But Salmon was the first to do so, as far as I know, and has pressed the objection most often and most forcefully.[3] Second, as I have here put the problem in my own words, there is some danger of my having inadvertently misrepresented Salmon.

This danger is more real, because Salmon's problem is certainly somewhat indefinite, or at least (as we will see) ambiguous. In this respect it resembles the 'groundlessness' objection, considered in the preceding chapter. But just as in that case, the indefiniteness of the objection does not make it unnecessary for me to try to meet it. On the contrary, it is imperative that I should do so. For it is Salmon's problem, along with the 'groundlessness' objection, which are the *real* objections that philosophers feel to the utility, or the credibility, of the theory of logical probability. The problem about 'grue', discussed in Chapter IX, and the objection that the theory of logical probability is not empirical, discussed in Chapter X, are by comparison only half-hearted objections.

(ii)

That it is easy to be mistaken as to what Salmon's problem is, is sufficiently proved by the fact that Salmon himself is so mistaken. For he has repeatedly asserted that his problem is '*Hume's problem about induction*',[4] yet it is certainly nothing of the kind.

The history of recent philosophy being what it has been, it is of course true that, when a philosopher discusses inferences which

---

[1] Kneale (1968), pp. 59–61.
[2] Blackburn (1973), p. 935.
[3] See Salmon (1965), pp. 265–70 and 277–80; Salmon (1967), pp. 75–9; . Salmon (1968), pp. 39–43 and 75–6.
[4] See Salmon (1967), pp. 52 and 79; Salmon (1968), p. 33.

are merely probable, the *examples* which nowadays come most easily to his mind are inductive ones. But the connection between Salmon's problem and induction is no closer than that. It is not only in induction, or in inferring the composition of populations from the composition of samples, that we are obliged to rely on invalid references, to some of which we ascribe high logical probability. We do the same in *direct* inference too (cf. Chapter VI section (i)); that is, in inferring the composition of a sample from the composition of a population. A proportional syllogistic example, then, such as the inference from 'Just 95% of ravens are black and *S* is a large sample of ravens', to 'Almost 95 per cent of the ravens in *S* are black', would have served, just as well as any example of *inductive* inference, to enable Salmon to press his problem upon us. Indeed, his problem, if it is a problem at all, would be quite unaffected even if we supposed that all inductive inferences are actually valid. Salmon's problem is one about *probable* inference, as such and in general, and as contrasted with valid inference. But Hume's 'problem about induction' is not: *it* is about *induction*.

There is, of course, in addition to these general considerations, a textual side to this matter. And the simple historical fact is, that there is nothing remotely like Salmon's problem anywhere in Hume's writings.

What Hume thought about inductive inference was (cf. Chapter III) that the conclusions *are not* highly probable in relation to the premisses, and indeed that they are not even more probable in relation to the premisses than they are *a priori*. It never occurred to him to ask, 'Granted that some of those conclusions *are* more probable in relation to the premisses than they are *a priori,* and granted that they are even highly probable, still, *why should I believe them?*' That, however, *is* Salmon's question; or rather, it is the special form which it assumes when the examples chosen, of merely probable inference, happen to be inductive ones. That Hume not only did not ask this question, but could not have done so, will be evident to anyone with a strong feeling for the history of thought. The question is in fact one which could have occurred to nobody before the present century. Any credit that is due, then, for the posing of Salmon's problem, is due to Salmon himself.

Salmon's mistaking his problem for Hume's is another instance of the confusion, often referred to in this book, of the two topics, probability and induction. It is also an instance of a deplorable tendency among twentieth-century philosophers, to which I have referred in Chapter VII (v), and of which I have elsewhere collected examples:[5] the tendency to exaggerate Hume's achievement, and to father on Hume the sprouts of their own brains, especially where these are of a 'sceptical' tendency.

Salmon's problem does, indeed, have a bearing on the arguments of Chapters V–VII. But this is *not* because those arguments happen to be arguments intended to prove that induction is justified. It is just because their premises, and conclusions, are *statements of logical probability*; or rather, because they are statements of logical probability other than extreme numerical equalities ('P(H/E)=1', etc.). For if there is anything at all in Salmon's problem, statements of logical probability, except the 'P(H/E)=1' kind, must be, unlike judgements of validity or 'P(H/E)=1', propositions of a peculiarly useless and pointless kind. For they cannot (so runs the charge) function as a guide of life: they cannot tell us what, on given evidence, we ought to believe.

I have implied that Hume, if someone had said to him, 'My total evidence is E, and P(H/E)=0·9; now, why should I believe H?', would have rejected the question out of hand as improper. So, surely would any person of sense, at any time: it must be a dull nose indeed that does not smell a pseudo-question here. I, however, situated where I am in intellectual history, cannot afford to be summary, but must rather treat the question with all seriousness. But I believe, and I will try to show that, although Salmon's problem is not 'Hume's problem about induction', it is *like* it in this respect: that there is absolutely nothing in it.

(iii)

We can, of course, make mistakes in assessing logical probability, as we can about anything else. We sometimes underestimate or overestimate the numerical value of P(H/E); or we believe that P($H/E.E'$)=P(H/E), when in fact E' is unfavourably relevant to H given E; and so on. There are even mistakes about the value of

[5] Stove (1973), pp. 125–32; Stove (1976c).

logical probabilities, or at least tendencies to mistake, which are (as we saw in Chapter VI (i)) common to the entire human race. So it is certainly possible for a proposition to *seem* to have a certain logical probability in relation to another, which it does not really have.

As well as this, we often say that a certain proposition *H seems* probable, when what we intend to convey is that *H* really *is* probable in relation to our present total evidence *E*; but we intend in addition to remind our hearers that *E* is consistent with some other evidence *E'*, such as we might come to know in the future, and such that in relation to our *then* total evidence *E.E'*. *H* is not probable at all, or is even impossible.

This manner of speaking is innocent enough, and even trivial, just because it is transparent enough what we really mean. Yet it has engendered a whole philosophy of probability, (the 'subjective theory' so-called), and even on the minds of people not influenced by that philosophy it has an unfortunate effect. For it tends to invest statements of logical probability with a subjective character: that is, it tends to blur the distinction between a statement of logical probability *being* true, and its *seeming* to be true, or its being generally or naturally *believed* to be true.

But that distinction is just as real, where statements of logical probability are concerned, as it is where any other class of propositions is concerned, and just as necessary to be insisted upon. And it is especially important to insist on it in the context of Salmon's problem. For, as will be obvious, nothing could be easier than for Salmon, or anyone, to set up an unfavourable comparison of probable inference with valid inference, *if probable inference is not distinguished from inference which seems probable*. All you would need to do would be to contrast valid inference with inference which seems probable (to some or all of us), but is not. (Perhaps, for example, what is called 'gamblers' inference' in Chapter VI.)

But this proceeding would evidently be as unfair as it would be easy. Salmon's problem arises, if it arises at all, from a comparison between valid inference, and inference which *really is* probable inference: not between valid inference and inference which passes with most of us for probable inference, or anything like that. In what follows, consequently, when a judgement of validity, or an extreme numerical quality $P(H/E) = 1$, is contrasted with,

say, 'P(H/E')=0·9', it is to be understood that the latter statement of logical probability, as well as the former, is *true*. Unless
this is understood, there is no 'Salmon's problem' at all.

(iv)

Salmon's problem, then, turns on a comparison between inference which is valid, and inference which is merely probable
(though really probable). Concrete examples are needed; and
non-inductive ones will be the least likely to introduce confusion
or irrelevance. So let us compare the inference from *F*, 'Just 95
per cent of ravens are black and Abe is a raven', to *H*, 'Abe is
black', with the inference to the same conclusion from *G*, 'All
ravens are black and Abe is a raven'.

Now, suppose Salmon's problem were expressed as follows.
'Admittedly, the inference from *F* to *H* has probability=0·9. But
of what value or use is this information? It tells us nothing about
the relative frequency with which truth is preserved by inference
like that from *F* to *H*. The inference from *G* to *H*, on the other
hand, is valid; and *this* information *is* of value. For it tells us that
this inference is an instance of a schema which always preserves
truth. Hence, if I am asked, where *G* is my total evidence, why I
should believe *H*, I can satisfactorily answer: because if *G* is
true, *H* is true. Whereas if I am asked, where *F* is my total evidence, why I should believe *H*, I cannot answer at all.'

Salmon's problem, if it were so expressed, would have to be
simply repudiated, on the ground that it incorporates a conception of validity which is utterly mistaken. For we saw in Chapter
X(v) that to call an inference valid is *not* to say that it is an
instance of a schema which always preserves truth. An inference
can be valid, yet not be an instance of any schema at all; and an
inference can be valid, and be an instance of a schema, yet not be
an instance of any schema which has a relative-truth-frequency;
and an inference can be an instance of a schema which always
preserves truth, and yet be invalid.

It would be far worse still, of course, if one were to say, in an
attempt to formulate Salmon's problem: 'The inference from *G* to
H always preserves truth; the inference from *F* to *H* does not.'
For this, it should be unnecessary to say, absolutely makes no
sense. The inferences from *G* to *H* and from *F* to *H* are *infer-*

ences; not inference-schema. And it is only of an inference-
schema, that it makes sense to say that it preserves truth always,
or not always, or with a certain relative frequency.

It may be worthwhile to point out that nonsense of precisely
this sort has not only been common coin of logicians' talk ever
since a Bolzano–Tarski account of validity became generally
accepted: it is nonsense which Bolzano himself systematically
and consistently insists upon. The validity of the inference from
G to *H*, Bolzano says, consists in the fact that every uniform
substitution which makes

All *M* are *N* and *x* is *M*

true, makes

x is *N*

true, too.[6] But of course this is quite literally nonsense. No substitutions can make such things true. Omnipotence itself could
not make such things true. They could not be made true by anything, because they are not the kind of thing which could *be* true.

(I do not say that this sort of nonsense is absolutely inseparable from a Bolzano–Tarski account of validity. It is not so. But
that account has other defects which are fatal to it, and it can
hardly be accounted one of its merits, that it makes talking nonsense so natural as to be almost irresistible.)

(v)

What *is* the difference between a valid inference and a merely
probable one: for example, between the inference from *G* to *H*,
and that from *F* to *H*?

It is mortifying to find ourselves driven back to a question so
elementary. Yet it is only too usual, as we have seen, for this simple question to be answered wrongly by implication at least. And
at the same time, unless it is answered rightly, Salmon's problem,
which turns precisely on the difference between valid and merely
probable inference, will be vitiated in its very formulation.

One difference between merely probable and valid inference is
this. In the former, the conjunction of the premiss with the nega-

---

[6] Bolzano (1837), p. 209 ff.

tion of the conclusion is logically possible; in the latter it is not. This is simply to say: all merely probable inferences are invalid.

A second difference, which is a consequence of this first one, is the following: that while validity is invariant under any addition to the premisses, logical probability, when it is not=1 or=0, is not so invariant. That is, if the argument from P to Q is valid, so is the argument from P-and-R to Q, whatever R may be: while the probability of Q in relation to P might be=0·9, say, without the probability of Q in relation to P-and-R being=0·9. Any logical probability whatever *is* invariant, of course, under all *necessarily-true* additional premisses; that is (generalizing (113)):

(179) $P(h(e.e')) = P(h/e)$ for all h, all e, and all necessarily true e'.

But no non-extreme logical probability is invariant under all additional premisses whatever.

The two characteristics, invalidity and variance under additional premisses, do not exhaust the difference between merely probable and valid inference. Obviously not, since they are characteristics shared by *all* invalid inferences which are not actually contravalid. Still, they are both features which are absolutely inseparable from merely probable inferences. If a person aspired to free all of his inferences from either of these two characteristics, he would be aspiring (whether or not he knew it) to dispense with probable inference altogether.

(vi)

Returning, then, to our concrete cases: in the one case our total evidence is G, 'All ravens are black and Abe is a raven', in the other our total evidence is F, 'Just 95 per cent of ravens are black and Abe is a raven'; in both, the conclusion is H, 'Abe is black'. The former inference being valid and the latter merely probable, the two differ in at least the respects mentioned in the preceding section. Salmon's problem is about the difference between the two inferences. But exactly what is the problem?

We all feel, at least after reading Salmon, that there *is* a problem: that the inference from F to H is not only of a lower degree of logical value than the inference to H from G, but that it is somehow of *no* value by comparison with that. But how? What is it that Salmon, and the Salmon in all of us, finds wanting in the merely probable inference? What is there, about a merely prob-able inference like that from *F* to *H*, which, if we knew it, would restore something like our pre-philosophical equanimity about relying on such inferences? What is the assurance that we would *like* to get?

'Well, where the premisses are true, there is, in every case of valid inference, a necessary connection between the validity of the inference and the truth of the conclusion. What we would *like* is to be assured of the truth of something corresponding to that: that where the premisses are true, there should be, in at least most cases of highly probable inference, a necessary connection between the high probability of the inference, and the truth of the conclusion.'

This is, I think, the true answer: this *is* what we hanker after, when we feel Salmon's problem.

If it is, however, then Salmon's problem is certainly a pseudo-problem. For, first, if we *could* get the assurance that we would like, we would be no better off than we were without it. And second, we could not possibly get it.

Our total evidence is *F*, 'Just 95 per cent of ravens are black and Abe is a raven', and Salmon has made us wonder what rea-son we have to believe *H*, 'Abe is black', even supposing that *F* is true. Well, suppose there *is* a necessary connection, in at least most cases of highly probable inference in which the premisses are true, between the high probability of the inference and the truth of the conclusion. Suppose, further, that we know this fact. Let us add it to our total evidence *F*. What have we gained by all this? Nothing: the inference to *H*, from *F*-and-this-fact, is a *merely probable inference still.* For any statement of a necessary connection—whether of a necessary connection between high probability and truth, or between whatever and whatever—will be a *necessary* truth; and all logical probabilities are, as (179) says, invariant under all necessarily true additional premisses. We might as well, therefore, have spared ourselves the trouble of seeking a necessary connection between high probability and truth; since even if we could get it, the probability of *H* in rela-tion to our total evidence would be only 0·95 still.

(A *merely probable* connection, as distinct from a necessary one, between high probability and truth—supposing such a con-ception were intelligible at all—would still more obviously leave us where we were. If it existed, and we knew it, and added it to our total evidence *F*, our inference to *H* would be merely probable still.)

Second, there cannot *be* a necessary connection, between the high probability of the inference and the truth of the conclusion, even where the premisses are true. Suppose there were such a connection, in even one case of merely probable inference from true premisses. Then, since by hypothesis the premisses *are* true and the inference *is* of high probability, if the truth of the conclusion were necessarily connected with these two things, that conclusion logically *must* be true. But in that case the inference would not be merely probable: it would be valid.

The assurance, then, which Salmon and the rest of us would *like* to get, about merely probable inferences, is the self-contradictory assurance that at least some of them are valid. What we have got *against* merely probable inferences, when we feel Salmon's problem, is not that their probability can vary under additional premisses: that we might acquire additional evidence which would change the probability of the conclusion. For we would feel Salmon's problem still, under *any* addition to our total evidence, *if it did not change the probability of our conclusion to 1*. In other words, what we have got against merely probable inferences, when we feel Salmon's 'problem', then, is just the *invalidity* of merely probable inferences, when we are made to feel this feature, inseparable from such inferences, as an alarming contingent defect in them.

We saw in Chapter VIII that, to generate the pseudo-problem of justifying induction, you must make a mere logical possibility *a source of anxiety*: you must make the fact, which is an inseparable feature of inductive inferences, that the conclusion *may* be false though the premiss be true, felt to be an alarming contingent defect of such inferences. What Salmon has done is simply to extend this process to *all* merely probable inferences. In the same way as Hume, and every philosophy teacher, generates in himself and others a spurious anxiety about inductive inference in particular, Salmon generates in himself and others a spurious anxiety about merely probable inference in general: namely, by rubbing away at that old and trivial sore, that the conclusion *may* be false though the premiss be true.

This is not a profitable occupation, or even a rational one. No doubt what we would *like* to get is an assurance that at least some merely probable inferences are valid; but where what we would like to get is logically impossible for anyone *to* get, our object should rather be to learn *not* to like to get it. We would be better employed in absorbing some words of Keynes, who said that

no knowledge of probabilities, less in degree than certainty, helps us to know what conclusions are true, and ... there is no direct relationship between the truth of a proposition and its probability. Probability begins and ends with probability. That a scientific investigation pursued on account of its probability will generally lead to truth, rather than false-hood, is at the best only probable. The proposition that a course of action guided by the most probable considerations will generally lead to success is not certainly true and has nothing to recommend it but its probability.[7]

Where our total evidence is *F*, 'Just 95 per cent of ravens are black and Abe is a raven', it may be false that *H*, 'Abe is black': *of course* it *may.* But in relation to our total evidence, *H probably* is *not* false, but true. And *this* statement, we recall from section (iii) above, is *true*: it is one of the elements of Salmon's problem, that what is being contrasted with valid inference is not, inference which seems probable, but inference which really is probable.

We also noticed in Chapter VIII an illusion which needs to be guarded against concerning inductive inference: that while the *probability* of the conclusion being true is unreal, impalpable, and un-reassuring, the *possibility* of its being false is real, pal-pable, and alarming. This is an illusion, for the simple reason that the invalidity of induction, (141), is nothing more than *a true statement of logical probability itself*. Exactly the same illusion needs to be guarded against here, where it is merely probable inference in general that is under discussion. In our minds, the fact that *H is* probable in relation to *F*, or that

(180) $P(H/F) = 0.95$,

is apt to go for nothing, just because it is *possible* for *H* to be false though *F* to be true. But *that fact itself* is nothing more than the truth of

(181) $P(H/F) < 1$;

[7] Keynes (1921), p. 322.

in other words, is nothing more than a true statement of logical probability.

(vii)

But Salmon, and the Salmon in all of us, is not easily repressed. Keynes's words, in particular, are bound to strike him as harsh and even superstitious; they will remind him irresistibly of the Stoic doctrine, that virtue is its own reward.

'I am asked', he will say, 'to accept an asymmetry which is quite unbelievable. Where G is my total evidence, we agree, I should believe H. The reason I should believe it is, that necessarily, if G is true, H is true. Valid inference, in other words, should be a guide of life, because it holds out the reward, concrete though conditional, of truth. Yet I am asked to accept merely probable inference, too, as a guide of life, although it is admitted that it *"has nothing to recommend it but its probability"*! Stoic doctrine indeed, of which the plain English is, that there is *no* reward for believing what is merely probable! I ask again, then: where my total evidence is F, what reason have I for believing H? It cannot be the fact, (though it *is* a fact), that

(180) $P(H/F) = 0.95$,

for *that* is a necessary truth, or is "analytic"; whereas H is a *contingent* proposition.'

Here the last sentence is right, of course. Nor do I know of anyone who has denied it. Where our total evidence is F, the reason, if any, that we have for believing H is at any rate not (180). On this point Carnap,[8] at least, to whom Salmon refers in this connection,[9] is perfectly clear.

But then, the third sentence of the above passage is simply false, and the asymmetry referred to in the first sentence is simply non-existent. Where my total evidence is G, the reason I should believe H is *not* the fact (though it *is* a fact) that

(182) Necessarily, if G is true then H is true,

or that

(183) G entails H,

⁸ See Carnap (1947).
⁹ Salmon (1968), pp. 39–43.

or that

(184) $P(H/G) = 1$.

For *these* propositions, just like (180), are necessary truths, or analytic, while H is contingent.

Where G is my total evidence, it is of course true that I *have* a reason to believe H; though it is not (182) or (183) or (184). What is that reason? The answer is obvious: G itself. Where one's total evidence is that all ravens are black and Abe is a raven, *that* proposition is the reason one has, to believe that Abe is black.

And we must give the same kind of answer in the case of the merely probable inference, from F to H. Where my total evidence is F, it is of course true that I *have* a reason to believe H. Salmon has never denied that: he has only insisted that that reason is not (180), and asked what it is. But the answer is obvious: F itself. Where one's total evidence is that just 95 per cent of ravens are black and Abe is a raven, *that* proposition is the reason one has, to believe that Abe is black.

Recall, once again, that it is one of the *elements* of Salmon's problem that

(180) $P(H/F) = 0.95$,

is *true*. The reader must therefore resist any temptation he may feel at this point, to doubt whether, after all, H really is highly probable in relation to F: there is no 'Salmon problem' at all, unless it is so. But, it being so, and my total evidence being F, the answer to the question, 'Why should I believe H?', is evidently: 'Because F'.

Concerning inductive inference, Hume and many others ask: 'Admittedly, all the many observed ravens have been black, but what reason have I to believe that nature is uniform with respect to the colour of ravens, or that *all* ravens are black?' The correct response to this, we saw in Chapter I, is simply to say: 'The reason you have, to believe that all ravens are black, is that all the many observed ravens have been black'. And as Salmon's 'problem' about merely probable inference is simply a generalization of Hume's 'problem' about inductive inference, when Salmon asks us, 'What reason have I to believe what is merely probable in relation to my total evidence?', our reply should similarly be: 'The reason you have is your total evidence'.

(viii)

Can Salmon's problem really be dissolved so easily and without residue? Philosophers will suspect not.

Let us (to vary the examples) compare the valid inference from

(*L*) All the balls in this urn are black, and Bob is a ball about to be drawn from it.

to

(*O*) Bob is black,

with the merely probable inference to the same conclusion from

(*M*) Most of the balls in this urn are black, and Bob is a ball about to be drawn from it.

(Here, 'most' is used in the sense which excludes 'all'.) Where *L* is one's total evidence, one has a reason to believe *O*, and even a completely conclusive reason to believe it; that reason is *L* itself. Salmon asks: where one's total evidence is *M*, what reason has one to believe *O*? I answer that one does have a reason, though of course not a completely conclusive reason, to believe *O*; that reason is *M* itself.

In real life, of course, our total evidence would never be so exiguous as *M*. But this does not matter, because it is not *only* where our total evidence is so exiguous, that Salmon's problem arises, if it arises at all. It would arise equally, for example, where there *are* other propositions beside *M* which we know or think we know, but where these are all *irrelevant to O*, in relation to *M*. And *this* is a situation which easily could arise in real life. In fact, if we are confronted, as we easily could be, with an urn of which all we know is *M*, then it almost certainly *will* be the case that, for every *K* which we know or think we know, $P(O/M.K) = P(O/M)$. Here too, then, Salmon could and would press his problem upon us, and ask: what reason have you to believe *O*? And here too our reply should simply be: *M*.

But can so ordinary an answer really be sufficient, to a question so extraordinary as Salmon's? Philosophers will suspect that, if I have succeeded in making it seem sufficient, that is only because of a tacit refusal on my part to think of any except ordinary circumstances: a refusal unworthy of a philosopher. And this suspicion is not without a certain plausibility in the present case.

In all ordinary circumstances, absolutely nothing would hang on whether O is true; that is, on whether Bob is black or not. In all ordinary circumstances, there is nothing which appals any of us in the difference between valid inference and inference which is merely probable. If all I know or think I know about the urn is M (or if everything else I know or think I know is irrelevant to O in relation to M), then I will cheerfully admit that I do not have *as much* reason to believe O, as I would have if I knew or thought I knew L. But I will also insist that I *do* have a reason to believe O. And if Salmon asks me what this reason is, I will with complete equanimity reply, 'M': that most of the balls in the urn are black, and Bob is one of them.

Suppose I learn, however, that I will be shot at once if Bob is not black. This addition to my total evidence does not (it should not be necessary to say) change the probability of O. But it is apt, all the same, to give a novel turn to my philosophy of probable inference. *Now*, for the first time, Salmon's problem suddenly 'comes alive' for me.

Now, of course, I desperately *want* to believe O, but, being rational, I equally desperately want to be reassured that O is what I should believe. Of course, if I knew or thought I knew L, that *all* the balls are black, there could not possibly be any anxiety. But it is now the *difference* between valid and merely probable inference, not the resemblance between them, which is painfully vivid to my mind. As my total evidence is in fact M, that *most* (not all) of the balls are black, why *should* I believe O? My old answer to this question, namely 'M', now seems to me no answer at all. 'Do not keep telling me', I will say, 'that most of the balls are black! I know that. I knew it all along. I am not interested in that. What is it to me that *most* of the balls are black? I am interested only in whether or not *Bob* is black.' If I am reminded that, in view of my total evidence, Bob is probably black, my language is likely to be intemperate: 'Do not give me this—about Bob being probably black! Nothing can be probably black. *Is Bob black?*'

My former Keynesian philosophy of probable inference will seem threadbare now. I will now hold that, if merely probable inference has indeed nothing to recommend it but its probability then Salmon's suggestion was right after all: it has *nothing* to recommend it. What is wanted concerning probable inference, I will now be convinced, is precisely what I had earlier argued (section (vi)) cannot be had, and would make no difference if it could be had: a connection between the probability of an inference, and the preservation of truth. It is *truth*, after all (I will now think), which matters in inference, and nothing else; and nothing less than its preserving truth can justify the reliance we place on merely probable inference. If anything can reassure me in my present extremity, if anything can answer the question 'Why should I believe *O*?', it must be that, just as valid inference always preserves truth, probable inference does so for the most part.

'And so it does', says Peirce, or Nagel. 'Help is at hand: you *should* indeed believe *O*. Your original inference was (essentially)

(A) Most of the balls are black
     Bob is one of the balls
     ———————————————
     Bob is black;

and you formerly thought that you had, simply in the premisses of (A), a reason to believe the conclusion of (A). You are wiser now: Salmon, plus the threat of death if *O* is false, have made you wonder whether you have any reason at all to believe the conclusion. You have. For the inference (A) is an instance of the inference-schema

(B) Most of the balls are black
     x is one of the balls
     ———————————————
     x is black;

and this schema is one which has the merit of preserving truth most of the time. Of course it does not preserve truth *all* the time; but, as you are rational, you cannot have meant, situated as you are, to ask for *that* degree of reassurance. Still, (B) *does* preserve truth *most* of the time; your (A) is an instance of (B), and an instance in which the premisses are true. *That* is why you should believe that the conclusion is true too; that is, that Bob is black.'

I think that, if I were confronted with an urn of which all I knew was *M*, my reaction to Salmon's problem *would* at first be as described above; that, if I then learnt that I was to be shot if Bob is not black, my reaction to Salmon's problem *would* then be the very different one which was also described above; and finally, that I *would* feel some reassurance, on its being pointed out to me that my original merely probable inference is an instance of a schema which preserves truth more often than not. I also believe, of course—since otherwise there could be no excuse for putting such things on paper—that all of this is true of a good many other philosophers as well.

If it is, however, then that only goes to show what fools a good many of us philosophers are. For there never was a grosser instance of a 'solution' which is nothing but the original 'problem' in different words, or a hollower reassurance than that which the truth-frequentist philosopher offers.

My inference,

(A) Most of the balls are black
     Bob is one of the balls
     Bob is black,

satisfied me well enough at first; then, under the threat of death, it no longer seemed to me that I had any reason at all to believe the conclusion; and finally I was reassured that I had, by the fact that (A) is an instance of an inference-schema which for the most part preserves truth, viz.

(B) Most of the balls are black
     x is one of the balls
     x is black.

What is that reasoning, by means of which the truth-frequentist philosopher succeeds in reassuring me, that I have a reason to believe that Bob is black? It is, evidently, this and nothing more:

(C) Most instances of (B) which have true premises have true conclusions
     (A) is an instance of (B) which has true premises
     (A) has a true conclusion.

But now, this inference (C) has absolutely nothing to recommend it which (A) does not have. (C) is a merely probable inference, just as (A) is. The degree of logical probability is evidently the same in both inferences. If, under threat of death if Bob is not

black, I require reassurances that I have reason to believe the conclusion of (A), that Bob is black, then under the same threat I
should equally require reassurance that I have reason to believe
the conclusion of (C). In other words, the reassurance afforded
by the premisses of (C), to one who already knows the premisses
of (A), is entirely spurious. Either I should never have felt
Salmon's problem about the inference (A), death-threat or not;
or I should feel it equally about the 'reassuring' inference (C).

Indeed, what is the inference (C), *except the inference (A), seen
through a haze of philosophers' words*?

The conclusion of (C) is just that the conclusion of (A) is true;
that is, that Bob *is* black; which is the conclusion of (A).

The minor premiss of (C) is just that the premisses of (A) are
true; that is, that most of the balls are black and that Bob is one
of the balls. So we retrieve from the minor premiss of (C) both
the premisses of (A).

Thus we have already retrieved from (C) the entire original
inference (A).

What is there left in (C)? Just the major premiss, that most
instances of (B) which have true premisses, have true conclusions. That is, that most of the uniform substitutions which
'make it true' that 'Most of the balls are black and x is one of the
balls', also make it true that 'x is black'. But as it is true (from the
minor premiss of (C)) that most of the balls *are* black, the substitutions which make it true that 'Most of the balls are black and x
is one of the balls', are necessarily, just the substitutions which
make it true that 'x is one of the balls'. The major premiss of (C)
says, then, beyond what the minor premiss already says, only that
most of the substitutions which make 'x is one of the balls' true,
make 'x is black' true. But that is just to say that most of the balls
are black. In other words, the major premiss of (C) says nothing,
beyond what the minor premiss already says.

The inference (C), then, is not only no better than the inference (A): it is no *other* than it, unless indeed we reckon the
inference,

(D) Most of the balls are black
     Most of the balls are black
     x is one of the balls

     x is black,

to be other than (A). But it can hardly need to be said that the first premiss in (D) is irrelevant to the conclusion, in relation to the other premisses.

Death-in-the-case-of-a-false-conclusion is, of course, only a device for bringing Salmon's problem vividly home to ourselves. Once we do that, then our merely probable inferences, to a particular conclusion from, say, the relative frequency of blackness among the balls in an urn, or from the relative frequency of blackness in the population of ravens, suddenly seem to us no longer of any logical value. What we really need to know, it then seems to us, is with what relative frequency the schema of our inference preserves truth. But this 'loop' in our thoughts is entirely hallucinatory. A knowledge of the relative frequency with which the schema of our merely probable inference preserves truth, even if we could get it, would leave us no better off than we originally were, with our knowledge of the relative frequency of blackness among balls or ravens. For we would at last have to be content with making, in connection with any particular inference, what we had earlier concluded we were unjustified in making in connection with any particular ball or raven: namely, *an inference which is merely probable.*

Keynes was essentially right: a merely probable inference has *nothing to recommend it but its probability.* Yet this slogan, for all its merits, does not strike *quite* the right note. For it is apt to suggest Stoicism: the voluntary renunciation of something which we could have got just by asking for it; which we could have been excused for asking for; and which would have bestowed some kind of advantage on us had we asked for it and got it. Any such suggestion, it should by now be unnecessary to say, is entirely out of place here. It is *not* true, as we saw in Chapter X, that there is, to be had, a corresponding (or any) relative-truth-frequency, for every logical probability. And we have now seen that there is never any excuse for asking for such a thing; for if there were such a thing, and we asked for it and got it, it would not bestow any kind of advantage on us.

(ix)

Valid inference differs from merely probable inference in other ways beside those mentioned in section (v) above, as I said at the time. One such difference concerns the degree of belief which it is rational to have in the conclusion; and this is a difference which touches the very essence both of valid inference and of merely probable inference.

Where a conclusion is entailed by one's total evidence, rationality prescribes not only that one *believe* the conclusion: it prescribes a unique *degree* of belief in it, namely a degree of belief which is a fraction $\frac{1}{1}$ of one's belief in the evidence. If, for example, we are *certain of* our total evidence, we should be certain of the conclusion too, where the inference is valid. Where a conclusion is merely probable in relation to our total evidence, rationality may still prescribe *belief* in the conclusion: it will, for example, if the probability of the conclusion in relation to the evidence is, say, 0·95. But in every case of merely probable inference, rationality prescribes a *lower* degree of belief in the conclusion than we have in the evidence. If, for example, the conclusion has probability = 0·95 in relation to our total evidence, and we are certain of that evidence, rationality prescribes a degree of belief in the conclusion which is a fraction 0·95 of certainty.

Since Salmon's problem concerns rational belief, and turns on the difference between valid and merely probable inference, one would have expected the difference which has just been mentioned to figure, and figure prominently, in the formulation of his problem. In fact, however, it never figures at all. Salmon's problem, as formulated by himself or others, is essentially just the one I have discussed so far: 'If I believe what is entailed by my total evidence, then I have a reason to believe what I do, and I believe as I rationally should; but what reason have I to believe what is merely probable in relation to my total evidence?' And there is nothing whatever in *this* problem, as we see, about the *degree* of belief which it is rational to have, in the conclusion of a valid inference, or in the conclusion of a merely probable one.

I have given in the preceding sections sufficient reasons for regarding Salmon's question as one to be repudiated rather than answered. But in addition to those reasons, the question itself is defective, as implying in its very formulation something false; and this is due to its omitting all reference to degrees of belief.

For it is *not* true in every case that, if I believe what my total evidence entails, then I believe as I rationally should. Suppose— to return to an earlier example—that my total evidence is *G*, 'All ravens are black and Abe is a raven', and the conclusion is H, 'Abe is black'; suppose that I am certain of G; and suppose that I believe H. It by no means follows that I believe as rationality prescribes. For I might have in H a degree of belief which is only, say, 0·9 of certainty, whereas rationality requires that I have the *same* degree of belief in H as I have in G.

In order to avoid implying the falsity just noticed, then, the part of Salmon's problem which concerns valid inference should have referred, not just to belief in the conclusion, but to a certain *degree* of belief in it, as being what rationality requires.

A fair statement of the problem would then call for the same kind of reformulation to be made of Salmon's question about the merely probable inference. Indeed, this is imperative anyway. For it is not enough to meet the requirements of rationality, where the conclusion is merely probable in relation to my total evidence, that I believe the conclusion with *some* degree of belief lower than that which I have in the evidence. Suppose the conclusion is H as before, but my total evidence is F, 'Just 95 per cent of ravens are black and Abe is a raven'; suppose I am certain of F, and believe H, though with a lower degree of belief than I have in F. It by no means follows that my belief in H is what rationality prescribes. For I might have in H a degree of belief which is only a fraction, say 0·85, of certainty whereas rationality prescribes that my degree of belief in H be 0·95 of certainty.

Salmon's question about merely probable inference, reformulated so as to take into account the fact that it is not belief, but a certain degree of belief, which rationality requires where an inference from total evidence is merely probable, would be, for example, this. 'My total evidence is F, that just 95 per cent of ravens are black and Abe is a raven; I am certain of F, the probability of H, "Abe is black", in relation to F, really is 0·95 (cf. section (iii)); now, what reason have I to have in H a degree of belief which is a fraction 0·95 of certainty?'

And the spuriousness of *this* question, I take it, is self-evident. It is one of those questions, like 'Who wrote the novels that Scott wrote?', or 'How many beans make five?', which supply, in the process of being asked, all the information that could possibly be needed in order to answer them.

The corresponding question, for the case of valid inference, would be, for example, this. 'My total evidence is *G*, that all ravens are black and Abe is a raven; I am certain of *G*; *G* entails *H*, "Abe is black", or, the probability of *H* in relation to *G* really is 1; now, what reason have I to have in *H* a degree of belief which is a fraction $\frac{1}{1}$ of certainty?' This question, too, evidently answers itself.

We have now formulated Salmon's problem as it must be formulated, in order to avoid implying something false: namely in terms of the *degree* of belief which rationality requires in the two cases, of valid and of merely probable inference from total evidence. And when we do this, the contrast between the two cases entirely vanishes: the question about merely probable inference, and the question about valid inference, are both transparently pseudo-questions.

It will be worthwhile to add that, when the question about valid inference is reformulated as it should be, in terms of degree of belief, there is no longer any temptation at all to think that the answer to it is, 'Because valid inference always preserves *truth*'. On the contrary: the question formulated two paragraphs back not only does not need, it does not even admit of that answer. What matters here, obviously, is an entirely different property of valid inference: that it always preserves, in a rational mind, the *same degree of belief* as there is in the total evidence.

The same thing happens with the question about merely probable inference. Once it is reformulated as it should be, in terms of degree of belief, there is no longer any temptation to think that the answer to it must be in terms of the relative frequency with which merely probable inference preserves *truth*. On the contrary: the question formulated five paragraphs back does not need, or even admit of, any such answer. What matters here, obviously, is an entirely different property of merely probable inference: that it always preserves in a rational mind, a lower degree of belief than there is in the total evidence, though still a positive degree of it.

(x)

Suppose that my total evidence is *F*, 'Just 95 per cent of ravens are black and Abe is a raven', but that I then learn that Abe's colour will be determined tomorrow, and that I will be shot at once if Abe is not black. This additional evidence (as I said in section (viii) above) does not change the probability of H, 'Abe is black', but it does (unless I am a most unusual person) change my philosophy of probability; and it does so in a way which is well worth attention.

It will be idle, now, for people to remind me that in relation to my total evidence it is extremely probable, indeed almost certain, that Abe is black. It is the *possibility* that he is not black, and that alone, which now occupies my mind. I can still acknowledge, *in words*, that the probability of Abe's being black is far greater than the probability of his not being so. But my degrees of belief refuse to flow with a corresponding inequality into these two alternatives, as they spontaneously did before, and as they would do still if nothing hung on the truth of H. When my friends insist that

(180) $P(H/F) = 0\cdot95$

I retort that it is, for all that, *possible* that Abe is one of the few non-black ravens; that is,

(181) $P(H/F) < 1$.

Notice this: that although (181) is in fact a *logical consequence of* (180), it now serves me as a *retort to* (180): as though the two propositions are actually *inconsistent*! The fact is, that while I can still employ, only too well, the concept of possibility, I cannot, at least for the time being, employ the concept of probability at all. I can still employ the *words*, of course, but they do not mean anything to me any more. It is as though I reasoned, 'Nothing is really probable, or even more probable than anything else, *because everything is possible*.'

That is certainly very peculiar, and very bad, reasoning. It is so, because the concept of probability not only carries the concept of possibility with it, but can in fact be built out of it in the following way: one alternative is more probable than another if, for every way in which the former can be realized, there is an equally possible way in which the latter can be realized, but not conversely. So little does it make sense, then, to *oppose* possibility to probability; and it is still worse to *reason*, to something's being not probable, from its opposite's being possible.

Yet there are other cases in which formally similar reasoning is by no means inexcusable. Most of us at the present day can no longer employ the concept of miracle, for example, and in the process of losing the ability to do so, many of us have reasoned, at least inwardly, somewhat thus: 'there is no such thing as a miracle, for everything is a miracle'. Indeed, at least one writer has so reasoned in print, in those very words.[10] Religious concepts, in fact, when religion is in decay, furnish many parallels to what happens to my concept of probability, when I learn that I will be shot tomorrow if Abe is not black.

Take for example the concept of the sacred. We, or our forebears, used to believe that a certain stone, or tree or statue, or place, or kind of animal, was sacred, and (what follows from that), that some other stones, etc., were not sacred, but 'ordinary'. By now, however, the concept of the sacred has simply departed from the minds of most of us: we *cannot* employ it. The nearest thing to it which we can employ is a sort of *epistemic* vestige of it: the concept of being *held to be* sacred (by someone). Among us, the word 'sacred' is now *always* enclosed in inverted commas, whether visible ones or not. This being so, it does not and cannot concern us, whether one says 'Nothing is sacred', or 'Everything is sacred': either is simply a way of attesting that the original concept now eludes us. And if some one goes so far as to reason from the latter saying to the former, even then we are conscious of a certain merit in his reasoning, for all its superficial absurdity.

A similar 'epistemization' overtakes my concept of probability when I learn that I will be shot tomorrow if Abe is not black. Talk about probability I now understand only as talk about what is *held to be* probable, or *seems* probable. The distinction between what is probable, and what is 'probable', is simply lost on me, at least temporarily. The high probability of Abe's being black now means to me literally no more than the profound sacredness of the oracle at Delphi does. The possibility that he is not black, on the other hand, is only too real, and all-absorbing. I am anaesthetized to differences of magnitude among probabilities, although hyper-aesthetized to certain possibilities.

This state of 'probability-numbness' afflicts most people only temporarily, if at all, and then only under the spur of some such

---

[10] Quoted in Robertson (1929), vol. I, p. 91.

painful circumstances as I have imagined above. But there is also an entire class of persons whom it afflicts all the time (at least in their professional capacity), and without being prompted by any particular source of anxiety. These are the philosophers of science of the last half-century.

Concerning any scientific theory, however probable, these philosophers, like the man who is to be shot if Abe is not black, display an exclusive and obsessive preoccupation with the possibility of a false conclusion from true premises. That some scientific theories are far more probable than others, they acknowledge, of course, in words, but this acknowledgement stays at the level of words. Differences in probability, with them, are only differences in 'probability', and correspond to nothing that is really felt. The *one* feature of scientific theories, to which philosophers' minds are now not numb, is that (being the conclusions of merely probable inferences) they *may* be false.

Popper, of course, is the most signal instance of this probability-numbness in recent philosophy of science. His entire philosophy, as is well known, is built around an obsessive preoccupation with the trivial truth that any scientific theory may be false. And that the probability of every scientific theory is *the same*, and the same in relation to any possible evidence as it is *a priori*, is something which (as we saw in Chapter III above) Popper expressly maintains.

But this is too perfect an instance of probability-numbness to be representative of the profession. The more typical state of mind is more negative. It is the sheer incapacity to feel the different degrees of probability which scientific theories can and do have; and a consequent inability to take probability seriously. Of this less overt but more typical probability-numbness, the purest expression is Salmon's problem. It is simply the philosophers' version, generalized to *all* merely probable inferences, of what is felt by the man who is to be shot tomorrow if Abe is not black: or rather, of that man's *inability to feel* differences in degree of probability. And no doubt the defect, noticed in the preceding section, in Salmon's very formulation of his problem, is a consequence of probability-numbness. The problem manifestly required to be formulated in terms of rational *degrees* of belief, but probability-numbness confined Salmon to the language of rational belief, instead.

We can all understand the probability-numbness of the man who is to be shot if Abe is not black, but whence has come the probability-numbness of our philosophers of science? It did not exist in the philosophy of science of the preceding two centuries (setting the solitary exception of Hume aside).

So far as its causes are strictly intellectual, the main cause of this probability-numbness is obvious enough: it is the fall of the Newtonian empire in physics, early in this century. It is that mighty subsidence of scientific confidence, and the dread of undergoing a similar retribution again, through again reposing over-much confidence in any scientific theory, which has frozen our philosophers into an exclusive preoccupation with the possible falsity of any theory.[11] But it is equally obvious that the causes of our probability-numbness are *not* only, or even mainly, intellectual. Probability-numbness in the philosophy of science is merely one facet of the wider phenomenon which Freud called modern nervousness: a phenomenon which is not the less real, for Freud's having offered a singularly improbable explanation of it.[12] Modern nervousness itself is evidently only one facet of that dissolution of Western Society which set in, rather suddenly, about the time of the First World War. And what the causes of *that* in turn are, is a question which it would be out of place to pursue here, even if I had, as I have not, anything to contribute towards answering it.

To lose the ability to employ a certain concept *can* be, of course, to make intellectual *progress*. For example, we are, I think, intellectually better off, other things being equal, when we become 'numb' to the concept of the sacred. (We might still, of course, be worse off, in non-intellectual respects.) But *probability*-numbness in the philosophy of science is not one of these progressive cases. The concept of probability and of possibility being connected in the way that they are, to be numb to the differences in magnitude between probabilities, while being hypersensitive to certain possibilities, is to be in a profoundly irrational mental state, and even a pathological one.

We all recognize this in the case of the man who learns that he is to be shot if Abe is black: no one would take a man in that situ-

---

[11] Cf. Stove (1982), pp. 50–4.
[12] Freud (1924), II, pp. 76–99.

ation as a model of how to distribute degrees of belief rationally. But we ought equally to recognize that, in the philosophy of science, the best model is not to be looked for in philosophers whose society is in an advanced stage of dissolution within, as well as under imminent sentence of death from without

(xi)

In the philosophy of logical probability, in non-deductive logic generally, and indeed in logic generally, the greatest single source of error and confusion is, in my opinion, the formalist tendency. I mean, for example, the hankering after relative-truth-frequency as a substitute, or a 'foundation', for merely probable inference; the tendency to identify the validity of an inference with truth always being preserved by a schema of which the inference is an instance; and, at the bottom of it all, the delusion that we gain something, or lose nothing, by making 'logical forms' or inference-schemas, rather than inferences themselves, the subject of our study.

Salmon, since he is evidently one of those who hanker after relative-truth-frequency as a foundation for merely probable inference, participates to some extent in the formalist tendency. To that extent, consideration of his problem has brought us back to the point at which we began this Part, and to the thing which is the source of most errors about logic whether deductive or non-deductive: the myth that logic is nothing if not formal.

But Salmon's problem is far more than an instance of the formalist tendency. It is an absolutely original contribution to the philosophy of probability, and, although it is so new, is a worthy addition to the old 'great problems' of philosophy: 'the problem of induction', 'the problem of universals', and so on. For it resembles these in the following decisive respects. First, there is absolutely nothing in it. Second, immense intellectual effort is required in order to satisfy oneself that there is nothing in it; far *more* intellectual effort, I may observe, than is required to invent the 'problem' in the first place, or to wrestle with it straight-facedly as though it really was a problem. Third, to consider the problem does no one any intellectual good, whatever may be the outcome of his consideration of it; for even when one has learnt that there is nothing in it, one has not learnt anything else.

Fourth, consideration of the problem, whatever its outcome, does extensive and irreversible intellectual harm. For Salmon's problem, like Hume's, can never be *entirely* dispelled. Just as, after Hume, there will always be, in the minds of even good philosophers, at least a residue of silly suspicion about induction, so there will always be, after Salmon, a residue of silly suspicion about merely probable inference. It should not be so: the 'problems' are mere nothings, built ulimately (as we saw in the case of induction in Chapter I) out of literary materials so trivial in themselves that even to catalogue them is a trial of anyone's patience. Still, it is so.

GLOSSARY OF NUMBERED ENTRIES
IN THE TEXT

(1) That all the many observed ravens have been black is not a completely conclusive reason to believe that all ravens are black.

(2) All the many observed ravens have been black.

(3) All ravens are black.

(4) p is not a completely conclusive reason to believe q.

(5) The inference from (2) to (3) is fallible.

(6) That all the many observed ravens have been black is a reason to believe that all ravens are black.

(7) The inference from (2) to (3) is rational.

(8) All ravens are observed.

(9) p is a reason to believe q.

(9a) p is a reason to believe that all ravens are black, if p is 'All the many observed ravens have been black.'

(10) Inductive inference presupposes that nature is uniform.

(11) That nature is uniform cannot be rationally inferred by induction.

(12) For all e and all h such that the inference from e to h is inductive, $P(h/e) \leq 0 \cdot 01$.

(13) For all e and all h such that the inference from e to h is inductive, $P(h/e) = P(\sim h/e)$.

(14) For all e and all h such that the inference from e to h is inductive, and for all tautological t, $P(h/t.e) = P(h/t)$.

(15) For any h which is contingent and unrestrictedly universal, and for all tautological t, $P(h/t) = 0$.

(16) If $P(q/p) = 0$, then, for all r, $P(q/p.r) = 0$.

(17) For all e and all h such that h is contingent and unrestrictedly universal, and the inference from e to h is inductive, and for all tautological t, $P(h/t.e) = P(h/t)$.

(18) For any two distinct non-overlapping individuals x and y, and for any predicate F such that the inference from Fx to Fy is inductive, $P(Fy/t.Fx) = P(Fy/t)$.

(19) p is not a reason to believe q.

(20) The premiss of an inductive inference is no reason to believe the conclusion.

(In entries (21)–(23), E is short for 'Abe is a raven'; H is short for 'Abe is black'; E' is short for 'More than half of all ravens are black'; and T is some tautology.)

(21) $P(H/T.E) > P(H/T)$ if and only if E'.

(22) $P(H/T.E.E') > P(H/T.E)$.

(23) $P(H/T.E) = P(H/T)$.

(24) P(Abe is black$/T$) < 1.

(25) P(Abe is black$/T$) $> P$(Abe is black. Abe is a raven$/T$).

(26) P(Abe is black$/T$) $< P$(Abe is black$/T$. Abe is a raven. Most ravens are black).

(27) $P(q/p) + P(\sim q/p) = 1$.

(28) $P(p.q/r) = P(p/r) \times P(q/r.p) = P(q/r) \times P(p/r.q)$.

(29) For all e, all e', all h, all h', such that the inferences from e to h and from e' to h' are both inductive, $P(h/e) = P(h'/e')$.

(In entries (30)–(33), Ba is short for 'Abe is black', Bb is short for 'Bob is black', and Bc is short for 'Charles is black'.)

(30) $P(Bb.Bc/Ba) = P(Bb/Ba)$.

(31) $P(Bb.Bc/Ba) = P(Bb/Ba) \times P(Bc/Ba.Bb)$.

(32) $P(Bc/Ba.Bb) = 1$.

(33) $P(Bc/Ba.Bb) < 1$.

(34) There are e, e', h, h', such that the inference from e to h and from e' to h' are both inductive, and $P(h/e) \neq P(h'/e')$.

(35) $P(p/r) \times P(q/r.p) = P(q/r) \times P(p/r.q)$.

(36) $P(p/T) \times P(q/T.p) = P(q/T) \times P(p/T.q)$.

(37) If $P(p/T)$ and $P(q/T)$ are each > 0, then $P(q/T.p) = P(q/T)$ if and only if $P(p/T.q) = P(p/T)$.

(38) $P(p/T.q) = P(p/T)$ if and only if $1 - P(\sim p/T.q) = 1 - P(\sim p/T)$.

(39) $P(p/T.q) = P(p/T)$ if and only if $P(\sim p/T.q) = P(\sim p/T)$.

(40) If $P(p/T)$ and $P(q/T)$ are each > 0, then $P(q/T.p) = P(q/T)$ if and only if $P(\sim p/T.q) = P(\sim p/T)$.

(41) If $P(\sim p/T)$ and $P(q/T)$ are each > 0, then $P(q/T.\sim p) = P(q/T)$ if and only if $P(\sim p/T.q) = P(\sim p/T)$.

(42) If $P(p/T)$, $P(\sim p/T)$, and $P(q/T)$ are each > 0, then $P(q/T.p) = P(q/T)$ if and only if $P(q/T.\sim p) = P(q/T)$.

(In entries (43)–(52), E is short for 'All the observed ravens have been black', and H is short for 'There are Australian ravens and all of them are black'.)

(43) If $P(E/T)$, $P(\sim E/T)$, $P(H/T)$ are each > 0, then $P(H/T.E) = P(H/T)$ if and only if $P(H/T.\sim E) = P(H/T)$.

(44) $P(E/T) > 0$.

(45) $P(\sim E/T) > 0$.

(46) $P(H/T) > 0$.

(47) $P(H/T.E) = P(H/T)$ if and only if $P(H/T.\sim E) = P(H/T)$.

(48) The inference from E to H is inductive.

(49) $P(H/T.E) = P(H/T)$.

(50) $P(H/T.\sim E) = P(H/T)$.

(51) $P(H/T.\sim E) = 0$.

(52) $P(H/T.\sim E) \neq P(H/T)$.

(In entries (53)–(63), H is short for 'There are Australian ravens and all of them are black'; E is short for 'All the Australian ravens observed between 1900 and 1980 were black'; E' is short for 'All the Australian ravens observed before 1900 were black'.)

(53) $P(H/T) \times P(E/T.H) = P(E/T) \times P(H/T.E)$.

(54) If $P(H/T)$ and $P(E/T)$ are each > 0, then $P(H/T.E) = P(H/T)$ if and only if $P(E/T.H) = P(E/T)$.

(55) $P(E/T) > 0$.

(56) The inference from E to H is inductive.

(57) $P(H/T.E) = P(H/T)$.

(58) $P(E/T.H) = P(E/T)$.

(59) $P(E/T.H) = 1$.

(60) $P(E/T) = 1$.

(61) If $P(q/p) = 1$ then, for any r, $P(q/p.r) = 1$.

(62) $P(E/T.E') = 1$.

(63) $P(E/T.E') < 1$.

(64) This coin will come up heads about half the time in 3000 tosses.

(65) The probability of heads at each toss with this coin is $\frac{1}{2}$.

(66) This coin will come up heads about half the time in 4 tosses.

(67) At all of the 20 tosses with this fair coin it has come up heads.

(68) It will not come up heads next time.

(69) At the 2 tosses with this fair coin it has come up heads.

(70) The probability$_2$ of heads with this coin is about $\frac{1}{2}$.

(71) This coin came up heads in half of 3000 tosses.

(72) This coin came up heads in half of 2 tosses.

(73) $\frac{m}{n}$ths of the F's are G

x is an F

——————————————

x is G.

(74) 95% of ravens are black

Abe is a raven
_____
Abe is black.

(75) At least $\frac{2}{3}$rds of ravens are black

Abe is a raven
_____
Abe is black.

(76) $\frac{n}{m}$ths of a large sample S of the F's are G
_____
About $\frac{n}{m}$ths of the population of F's are G.

(77)

Any F $\left\{\begin{array}{l} \text{has a probability 0·9 of being} \\ \text{has a high probability of being} \\ \text{is very probably a} \\ \text{is almost certainly} \\ \text{is almost certain to be} \end{array}\right\}$ G.

(78) Any mutation is almost certain to be harmful.

(79) M is a mutation.

(80) M is almost certain to be harmful.

(81) M is a beneficial mutation.

(82) M is beneficial and almost certain to be harmful.

(83) For all x, all $\frac{n}{m}$, all $r > 3000$,
P(x is a near-Pop-matcher/x is an r-fold sample of Pop, and at least $\frac{n}{m}$ths of the 3000-or-more-fold samples in Pop are near-Pop-matchers) $\geq \frac{n}{m}$.

(84) At least $\frac{n}{m}$ths of the 3000-or-more-fold samples in Pop are near-Pop-matchers

x is an r-fold sample of Pop
_____
x is a near-Pop-matcher.

(85) P(S is near-Pop-matcher/S is a 3020-fold sample of Pop, and at least $\frac{9}{10}$ of the 3000-or-more-fold samples in Pop are near-Pop-matchers) $\geq 0·9$.

(86) P($C/A.B$) $\geq 0·9$.

(87) Necessarily, if Pop is finite, and large enough to contain ten 3000-or-more-fold samples, then at least $\frac{9}{10}$ of the 3000-or-more-fold samples in Pop are near-Pop-matchers.

(88) Necessarily, Pop is finite.

(89) Necessarily, if Pop is large enough to contain ten 3000-or-more-fold samples, then at least $\frac{9}{10}$ of the 3000-or-more-fold samples in Pop are near-Pop-matchers.

(90) Necessarily, if A then Pop is large enough to contain ten 3000-or-more-fold samples.

(91) Necessarily, if A then at least $\frac{9}{10}$ of the 3000-or-more-fold samples in Pop are near-Pop-matchers.

(92) Necessarily, if A then B.

(93) If necessarily if p then r, $P(q/p.r)=P(q/p)$.

(94) $P(C/A)\geq 0.9$.

(95) $P(C/A.D)\geq P(C/A)$.

(96) $P(C/A.D)\geq 0\cdot 9$.

(97) $P(q/p.r)=P(q.r/p.r)$.

(98) $P(C/A.D)=P(C.D/A.D)$.

(99) $P(C.D/A.D)\geq 0\cdot 9$.

(100) Necessarily, if $C.D$ then E.

(101) $P(r/p)\geq P(q/p)$, if necessarily if q then r.

(102) $P(E/A.D)\geq 0\cdot 9$.

(103) The inference from $A.D$ to E is inductive.

(104) The inductive inference from $A.D$ to E has high probability.

(105) $P(H/E)=0\cdot 95$.

(106) $P(\sim H/E)=0\cdot 4$.

(107) $P(q/p)+P(\sim q/p)\leq 1$.

(108) $P(G/E.F)\geq 0\cdot 9$.

(109) $P(G/E.F.A.D)\geq P(G/E.F)$.

(110) $P(G/E.F.A.D)\geq 0\cdot 9$.

(111) $P(E/A.D.F)\geq P(E/A.D)$.

(112) The inference from $A.D$ to E, and the inference from $A.D.F$ to E, are both inductive.

(113) $P(h/e.e')=P(h/e)$, for all h, all e, and all tautological e'.

(114) $P(E/A.D.F)=P(E/T)=P(E/A.D)$.

(115) $P(E/A.D.F.G)<1$.

(116) $P(E.G/A.D.F) = P(E/A.D.F) \times P(G/A.D.F.E) = P(G/A.D.F) \times P(E/A.D.F.G)$.

(117) $P(G/A.D.F)>0\cdot 81$.

(118) The inference from $A.D.F$ to G is inductive.

(119) The inductive inference from $A.D.F$ to G has high probability.

(120) P(Abe is black/Abe is a raven and just 95% of ravens are black) = $0\cdot 95$.

(In entries (121)–(138), H is short for 'Just two of the individuals Abe, Bob, Charles are black'; I is short for 'Abe is black'; Ba is short for 'Abe is black'; Bb for 'Bob is black'; Bc for 'Charles is black'.)

(121) $P(I/H) = \frac{2}{3}$.

(122) $P(H.I/T) = P(H/T) \times P(I/T.H)$.

(123) $P(I/T.H) = \dfrac{P(H.I/T)}{P(H/T)}$.

(124) $P(I/H) = \dfrac{P(H.I/T)}{P(H/T)}$.

(125) H is logically equivalent to: $(Ba.Bb.\sim Bc) \vee (Ba.\sim Bb.Bc) \vee (\sim Ba.Bb.Bc)$.

(126) If p is logically equivalent to p', and q logically equivalent to q', then $P(q/p) = P(q'/p')$.

(127) $P(I/H) = \dfrac{P(Ba.((Ba.Bb.\sim Bc) \vee (Ba.\sim Bb.Bc) \vee (\sim Ba.Bb.Bc))/T)}{P((Ba.Bb.\sim Bc) \vee (Ba.\sim Bb.Bc) \vee (\sim Ba.Bb.Bc)/T)}$.

(128) The conjunction in (127) of Ba with the long disjunction is logically equivalent to:
$(Ba.Ba.Bb.\sim Bc) \vee (Ba.Ba.\sim Bb.Bc) \vee (Ba.\sim Ba.Bb.Bc)$.

(129) The proposition after the colon in (128) is logically equivalent to:
$(Ba.Bb.\sim Bc) \vee (Ba.\sim Bb.Bc) \vee (Ba.\sim Ba.Bb.Bc)$.

(130) $P(I/H) = \dfrac{P((Ba.Bb.\sim Bc) \vee (Ba.\sim Bb.Bc) \vee (\sim Ba.Ba.Bb.Bc)/T)}{P((Ba.Bb.\sim Bc) \vee (Ba.\sim Bb.Bc) \vee (\sim Ba.Bb.Bc)/T)}$.

(131) If $P(q.r/p) = P(q.s/p) = P(r.s/p) = 0$, then $P(q \vee r \vee s/p) = P(q/p) + P(r/p) + P(s/p)$; whence, if three propositions are pairwise-exclusive, then the probability of their disjunction is the sum of the probabilities of the disjuncts.

(132) All the disjuncts in each long disjunction in (130) are pair-wise-exclusive.

(133) $P(I/H) = \dfrac{P(Ba.Bb.\sim Bc/T) + P(Ba.\sim Bb.Bc/T) + P(\sim Ba.Ba.Bb.Bc/T)}{P(Ba.Bb.\sim Bc/T) + P(Ba.\sim Bb.Bc/T) + P(\sim Ba.Bb.Bc/T)}$.

(134) $P(\sim Ba.Ba.Bb.Bc/T) = 0$.

(135) $P(I/H) = \dfrac{P(Ba.Bb.\sim Bc/T) + P(Ba.\sim Bb.Bc/T)}{P(Ba.Bb.\sim Bc/T) + P(Ba.\sim Bb.Bc/T) + P(\sim Ba.Bb.Bc/T)}$.

(136) $P(Ba.Bb.\sim Bc/T) = P(Ba.\sim Bb.Bc/T) = P(\sim Ba.Bb.Bc/T)$.

(137) $P(Ba.Bb.\sim Bc/T) > 0$.

(138) All the probabilities mentioned in the right-hand side of (135) are > 0 and equal to one another.

(139) $P(G/T) \leq 0\cdot81$.

(140) $P(G/A.D.F.T) > P(G/T)$.

(141) $P(h/e) < 1$, for all e, all h, such that the inference from e to h is inductive.

(142) 'All the emeralds observed before AD 2000 are grue' confirms 'Any emerald observed after AD 2000 is grue.'

(143) 'All the emeralds observed before AD 2000 are green' confirms 'Any emerald observed after AD 2000 is blue.'

(144) 'All the F observed before t are G' confirms 'Any F observed after t is G'.

(142′) 'All the emeralds observed before 2000 are grue' is initially favourably relevant to 'Any emerald observed after 2000 is grue.'

(143′) 'All the emeralds observed before 2000 are green' is initially favourably relevant to 'Any emerald observed after 2000 is blue'.

(144′) 'All the F observed before t are G' is initially favourably relevant to 'Any F observed after t is G.'

(145) $P(\text{Abe is black}/T) < 1$.

(146) $P(\text{Abe is black}/T) = P(\text{Bob is black}/T)$.

(147) 'Abe is black and Bob is black' entails 'Abe is black.'

(148) 'Abe is a raven and all ravens are black' entails 'Abe is black.'

(149) 'x is F and all F are G' entails 'x is G', for all x, all F, all G.

(150) 'Abe is a person now in this room and all persons now in this room are black' entails 'Abe is black.'

(151) Abe is black and Abe is a person now in this room and all persons now in this room are black.

(152) $P(x \text{ is } G/x \text{ is } F \text{ and just } \frac{m}{n}\text{ths of } F \text{ are } G) = \frac{m}{n}$, for all $n > m > 0$, all x, all F, all G.

(153) Abe is not black and Abe is a person now in this room and just $\frac{2}{3}$ of persons in this room are black.

(154) For any contingent p and any necessarily-true q, p does not entail q.

(155) $P(h/e) < 1, > 0$, for all tautological e and all contingent non-quantified h.

(156) $P(h/e) = P(h'/e')$, for all e, e', h, h', such that e' can be generated from e, and h' from h, by mere uniform replacement of one individual constant by another.

(157) 'All F are G and x is G' does not entail 'x is F', for any x, any F, any G.

(158) 'All men are mortal and x is mortal' does not entail 'x is a man', for any x.

(159) Popper's cat 'Socrates' is not a man and Popper's cat 'Socrates' is mortal and all men are mortal.

(160) 'P' does not entail 'Q'.

(161) 'Popper's cat "Socrates" is mortal and all men are mortal' does not entail 'Popper's cat "Socrates" is a man'.

(162) '*p*' entails 'It is possible that *p*', for all *p*.

(163) '*P*-and-not-*Q*' entails 'It is possible that *P*-and-not-*Q*'.

(164) For all *x*, all *F*, all *G*, an argument from '*x* is *F* and all *F* are *G*' to '*x* is *G*' is valid.

(165) For all *x*, all *F*, all *G*, it is not the case that '*x* is *F* and all *F* are *G*' is true and '*x* is *G*' is false.

(166) For all *x*, all *F*, all *G*, either '*x* is *F* and all *F* are *G*' is false or '*x* is *G*' is true.

(167) (151) confirms (149).

(168) O_1.

(169) (168) confirms (167).

(170) O_2.

(171) (170) confirms (169).

(172) If all ravens are black, then
　　　P(Abe is black/Abe is a raven)
　　=P(Abe is black/Abe is a raven and all ravens are black).

(173) 　　P(Abe is black/Abe is a raven and all ravens are black)
　　> P(Abe is black/Abe is a raven).

(174) Intuition tells us that (145).

(175) Everyone knows that (146).

(176) How do you know that (120)?

(177) ....

(178) How do you know that (177)?

(179) P(*h*/*e*.*e'*)=P(*h*/*e*) for all *h*, all *e*, and all necessarily true *e'*.

(180) P(*H*/*F*)=0·95.

(181) P(*H*/*F*)< 1.

(182) Necessarily, if *G* is true then *H* is true.

(183) *G* entails *H*.

(184) P(*H*/*G*)=1.

BIBLIOGRAPHY

Aristotle, *Prior Analytics.*

Armstrong, D. M. (1983). *What is a Law of Nature?* (Cambridge: Cambridge University Press).

Barker, S. (1957). *Induction and Hypothesis* (Ithaca, NY: Cornell University Press).

Blackburn, S. (1973). Review of Stove (1973). *Times Literary Supplement,* 10 August, p. 935.

Bolzano, B. (1837). *Theory of Science,* trans. R. George (Oxford: Blackwell, 1972).

Bradley, M. C. (1977). 'Stove on Hume', *Australasian Journal of Philosophy,* 55, no. 1.

Burks, A. W. (1977). *Chance, Cause, Reason* (Chicago, Ill.: University of Chicago Press).

Butler, S. (1923). *A First Year in Canterbury Settlement,* first edn. 1863 (London: Jonathan Cape).

Carnap, R. (1947). 'Probability as a Guide of Life', *Journal of Philosophy,* XLIV, no. 6.

—— (1962). *Logical Foundations of Probability,* first edn. 1950 (Chicago, Ill.: University of Chicago Press).

Cohen, M. and Nagel, E. (1934). *An Introduction to Logic and Scientific Method,* complete edn. (London: Routledge & Kegan Paul).

Copi, I. M. (1954). *Symbolic Logic* (New York: Macmillan).

Freud, S. (1924). 'Civilized Sexual Morality and Modern Nervousness', in *Collected Papers,* trans. Riviere (London: International Psycho-Analytical Press).

Goodman, N. (1954). *Fact. Fiction and Forecast* (London: University of London, Athlone Press).

Hacking, I. (1975). *The Emergence of Probability* (Cambridge: Cambridge University Press).

Hanson, N. R. (1969). *Perception and Discovery,* ed. Humphreys (San Francisco Calif.: Freeman & Cooper Co.).

Hempel, C. G. (1943). 'A Purely Syntactical Definition of Confirmation', *Journal of Symbolic Logic.* 8, no. 4.

—— (1965). *Aspects of Scientific Explanation* (New York: Free Press).

Hume, D. (1739). *A Treatise of Human Nature,* ed. Selby-Bigge (Oxford: Oxford University Press, 1888) and ed. Nidditch (Oxford: Oxford University Press, 1978).

—— (1740). *An Abstract of . . . a Treatise of Human Nature,* reprinted in the edition of Hume (1739) referred to above.

—— (1748). *An Enquiry concerning Human Understanding,* ed. Selby-Bigge, Oxford University Press, 1893; ed. Nidditch, 1975.

—— (1882). *The Philosophical Works,* ed. Green and Grose (London: Longmans, Green & Co.).

Keynes, J. M. (1921). *A Treatise on Probability* (London: Macmillan).

Kneale, W. (1949). *Probability and Induction* (Oxford: Clarendon Press).

—— (1949). 'Confirmation and Rationality', in Lakatos (1968).

Koopman, B. (1940). 'The Axioms and Algebra of Intuitive Probability', *Annals of Mathematics.* 41, no. 2.

Kuhn, T. S. (1970). 'Reflections on my Critics', in Lakatos and Musgrave (eds.), *Criticism and the Growth of Knowledge* (Cambridge: Cambridge University Press).

Lakatos, I. (1968) (ed.). *The Problem of Inductive Logic* (Amsterdam: North-Holland Publishing Co.).

Mill, J. S. (1843). *A System of Logic,* first edn. 1843; 8th edn. 1941 (London: Longmans Green).

Mortensen, C. (1977). 'Koopman, Stove and Hume', *Australasian Journal of Philosophy,* 55, No. 1.

Peirce, C. S. (1932). *Collected Papers of C. S. Peirce,* eds. Hartshorne and Weiss, vol. 2 (Cambridge, Mass.: Harvard University Press).

Popper, K. R. (1959). *The Logic of Scientific Discovery* (London: Hutchinson).

—— (1968). 'Theories, Experience, and Probabilistic Intuitions', in Lakatos (1968).

—— (1974). Contributions to *The Philosophy of Karl Popper,* ed. Schilpp (La Salle, Ill.: Open Court).

Robertson, J. M. (1929). *A History of Freethought in the Nineteenth Century* (London: Dawsons of Pall Mall).

Salmon, W. C. (1965). Contributions to a symposium in *American Philosophical Quarterly,* 2, No. 4.

—— (1967). *The Foundations of Scientific Inference* (Pittsburgh, Pa.: University of Pittsburgh Press).

—— (1968). 'The Justification of Inductive Rules of Inference', in Lakatos (1968).

—— (1982). 'Further Reflections', in McLaughlin ed., *What? Where? When? Why?* (Dordrecht: Reidel).

Stove, D. C. (1965). 'Hume, Probability, and Induction', *Philosophical Review,* LXXIV, no. 2.

—— (1966). 'On Logical Definitions of Confirmation', *British Journal for the Philosophy of Science,* XVI, no. 64.

—— (1972). 'Misconditionalization', *Australasian Journal of Philosophy,* 50, no. 2.

—— (1973). *Probability and Hume's Inductive Scepticism* (Oxford: Clarendon Press).

—— (1975). 'Hume, the Causal Principle, and Kemp Smith', *Hume Studies*, I. no. 1.

—— (1976a). 'Hume, Induction, and the Irish', *Australasian Journal of Philosophy*, 54, no. 2.

—— (1976b). 'Why Should Probability be the Guide of Life?', in *Hume, a Re-Evaluation*, eds. Livingston and King, Fordham University Press, 1976; reprinted in McLaughlin, ed. *What? Where? When? Why?* (Dordrecht: Reidel, 1982).

—— (1976c). Review of *Hume*, by T. Penelhum, *Dialogue*.

—— (1979). 'The Nature of Hume's Scepticism', in *McGill Hume Studies*, eds. Norton, Capaldi, and Robison (San Diego, Calif.: Austin Hill Press).

—— (1982). *Popper and After: Four Modern Irrationalists* (Oxford: Pergamon Press).

Stroud, B. (1977). *Hume* (London: Routledge & Kegan Paul).

Tarski, A. (1956). *Logic, Semantics, Meta-Mathematics* (Oxford: Clarendon Press).

Todhunter, I. (1865). *A History of the Mathematical Theory of Probability* (Cambridge and London), reprinted Chelsea Pub. Co., New York, 1965.

von Wright, G. H. (1957). *The Logical Problem of Induction* (Oxford: Blackwell).

Williams, D. C. (1947). *The Ground of Induction* (Cambridge, Mass.: Harvard University Press).

Wisdom, J. O. (1952). *Foundations of Inference in Natural Science* (London: Methuen).

INDEX OF PERSONS

INDEX OF SUBJECTS